John Gerstner and the Renewal
of Presbyterian and Reformed
Evangelicalism in Modern America

Princeton Theological Monograph Series

K. C. Hanson, Charles M. Collier, D. Christopher Spinks,
and Robin A. Parry, Series Editors

Recent volumes in the series:

Koo Dong Yun
*The Holy Spirit and Ch'i (Qi):
A Chiological Approach to Pneumatology*

Stanley S. MacLean
*Resurrection, Apocalypse, and the Kingdom of Christ:
The Eschatology of Thomas F. Torrance*

Brian Neil Peterson
*Ezekiel in Context: Ezekiel's Message Understood in Its Historical
Setting of Covenant Curses and Ancient Near
Eastern Mythological Motifs*

Amy E. Richter
Enoch and the Gospel of Matthew

Maeve Louise Heaney
Music as Theology: What Music Says about the Word

Eric M. Vail
Creation and Chaos Talk: Charting a Way Forward

David L. Reinhart
*Prayer as Memory: Toward the Comparative Study of Prayer
as Apocalyptic Language and Thought*

Peter D. Neumann
Pentecostal Experience: An Ecumenical Encounter

Ashish J. Naidu
*Transformed in Christ:
Christology and the Christian Life in John Chrysostom*

John Gerstner and the Renewal
of Presbyterian and Reformed
Evangelicalism in Modern America

Jeffrey S. McDonald

PICKWICK *Publications* · Eugene, Oregon

JOHN GERSTNER AND THE RENEWAL OF PRESBYTERIAN AND RE-
FORMED EVANGELICALISM IN MODERN AMERICA

Princeton Theological Monograph Series 226

Pickwick Publications
An Imprint of Wipf and Stock Publishers
199 W. 8th Ave., Suite 3
Eugene, OR 97401

www.wipfandstock.com

PAPERBACK ISBN: 978-1-4982-9631-1
HARDCOVER ISBN: 978-1-4982-9633-5
EBOOK ISBN: 978-1-4982-9632-8

Cataloguing-in-Publication data:

Names: McDonald, Jeffrey S.

Title: John Gerstner and the renewal of Presbyterian and Reformed Evangelicalism in
modern America / Jeffrey S. McDonald.

Description: Eugene, OR: Pickwick Publications, 2017 | Series: Princeton Theological
Monograph Series 226 | Includes bibliographical references and index.

Identifiers: ISBN 978-1-4982-9631-1 (paperback) | ISBN 978-1-4982-9633-5 (hardcover)
| ISBN 978-1-4982-9632-8 (ebook)

Subjects: LCSH: Gerstner, John H. (John Henry) 1914–1996 | Theology | Reformed
church—doctrines | Evangelicalism—United States

Classification: BR50.M92 2017 (paperback) | BR50.M92 (ebook)

Manufactured in the U.S.A.   12/18/17

To Krista

Contents

Acknowledgments

I would like to thank Bradley Longfield for his helpful advice and for his courses on religious biography and church history at the University of Dubuque Theological Seminary. Moreover, I express my gratitude to two Dubuque theologians who encouraged me along the way—Elmer Colyer and the late Donald G. Bloesch. Other scholars who have provided help through the years include: Mark Noll, Richard Burnett, Kermitt Staggers, Gary Hansen, Dennis Roark, Charles Herman, Dean Rapp, Charles Weber, Edith Blumhofer, Oliver B. Pollak, John Grigg, Bruce Garver, Ben Brick, and Mary Lyons-Carmona. In addition, Darryl G. Hart and Ken Stewart have provided me with key insights into Presbyterian history. Warm thanks also go to Jonathan Gerstner for answering so many questions and allowing me complete access to his father's papers and personal material.

I also want to express my gratitude to Marlin Schiach for his conscientious comments on various drafts. I offer a special thank you to Professor A. Donald MacLeod of Brighton, Ontario, for his friendship, mentoring, and inspiring models of Christian biography. My supervisor, Professor David W. Bebbington, provided wise counsel, careful reading, and astute criticisms. It has been a real blessing to have the opportunity to work with such a caring person and talented historian.

I would also like to extend my appreciation to the members of Avery Presbyterian Church, Bellevue, Nebraska, Murray Presbyterian Church, Murray, Nebraska, and Covenant Presbyterian Church, Omaha, Nebraska. My sincere thanks also go out to my family: John McDonald, Jimmy McDonald, Judge Stanley and Ramona Brinkley, and Jason and Sara Brinkley. My parents, Jan and Kevin McDonald, have been great encouragers throughout my life, and I am appreciative of all they have done for me. I would also like to thank my children, Katie, Meredith, and Parker for allowing their dad to devote so much time to this project. Perhaps someday they will find John Gerstner interesting as well. Lastly, I am grateful for the constant love, patience and support of my wife, Krista. She is a terrific mother and a wonderful partner on life's journey. This work is dedicated to her.

I

Introduction

JOHN HENRY GERSTNER JR. WAS BORN IN 1914 AND RAISED PRIMARILY IN Philadelphia, Pennsylvania. As a young adult he became a member of the United Presbyterian Church of North America (UPCNA) and was actively engaged in Christian ministry, but he also pursued scholarship. He excelled in his academic studies. In 1945 he received a PhD from Harvard University and then began to devote energy to stimulating evangelical thinking in the church and in the academy. He published widely in various journals and periodicals; moreover, he authored numerous books. In his later years the lectures that Gerstner delivered for a para-church ministry were recorded and transmitted through new forms of multimedia. His specialty was Jonathan Edwards (1703–1758), the great colonial American theologian and philosopher. Today he is perhaps best remembered in academic circles for his voluminous writings on Edwards's theology. Yet Gerstner is also known for his work on Reformed apologetics, the cults, and biblical inerrancy. In addition, he wrote on the history of Presbyterianism and evangelicalism. He was an active and well-known writer and churchman, but this study represents the first comprehensive analysis of his life and thought.

During Gerstner's career he involved himself in various Presbyterian and evangelical events and controversies that shaped his reputation. The main impulse in Gerstner's career was injecting conservative evangelical Presbyterian modes of thought into the mainline northern Presbyterian church, but Gerstner also directed efforts more broadly and became a leader in the evangelical movement at large. This study will demonstrate just how much the Pittsburgh professor achieved in his career. He was a strong advocate for his views. Expressions of Gerstner's resolution revealed both personal strengths and weaknesses and this book will identify the ways in which Gerstner's militancy both helped and hurt his career and scholarly reputation. Analyzing the scholar's setbacks and disappointments yields particularly cogent insights into Gerstner's life experiences. Gerstner's tireless work was ended only by his death in 1996.

In 1993, three years before John Gerstner died, a friend wrote a letter to him asking for a "status report from your perspective" on the future of classical Reformed "apologetics."[1] Gerstner responded by saying that while he was "disappointed" with the progress, " [w]e dare never underestimate our sovereign God, or rely much on our own very limited vision."[2] Gerstner's foresight may have had limits, but his large vision of the Reformed faith was realized in significant ways through his many years of energetic teaching, preaching, and writing. Indeed, for over fifty years, he had labored to revitalize and strengthen Presbyterian and Reformed evangelicalism. Even though the influence of the movement had waned in the northern Presbyterian Church (USA) during the 1920s, Presbyterian and Reformed evangelicalism remained within the mainline church and thrived in some older and newly founded Reformed denominations, ministries and schools. Gerstner played a leading role in propelling this Calvinist-orientated evangelicalism into the future. His efforts in this endeavor have been largely ignored, however, and his significance has not been realized. This study analyzes Gerstner's life and thought in relation to the history of the mainline Northern Presbyterian church and the burgeoning evangelical movement and reveals his importance in pre- and post- World War II American religion.

The church historian played a leading role in the post-World War II expansion of evangelicalism through his teaching in both mainline and non-mainline Protestant schools. Unlike most other evangelical scholars who associated themselves with the neo-evangelical movement, Gerstner spent the majority of his career at a mainline Protestant seminary, which during the 1960s and 1970s had a largely progressive ethos. Gerstner's strategy was to provide an evangelical voice in this context and to spread his influence to the other evangelical schools in which he taught. Many students viewed him as a challenging professor as he used the Socratic method to ensure that students had mastered their assigned coursework. Throughout his career he was a dynamic preacher, lecturer, and speaker who spoke forcefully. He had a somewhat gruff voice, which was caused by an asthmatic condition that made him strain as he talked. His fervent messages and his reputation as an excellent speaker allowed him to gain a hearing for conservative theology. As a strong proponent for evangelical beliefs he was not easily dismissed and his opponents knew that he had a sharp intellect.

1. Bogue, Letter to Gerstner.
2. Gerstner, Letter to Bogue.

Gerstner eschewed liberal and neo-orthodox theology in an era when these two theological viewpoints dominated mainline Presbyterian seminary faculties.[3] He could be gracious and charitable, but was uncompromising in his evangelical stance. His conservatism was not always appreciated by others. As a professor of church history and as an evangelical Presbyterian, he stood squarely for what he regarded as the classical Reformed and evangelical position. Comparatively, his life and thought are similar to those of W. Stanford Reid (1916–1996), the stalwart evangelical Canadian Presbyterian historian and renewal leader.[4] Both men were graduates of Westminster Theological Seminary (Pennsylvania), church historians, and mainline evangelical Presbyterian leaders. During Gerstner's long career, he sought to pass on to his readers, students, hearers, and followers a blend of the conservative Calvinist Old Princeton theology combined with the powerful thought of Jonathan Edwards (1703–1758).[5] While many today likely regard this as a strange mixture of differing theological viewpoints, Gerstner attempted to argue for continuity between the legendary New England theologian and the doctrinal doyens of Old Princeton. As an evangelical scholar, he set forth his views in print and refused to allow his beliefs to be marginalized by the mainline northern Presbyterian Church. He engaged in open debate with the leading Presbyterian theologians challenging their agenda for the church. Gerstner also stirred up excitement for Reformed theology in small Presbyterian denominations and in the wider evangelical movement. He helped to create new evangelical renewal organizations and institutions. Gerstner becomes a fascinating historical figure of study partly because he had an uncanny ability to extend his influence into so many different realms of American Protestantism. During his long career the historian was involved with a myriad of denominations, para-church agencies, and educational institutions.

Understanding the distinct Presbyterian tradition in which Gerstner's mind and spiritual life were formed is essential for grasping Gerstner as a young student and scholar. Quentin Skinner, a leading British political theorist and intellectual historian, has emphasized the importance of historians analyzing the intellectual context in which a person lived. Skinner's scholarly goal is to "use the ordinary historical techniques of historical enquiry to grasp [past thinkers'] concepts, to follow their distinctions, to

---

3. Coalter, Mulder, and Weeks, *The Re-Forming Tradition*.

4. On Reid, see MacLeod's ground-breaking biography *W. Stanford Reid*.

5. Old Princeton theology refers to the doctrinal stance of Princeton Theological Seminary (NJ) as it existed from 1812 to 1929.

appreciate their beliefs, and so far as possible to see things their way."[6] To describe Gerstner's life and thought accurately, one must understand the details of the intellectual context in which he emerged. The earliest religious contacts of Gerstner's young life were with a congregation that was part of the United Presbyterian Church in North America (UPCNA). This Presbyterian body had its own distinct history, institutions, and traditions. The denomination was an evangelical Calvinist church, which combined two different Scottish Presbyterian traditions. The UPCNA had its origins in the Scottish Covenanter tradition of the seventeenth century and the Scottish Seceder movement of the eighteenth century.[7] After members of these two church groups migrated to North America, they remained separate entities. However, in 1782 the vast majority of the churches in these two denominations merged to form the Associate Reformed Church. In 1858 the Associate Reformed Church joined with the Associate Synod (a continuing group that did not participate in the church union of 1782) to form the United Presbyterian Church in North America (UPCNA).[8] Throughout the late nineteenth and early twentieth centuries the UPCNA retained an evangelical Reformed theological stance and the church had a robust missionary impulse.[9] Significantly, many UPCNA scholars and institutions were involved in the fundamentalist and evangelical movements. Gerstner, as this book will reveal, emerged out of the world of *evangelical* United Presbyterianism.

The Reformed Protestant tradition has its origins in Switzerland during the great sixteenth century Protestant Reformation and developed under the leadership of Ulrich Zwingli (1484–1531) and John Calvin (1509–1564). While Martin Luther's Reformation movement in Germany influenced the Swiss Reformation, the Swiss developments were not directly dependent on Lutheranism.[10] The Reformed tradition had objections to some parts of the Roman Catholic Church's theology and its worship practices. Instead, it emphasized the need for the church to purify itself by the study and preaching of the Scripture. The Reformed wanted a gospel-centered church that was not beholden to human tradition. The Swiss Reformation had a humanist dimension that stressed *ad fontes*, a return to the

6. Skinner quoted by Coffey and Chapman, "Introduction," 2.

7. Vandoodewaard, *The Marrow Controversy and Seceder Tradition.*

8. Fisk, "United Presbyterian Church in North America," 264–65.

9. Jamieson, *The United Presbyterian Story*; McNaugher, *Theological Education in the United Presbyterian Church and Its Ancestries*; McCulloch, *The United Presbyterian Church and Its Work in America.*

10. Leith, *Introduction to the Reformed Tradition*, 33.

original sources.[11] Reformed scholars studied the Bible's original languages and sought to formulate theology according to God's word. They wanted the church's teachings and worship to have biblical warrant. As Protestants they stressed that salvation was not based on human merit, but rather that one was justified by faith. The Reformed movement spread to France, the Netherlands, Germany, Hungary, the British Isles, and elsewhere. After studying in Geneva, John Knox (1514–1572) returned to Scotland and successfully spread the Reformed tradition in his homeland.[12] The Reformed movement in Britain was referred to as Presbyterian, whereas on the continent it was called Reformed. Calvinists from Scotland and Ireland who immigrated to North America established various Presbyterian denominations in the new land. Presbyterians sought to adhere to Reformed theology and a form of church government where elders ruled over their congregations.

Evangelicalism is a Protestant movement that traces its origins to Great Britain in the 1730s and to the preaching ministries of Howell Harris (1714–1773) and Daniel Rowland (1713–1790). The movement gained phenomenal strength under the gospel preaching ministries of John Wesley (1703–1791) and George Whitefield (1714–1770), and Whitefield helped expand evangelicalism in colonial America.[13] In the new land evangelicalism grew and has come to involve churches from virtually all the American Protestant traditions: Reformed, Methodist, Holiness, Baptist, Episcopal Pentecostal, Lutheran, Mennonite, Plymouth Brethren, and the Scandinavian-American Free Churches. Fundamentalism, which appeared in the late nineteenth and early twentieth centuries, is a form of evangelicalism that is more rigid and less open to mainstream culture.[14] The evangelical movement has been a pan-denominational movement that has involved churches with denominational affiliations, as well as independent churches, and still others that are only loosely affiliated or connected. American evangelicalism has also been deeply influenced by evangelicals in other parts of the world, especially Canada and Great Britain.[15] Evangelicals have differed on various practices and doctrines and yet it is an historically observable coalition, involving both formal and informal connections. David Bebbington, a British historian, offers the most serviceable and best phenomenological definition of the historic evangelical movement in his study *Evangelicalism in Modern Britain* (1989). Bebbington identifies four key characteristics of

11. Ibid., 33–34.
12. Kyle and Johnson, *John Knox*.
13. Bebbington, *Evangelicalism in Modern Britain*, 20–21.
14. Marsden, *Fundamentalism and American Culture*, 3–4.
15. Noll and Rawlyk, eds., *Amazing Grace*.

evangelicalism, which include: conversionism, activism, Biblicism, and cru-cicentrism.[16] Firstly, conversionism is the belief that people need to make a commitment to Christ. Secondly, evangelicals are known for activism because they have been keenly interested in efforts to reach the world with the gospel message and social action. Thirdly, evangelical biblicism reflects the belief that the Bible is the supreme religious authority, God's inspired word. Fourthly, the movement is crucicentric as it stresses Christ's death on the cross as an atonement for sin. Gerstner's life was greatly shaped by the forms of evangelicalism he encountered early in his life and he bore the appellation "evangelical" proudly seeking to be a molder of the movement throughout his career.

The term neo-evangelical is sometimes used to describe evangelicals who emerged from the 1930s seeking to reform fundamentalism and stimu-late fresh evangelical engagement with the broader culture and mainstream intellectual life.[17] Significant scholarly leaders in the neo-evangelical move-ment included Carl F. H. Henry (1913–2003), Edward Carnell (1919–1967), and George Eldon Ladd (1911–1982). These neo-evangelicals pursued a less sectarian approach and fostered dialogue with theological voices outside evangelicalism. Henry, Carnell, and Ladd served as professors at Fuller Theological Seminary in Pasadena, California, which was founded in 1947 and was the chief institutional headquarters for neo-evangelical-ism.[18] Harold John Ockenga (1905–1985), another leader in this evangeli-cal movement, was simultaneously pastor of Park Street Congregational Church (Boston, Massachusetts) and twice president of Fuller (1947–1954, 1960–1963). Billy Graham, the famed evangelist, also had a leadership role in neo-evangelicalism. The movement's mouthpiece was the well-funded periodical *Christianity Today*, which was founded in 1956. This reformist evangelical movement tried to forge an orthodox middle path between conservative evangelicalism and liberal Protestantism. One of Gerstner's former students, Jack Rogers would play a key role, as a Fuller Seminary theologian, in trying to move the neo-evangelical movement in a more pro-gressive direction. Neo-evangelicalism had a prominent role in American Protestantism in the second half of the twentieth century and Gerstner's response to this strategic evangelical initiative will be evaluated.

The dominant mainline Presbyterian body, the Presbyterian Church U.S.A., was also a major factor in Gerstner's life and thought. The origins of the PCUSA can be traced to the first Presbyterians who arrived in North

16. Bebbington, *Evangelicalism in Modern Britain*, 1–19.

17. Noll, *A History of Christianity in the United States and Canada*, 523.

18. On Fuller's history see Marsden's excellent study *Reforming Fundamentalism*.

America in the seventeenth century. In 1706 the first presbytery was formed in the new land and later the first synod was founded in 1716. The denomination's first general assembly was held in 1788.[19] The PCUSA remained the largest American Presbyterian body, but experienced a major split in 1837 when New School and Old School Presbyterians divided over the issue of revivals. New School Presbyterians were pro-revivalists and held to a less strict understanding of the Westminster Confession, whereas members of the Old School were troubled by the tactics of revivalists and maintained a more conservative view of the Westminster Confession.[20] The New School began as a separate denomination in 1837 after Old School Presbyterians were able to eject four New School Synods at that year's General Assembly. The Old School body divided into northern and southern churches at the outbreak of the Civil War in 1861. In the American south the Old and New School churches reunited in 1864. In the north, the Old and New Schools reconciled their theological differences and merged in 1869. The northern mainline church was known as the PCUSA and after the Civil War the southern denomination was named the Presbyterian Church U.S. (PCUS).[21] By the 1930s the PCUSA and the PCUS were the two largest Presbyterian bodies in the United States and John Gerstner's UPCNA ranked third in membership, but far behind.

From 1950 to 1960 Gerstner served as a professor of church history at the UPCNA's only seminary: Pittsburgh-Xenia Theological Seminary (PXTS), located in Pittsburgh, Pennsylvania. Upon a denominational merger, he then taught at the newly consolidated Pittsburgh Theological Seminary (PTS) until his retirement in 1980. Furthermore, he taught as a visiting professor or guest instructor in numerous other academic institutions. Over the course of his life, he was an ordained minister in a number of different denominations. From 1940 to 1958 he served as a UPCNA clergyman. After the historic 1958 church union of the UPCNA and the PCUSA, he then served in the newly formed UPCUSA. When the UPCUSA and the southern PCUS reunited in 1983, Gerstner maintained his ordination in that church for seven years. Lastly, from 1990 to his death in 1996 he was a minister in the PCA, a denomination that split off from the PCUS in 1973.

In order to make sense of Gerstner's intellectual outlook and the trajectory of his career, one must understand the ideological context in which

19. Weeks, "Presbyterian Church (U.S.A.)," 931–32.

20. Marsden, *The Evangelical Mind and the New School Presbyterian Experience*; Gutjahr, *Charles Hodge*; Hoffecker, *Charles Hodge*; Stewart and Moorhead, eds., *Charles Hodge Revisited*.

21. On the history of southern Presbyterianism, see Thompson, *Presbyterians in the South*.

he emerged. Even though Gerstner came of age in the UPCNA, he was affected by an acute crisis that occurred from 1922 to 1936 in the much larger PCUSA. This event, which became known as the "Presbyterian Controversy" or the "Fundamentalist-Modernist Conflict," made a lasting impression on the young Gerstner.[22] His life was largely an extension of this earlier internecine hostility. Grasping the basic history of this momentous Presbyterian episode is essential for understanding Gerstner's career and mind. The great "Presbyterian Controversy" touched the PCUSA in a myriad of ways, from contentious general assemblies to an investigation and reorganization of the PCUSA's flagship theological school, Princeton Theological Seminary. Evidence indicates that the root of the division was doctrinal. Progressive and moderate Presbyterians had resisted conservative policies that required ministers to affirm five doctrines that the general assemblies of 1910, 1916, and 1923 had determined to be "essential and necessary."[23] The five fundamental theological points were the inerrancy of Scripture, the virgin birth, substitutionary atonement, bodily resurrection, and the miracle-working power of Christ. The PCUSA's relative theological conservatism had developed in the 1890s in response to the liberal biblical criticism of Charles Briggs (1841–1913) and Henry Preserved Smith (1847–1927). In an 1892 general assembly statement known as the Portland Deliverance, the PCUSA had affirmed that "[o]ur church holds that the inspired Word, as it came from God, is without error."[24] From the 1890s to the 1920s many Presbyterians campaigned vigorously to ensure that the PCUSA affirmed fundamental Christian doctrine and to reject modernist theology and progressive methods of biblical scholarship.

From 1892 to 1925 Presbyterian traditionalists upheld conservative theological subscription to the defined fundamentals for PCUSA ministers. In reaction to what they considered to be the doctrinal rigidity of their denomination, liberal and moderate Presbyterians mobilized and fought for broader theological tolerance. In 1924 this party within the church created its own statement of belief, which became known as the Auburn Affirmation and declared that the five points were "not the only theories allowed by the Scriptures and our [church's theological] standards."[25] The Auburn Affirmationists argued persuasively for doctrinal liberty and Christian unity. They rejected what they perceived as theological precisionism on the

22. On the history of this significant PCUSA conflict, see Longfield, *The Presbyterian Controversy*; Weston, *Presbyterian Pluralism*.

23. Longfield, *The Presbyterian Controversy*, 25.

24. Portland Deliverance quoted by Longfield, *The Presbyterian Controversy*, 23.

25. Auburn Affirmation quoted by Longfield, *The Presbyterian Controversy*, 79.

grounds that it disrupted the life, mission, and witness of the church. By 1925 conservative Presbyterians had lost control of the PCUSA and previous doctrinal requirements were nullified by the 1926 General Assembly. The Auburn Affirmationists' theological vision was realized at the 1926 General Assembly because that denominational meeting approved a special commission report which made adherence to the five fundamentals non-binding.[26] The 1925 Special Commission had been formed to investigate the cause of unrest within the PCUSA.[27] An alliance of modernist and moderate evangelical Presbyterian forces now provided leadership for the denomination's future. Ultimately, the momentous ecclesiastical conflict became focused primarily on one individual, J. Gresham Machen (1881–1937), who was a distinguished New Testament professor at Princeton Seminary.[28] The 1925 Special Commission determined that Machen, the leader of the conservative Princeton faculty majority, had been the source of conflict within the seminary.

Machen, who had begun teaching at Princeton in 1906, had become known as one of the most cogent conservative Presbyterians. He had achieved initial fame as a result of the incisive arguments he had marshalled against modernist theology in his classic work *Christianity and Liberalism* (1923).[29] The crux of Machen's argument was not that liberals were not Christians, but rather that naturalistic liberalism is not Christianity.[30] He became an ardent supporter of conservative doctrine and a sharp critic of the Auburn Affirmation. In order to limit Machen's influence, the 1929 PCUSA General Assembly voted to reorganize Princeton Seminary and placed two signatories of the Auburn Affirmation on the school's newly formed board of trustees.[31] Incensed by this action, Machen and three other Princeton professors resigned and founded Westminster Theological Seminary in Philadelphia, Pennsylvania. Machen was eventually suspended from the ministry of the PCUSA in 1936 for helping to create a new mission board that would rival what he felt was the liberalized PCUSA's mission board.

Even though Gerstner never studied with Machen, Gerstner was shaped by the controversy in which Machen was engaged. Gerstner entered Westminster Seminary in 1937 and experienced first-hand the aftermath of

26. Longfield, *The Presbyterian Controversy*, 159–60.

27. Ibid., 156–61; Weston, *Presbyterian Pluralism*, 72–81.

28. On Machen's life and thought, see Hart, *Defending the Faith*; Chrisope, *Toward a Sure Faith*.

29. Machen, *Christianity and Liberalism*.

30. Ibid., 2, 160.

31. Longfield, *The Presbyterian Controversy*, 173.

the great Presbyterian conflict. His education in this institution that Machen helped to found reinforced in his mind the need for solid Reformed theology and Gerstner's anti-modernism. In 1940 he earned two degrees from the seminary. Moreover, a few years earlier at Westminster College Gerstner studied under one of Machen's former students, John Orr (1893–1983), who subsequently became Gerstner's mentor and spiritual father. Orr was an advocate of the Old Princeton theology and had been involved in a key scholarly organization that Machen had founded. The evangelical UP subculture, to which Machen had connected himself, also played a part in Gerstner's life and thinking. The Pittsburgh church historian's evangelical churchmanship has its origins in these earlier disputes and the Presbyterian and Reformed evangelicalism Machen had worked diligently to foster.

A very influential system of thought in American Presbyterianism, evangelicalism, and Gerstner's life was the Old Princeton theological tradition. Princeton Seminary had been founded in 1812 and was a bastion of Reformed orthodoxy and doctrinal conservatism until 1929 when the school faced the major disruption headed by Machen and the Old Princeton tradition was largely moved to Westminster Seminary.[32] Old Princeton refers to the seminary and its theological/biblical scholarship as it existed from 1812 to 1929. Old Princeton scholars considered themselves to be the heirs of Calvinism as set down by the Westminster standards and the Swiss theologian Francis Turretin (1623–1687).[33] They held to a strict confessional stance, had a high view of the Bible and maintained a vital piety.[34] Its leaders at the seminary included Archibald Alexander (1772–1851), Charles Hodge (1797–1878), A. A. Hodge (1823–1886), B. B. Warfield (1851–1921), and lastly J. Gresham Machen. Numerous other scholars at the school during this period were also a part of this learned tradition. In the nineteenth century Princeton Seminary taught more students than any other theological institution in America.[35] One point that is sometimes missed is that the Old Princeton tradition lived on at Princeton after 1929 in the work of William Park Armstrong (1874–1944), Casper Wistar Hodge (1870–1937), Geerhardus Vos (1869–1942), and Andrew Blackwood (1882–1956).[36] Under

32. Moorhead, *Princeton Seminary in American Religion and Culture*; Calhoun, *Princeton Seminary*, vols. 1–2.

33. Hoffecker, "Princeton Theology," 202.

34. Hoffecker, *Piety and the Princeton Theologians*.

35. Noll, "Princeton Theology," 19.

36. Armstrong, Hodge, and Vos had great sympathy for Machen's position, but decided to stay at Princeton Seminary. Blackwood came to Princeton the semester after Machen left and was a strong evangelical voice at the school who admired the Old Princeton legacy. On this point, see Adams, *The Homiletical Innovations of Andrew*

the leadership of John Mackay (1889–1983), who served as president of the school from 1936 to 1959, Princeton Seminary had for the most part moved away from the Old Princeton tradition.[37] Nevertheless, Old Princeton continues to attract attention from both detractors and proponents to this very day. Debates about its theological legacy are signs of its continued vitality.

Even though Gerstner had high-profile involvement in numerous well-known and often analyzed UPCUSA events and disputes, he has been astonishingly overlooked. Scholars examine the various church controversies and mention a host of individuals, but not Gerstner. Maybe this is because Gerstner is a recent figure. It remains unclear why scholars have failed to examine the indefatigable Pittsburgh church history professor. Perhaps historians have disregarded him because he represented what is considered to be an ideological extreme, or because he is seen on the losing side in the battles that he fought in the mainline Presbyterian church. It appears that his lack of conformity to the newly-merged entity, the UPCUSA, has largely eliminated Gerstner from Presbyterian history. The UPCNA's 1958 merger with the larger PCUSA has served to obscure the UPCNA's history and the former UPCNA churchman. Indeed, since the merger of the UPCNA and the PCUSA in 1958, very few historical studies of the UPCNA church, or of any UPCNA figures, have been published. Moreover, after church union it seems apparent that UPCNA history was viewed as too backward looking for those who were now members of the new UPCUSA (after 1983 the PCUSA). Church union made previous denominational identity murky. An added problem is that in the 1958 merger the newly combined church took the "U" from UPCNA to create the UPCUSA and this seems to have led to general confusion and to a blurring of backgrounds in the history of the UPCNA. Presbyterian mergers and the allegiance expected to the newly formed communions (the UPCUSA and the PCUSA) have served to consign the UPCNA and Gerstner to near oblivion.

Yet there are some shafts of light in the cloudy history of the UPCNA. In a 1994 edited volume on the history of Pittsburgh Theological Seminary, *Ever a Frontier*, some significant essays are offered on the history of UPCNA seminaries.[38] Another notable exception to UPCNA neglect is A. Donald MacLeod's biography of George Murray, a Boston evangelical UPCNA minister.[39] In addition, Charles Partee's biography of a key UPCNA and

---

Blackwood. Blackwood had a UPCNA background.

37. On Mackay, see Metzger's *The Hand and the Road.*

38. Walther, ed., *Ever a Frontier.*

39. MacLeod, *George Murray of the "U.P."* Two helpful, but older dissertations on the UPCNA are Coleman's "The Life and Works of John McNaugher" and Kelly's "The

later UPCUSA missionary Don McClure does highlight UPNCA mission-ary activity abroad.[40] Joseph Moore has produced a fine study that deals with the political ideology of the UP and the larger Covenanter/Seceder Presbyterian tradition.[41] Jim Dennison and Albert Stuart have also offered some illuminating essays on the UPCNA's 1925 confessional change and the church's evangelical Calvinism.[42] In 2008, on the one hundred and fiftieth anniversary of the founding of the UPCNA, Thomas Gilliland produced a self-published, popular and brief survey of the UPCNA, which Gilliland claimed was "intentionally a sketch rather than a history, a tribute rather than an analysis."[43] More general treatments of American Presbyterians have not been too kind to the UPCNA. In Darryl Hart's 2013 noteworthy history of Calvinism, the UPCNA is mentioned only once in a reference to its merger with the PCUSA.[44] In Bradley Longfield's excellent study entitled *Presbyterians and American Culture* (2013), the UPCNA is discussed on two pages, but here again only in reference to church union negotiations.[45]

Ernest Sandeen, in *The Roots of Fundamentalism* (1970), does devote several discussions to the millenarian strain among UPCNA professors and seminaries.[46] Tyler Flynn's 2007 dissertation on Calvinism and public life in western Pennsylvania also reveals some links among the UPs, Gerstner, and the broader evangelical movement.[47] George Marsden makes no mention of UPCNA conservatives in his magisterial *Fundamentalism and American Culture* (1980, revised 2006).[48] In his study, Marsden neglected UPCNA involvement in the writing of *The Fundamentals*, the League of Evangelical Students, and in the founding of a South Carolina Bible college.[49] This mi-

---

History of Religious Instruction in United Presbyterian Colleges." Older works and essays that are also helpful include McCulloch's *The United Presbyterian Church and Its Work In America*; Jamison, *The United Presbyterian Story*; and Gerstner, "The United Presbyterian Church," 86–101.

40. Partee, *Adventure in Africa*.

41. Moore, *Founding Sins*.

42. Dennison Jr., "John McNaugher and the Confessional Revision of 1925," 221–231; Stuart, "Diminishing Distinctives."

43. Gilliland Jr., *Truth and Love*.

44. Hart, *Calvinism*, 292.

45. Longfield, *Presbyterians and American Culture*.

46. Sandeen, *The Roots of Fundamentalism*.

47. Flynn, "Calvinism and Public Life: A Case Study of Western Pennsylvania 1900–1955."

48. Marsden, *Fundamentalism and American Culture*.

49. Marsden does note that Robert McQuilkin founded the Columbia Bible College in South Carolina, but there is no mention that McQuilkin was a UPCNA minister

nor criticism aside, Marsden's work has been enormously helpful in trying to understand the history of Reformed evangelicalism in American history. His books on New School Presbyterianism, Fundamentalism, the history of Fuller Seminary and, Jonathan Edwards are indispensable resources for grasping key theological and ecclesiastical developments.[50] Moreover, the work of D. G. Hart has been crucial for the historical study of twentieth-century Reformed evangelicalism because it highlights the beginnings of conservative dissent within the mainline Presbyterian Church. Hart has written an illuminating biography of J. Gresham Machen and provided valuable histories of the OPC and American Presbyterianism.[51] Bradley Longfied's *The Presbyterian Controversy* also provides a thorough evaluation of conservative dissent, differences among evangelical Presbyterians, and the ecclesiastical pyrotechnics that resulted.

Barry Hankins's biography of Francis Schaeffer, the conservative Presbyterian thinker, illustrates how strongly the earlier conflict could affect someone's subsequent career and their attempt to shape the modern evangelical movement.[52] In addition, William R Glass' *Strangers in Zion* highlights the Presbyterian contribution to fundamentalism in the American south.[53] Glass' book rightly emphasizes the momentous role Robert McQuilkin played in developing southern fundamentalism. Unfortunately, Glass does not mention that McQuilkin was ordained in the UPCNA and was privately educated by a UPCNA seminary professor before founding Columbia Bible College (SC). Dale Soden's biography of Mark Matthews (1867–1940) is an intriguing account of an evangelical Presbyterian minister in Seattle, Washington, who sought to transform his city with progressive social reform.[54] Despite these studies a comprehensive historical analysis of twentieth-century Presbyterian and Reformed evangelicalism in America has not yet been written.

---

trained by the UPCNA archaeologist Melvin Grove Kyle. See Marsden, *Fundamentalism and American Culture*, 96.

50. Marsden, *The Evangelical Mind and the New School Presbyterian Experience*; *Fundamentalism and American Culture*; *Reforming Fundamentalism*; *Jonathan Edwards*.

51. Hart, *Defending the Faith*; *Seeking a Better Country*; *Between the Times*; and Hart and Muether, *Fighting the Good Fight*.

52. Hankins, *Francis Schaeffer*.

53. Glass, *Strangers in Zion*.

54. Soden, *Reverend Mark Matthews*. Schlect's MA thesis on Roy Brumbaugh, an evanlgelical Presbyterian pastor, is also a helpful study on how the Fundamentalist-Modernist conflict affected the Pacific Northwest. See Schlect, "J. Gresham Machen, Roy T. Brumbaugh, and the Presbyterian Schism of 1934–1936."

Another curious fact is that Gerstner barely appears in the secondary literature on the history of American evangelicalism. He is not mentioned in Brian Stanley's masterly *The Global Diffusion of Evangelicalism* (2013), nor is he listed in the *Biographical Dictionary of Evangelicals* (2003). The Pittsburgh church historian is also not found in Molly Worthen's landmark study of evangelical intellectual life, *Apostles of Reason* (2014).[55] In their helpful studies of evangelicalism, Joel Carpenter and Rudolph Nelson only briefly identify Gerstner as one among the Harvard evangelicals of the 1940s.[56] Moreover, Gary Dorrien, the eminent historian of liberal theology, offers only scant mention of Gerstner in his *The Remaking of Evangelical Theology* (1998).[57] In a 2011 essay, Philip Eveson, an English scholar, does point out Gerstner's British connection by noting that Carl Henry and Gerstner spoke at the London Theological Seminary.[58]

The one area in which Gerstner's efforts have not been ignored is in the field of Jonathan Edwards studies. Yet here again D.G. Hart spends only two and one-half pages explaining Gerstner's role in reviving Edwards amongst evangelicals.[59] Douglas Sweeney in *The Cambridge Companion to Jonathan Edwards* offers a paragraph on Gerstner as the "leading pioneer in the evangelical Edwards renaissance."[60] In the same volume Stephen Crocco, a former Gerstner student, offers some brief discussion of Gerstner's early work with the esteemed Yale works of Jonathan Edwards.[61] In *The Princeton Companion to Jonathan Edwards*, Mark Noll mentions Gerstner as someone who "introduced thousands of students to Edwards' theology as an impeccable version of classical Calvinism."[62] Kenneth Minkema comments on Gerstner in his essay "Jonathan Edwards in the Twentieth Century."[63] While the above scholars write within the mainstream of Edwards scholarship, Gary Crampton's work on Gerstner represents an important contribution from within the conservative Reformed community. Crampton's *Interpreting Jonathan*

55. Worthen, *Apostles of Reason*.

56. Carpenter, *Revive Us Again*, 191; Nelson, *The Making and Unmaking of an Evangelical Mind*.

57. Dorrien, *The Remaking of Evangelical Theology*.

58. Eveson, "Lloyd-Jones and Ministerial Education," 194.

59. Hart, "Before the Young, Restless, and Reformed," 239–42. There has also been some analysis of Gerstner's apologetic position. See, Juha, *Theological Epistemology of Contemporary American Confessional Reformed Apologetics*; and Lewis, *Testing Christianity's Truth Claims*, 60–71.

60. Sweeney, "Evangelical Tradition in America," 230.

61. Crocco, "Edwards Intellectual Legacy," 314–16.

62. Noll, "Edwards Theology After Edwards," 305.

63. Minkema, "Jonathan Edwards in the Twentieth Century," 659–87.

Edwards (2011) is a large-scale overview and analysis of Gerstner's three-volume study of Edwards' theology.[64] The present thesis provides a more detailed historical evaluation of Gerstner's work on Edwards and shows that Gerstner was indeed a long-time promoter of the colonial theologian.

In order to understand Gerstner it is necessary to have some knowledge of the cultural context in which he lived. The twentieth century was a time of great change in American society. From 1920 to 1976 the Gross National Product of the United States grew from $88.9 billion to $1.69 trillion.[65] The country experienced economic gains, but it also advanced in the areas of race and gender equality. In the middle of the century African-Americans engaged in the struggle for civil rights and effectively used a strategy of non-violent resistance.[66] In 1954 the US Supreme Court ruled in *Brown v. Board of Education* that segregation was unconstitutional, and Chief Justice Earl Warren stated that all people "are entitled to exactly the same treatment as all the others."[67] The 1964 Civil Rights Act also put an end to enforced segregation. In addition, the number of women in the workforce rose steadily during the century and illustrated a major social shift. From the beginning of World War II to the mid-1980s the number of women in the workforce jumped from one-quarter to nearly two-thirds.[68] These dramatic advances in economics, civil rights, and occupational opportunities for women coincided with serious change within American religion. As Americans grew in prosperity, achieved civil rights and moved away from traditional gender roles in the workplace the country became more focused on ordinary citizens. In the sphere of religion this meant that the older established mainline churches went into a period of membership loss, whereas evangelical Protestantism (largely populist) experienced growth. From 1966 to 1987 the PCUSA lost over 1.2 million members.[69] Evangelical Protestantism, however, during this period grew exponentially. For example, from 1960 to 1997 the Southern Baptist Convention grew by almost 6 million members.[70] Between 1965 and 1989 the Assemblies of

64. Crampton, *Interpreting Jonathan Edwards.*

65. Snowman, *America Since 1920.*

66. White, *Black Leadership in America 1895–1968.*

67. Warren quoted by Abraham in *America Transformed*, 123.

68. Chafe, *The Paradox of Change*, 221.

69. Longfield, *The Presbyterian Controversy*, 3.

70. Noll, *The Old Religion in the New World*, 178. Noll, an American historian, identifies conservative Protestants as members of fundamentalist, evangelical, holiness, or Pentecostal churches.

God expanded 121 percent.[71] By 1996, the year of Gerstner's death, about one in four Americans was affiliated with a conservative Protestant church, whereas not quite one in six Americans identified as a mainline Protestant.[72] American Protestantism changed dramatically after World War II and the old Protestant mainline faced staggering losses. A study of Gerstner's life and career offers important insights on conservative dissent within this dramatic period of mainline Presbyterian decline.

This book will now provide a survey of the chapters that will follow. Chapter 2 analyzes Gerstner's early years and education. Gerstner was not raised in a Christian home, nor did Gerstner receive religious instruction as a child or youth. In high school Gerstner was exposed to Christianity at a UPCNA church, but it was not until after high school that Gerstner had a conversion to Christ. This chapter will investigate Gerstner's academic training at the Philadelphia School of the Bible, Westminster College (Pennsylvania), Pittsburgh-Xenia Theological Seminary, the University of Pittsburgh, Westminster Theological Seminary (Pennsylvania), and Harvard University. Gerstner's experiences in these schools, along with the theological controversy in the PCUSA, proved pivotal in his theological and intellectual development. This chapter will examine the religious context, evangelical United Presbyterianism, and its relation to Machen and the conservatives in the PCUSA.

Chapter 3 shows Gerstner as an emerging Reformed scholar at the UPCNA's Pittsburgh-Xenia Theological Seminary. During the 1950s Pitt-Xenia had become a more explicit evangelical center of scholarship, and Gerstner was helping to strengthen the school's ties to the wider evangelical world. He did this primarily through his involvement with a new evangelical periodical *Christianity Today*. Gerstner's book reviews and articles reveal Gerstner's early thinking. His participation in the nascent evangelical movement and his association with smaller Reformed bodies reveals that, early in his career, Gerstner had the ability to speak to a wide audience. By the end of the 1950s, however, the UPCNA had merged with the PCUSA to form the UPCUSA, and, as a result, Pitt-Xenia consolidated with the PCUSA's seminary in Pittsburgh—Western Theological Seminary. The loss of Gerstner's institutional and denominational identity was traumatic for the young historian.

Chapter 4 reveals Gerstner's role as an author and defender of evangelical beliefs. During this period he established himself as a writer and continued his work with *Christianity Today*. He faced struggles at the newly

71. Reeves, *Twentieth-Century America*, 284.
72. Noll, *The Old Religion in the New World*, 179.

created Pittsburgh Theological Seminary and in the recently created UP-CUSA. He opposed the development of a new confession and the making of a new *Book of Confessions*. Among UPCUSA scholars Gerstner stood virtu-ally alone in his criticisms of these important doctrinal changes. Moreover, he continued to write on Edwards, and, by the end of the decade, was given a key role in the field of Edwards studies. He also began work as an adjunct professor at a strictly evangelical seminary, Trinity Evangelical Divinity School (TEDS). Another area that will be analyzed is Gerstner's role in lead-ing an evangelical student group at PTS.

Chapter 5 examines Gerstner's work as a shaper of modern evan-gelicalism. He continued to teach at PTS and TEDS and became involved in a new study center that had been founded by his protégé, R. C. Sproul. Gerstner sided with those who sought to defend the doctrine of biblical inerrancy, and he helped create an important organization to defend iner-rancy. The church historian experienced professional disappointment, but he carried on with his writing and teaching ministry. A key setback will be analyzed. He also became embroiled in a major UPCUSA church court case involving one of his students and this will also be examined.

Chapter 6 traces Gerstner's career in the decade after his 1980 retire-ment from PTS. In this period he became involved in a nationally known heresy case, which thrust the church historian into a fierce denominational showdown. His role as a theologian-in-residence at a large Midwestern PCUSA church will also be evaluated. He continued to write, producing a key work that defended what he labeled as classical Reformed apologetics.

Chapter 7 analyzes Gerstner's final years as a teacher, lecturer, and writer. In the last six years of his life, he produced several polemical works that addressed issues that he thought had the power to weaken the evan-gelical movement. During this phase of his career, he also published his three-volume survey of Jonathan Edwards' theology. These writings will be analyzed along with Gerstner's departure from the PCUSA and the criti-cisms he made of the denomination and its seminaries.

The goal of this book is to offer a critical evaluation of Gerstner's life and thought. Gerstner's career was one of challenge *and* opportunity. Re-markably, some of his failures led to successes in alternative areas. In other respects Gerstner did face rejection, both academic and ecclesiastical. Con-ceivably the reason why historians have neglected Gerstner is that some of his failures were quite visible and this led him to move increasingly outside mainstream scholarship and church life. This viewpoint is understand-able, but it is misguided and lacks historical awareness. Gerstner, as this study will show, was an important Presbyterian and evangelical leader in the twentieth century and his vision lives on in contemporary Presbyterian and Reformed evangelicalism. A study of Gerstner's life and thought provides a much-needed corrective to American Presbyterian history because it offers the analysis of someone who came from the evangelical UPCNA tradition and then experienced the post-World War II decline of mainline Presbyterianism and the rise of latter day Presbyterian and Reformed evangelicalism. This book sheds much-needed light on mainline evangelical Presbyterianism and on the Reformed wing of American evangelicalism. Just as Glen Scorgie's fine study of James Orr (1844–1913), a Scottish Presbyterian theologian, revealed Orr's desire for the theological continuity of evangelical Calvinism, this study will show that in America that kind of continuity, in a slightly more conservative form, existed in Gerstner.[73] The Pittsburgh church historian, perhaps more than anyone else, transmitted the Presbyterian and Reformed evangelicalism of his young adult years to the present-day expressions of the movement.

73. Scorgie, *A Call for Continuity.*

The Making of an Evangelical Scholar
(1914–1949)

JOHN GERSTNER'S LIFE AND THOUGHT WERE SIGNIFICANTLY SHAPED BY the experiences and influences of his early life. Growing up in Philadelphia, Pennsylvania, he was shaped by religious movements that had touched the city of brotherly love. Gerstner's parents and a high school sweetheart played critical roles in his formative years. His conversion in 1932 changed his life forever. Another seminal factor in his development was the variety of his education. He studied at a wide variety of institutions which all affected him in different ways. Exactly how Gerstner's diverse educational experiences transformed him is a major issue to be analyzed. The young scholar's mind and church commitment were also shaped by the world of *evangelical* United Presbyterianism. The theological character and evangelical impulse of the United Presbyterian Church of North America (UPCNA) form another key issue to be investigated. The influence of Gerstner's academic preparation and religious commitment was immense and must be evaluated in order to understand Gerstner's life and thought.

John Henry Gerstner Jr. was born on November 22, 1914 in Tampa, Florida. His father John Sr. had immigrated to the United States from Darmstadt, Germany, when he was six years old. His mother Margie Wilson had grown up a southerner in Macon, Georgia, where her father was in charge of a turpentine factory.[1] John Sr. was working as a waiter in Tampa when his son was born; their son would be the couple's only child. Shortly after John Henry came into the world, Gerstner's parents decided to move the family to Baltimore, Maryland, and then shortly thereafter to Philadelphia, Pennsylvania. Gerstner spent his childhood and early teenage years living in Philadelphia. Even though Gerstner's parents had had some

1. Gerstner, Interview with Coffin.

earlier connection in their lives to a church, Gerstner often repeated that it was the church that they "stayed away from."[2] His father had a Lutheran background, but did not attend. Gerstner commented that his mother "was equally apathetic about her Methodism." Looking back on his early years, Gerstner noted, "I had no religious rearing."[3] Gerstner recalled that he had loving parents who taught him cleanliness and respect for women. Yet the 1930 US Census reveals that Gerstner's parents had divorced and that the father and son were lodgers in a family home owned by J. Louis Barrick, a Philadelphia attorney.[4] In retrospect Gerstner described his relationship with his father as "friendly with each other, but nothing intimate." While Gerstner's parents were not hostile to religion, his childhood was void of any familial Christian influences. Gerstner appears to have had a somewhat challenging childhood.

It seems most likely that Gerstner attended Shaw Junior High School, which was just a few blocks from the home he lived in. Gerstner then enrolled in the West Philadelphia High School, a large public school that had been built in 1912 and took up an entire city block.[5] At West Philadelphia, Gerstner "edited the school newspaper and was active in bowling and debate." Academically the young high school student excelled, and in 1932 he graduated eighth in a class of 300.[6] Gerstner lived a lower-middle class lifestyle in Upper Darby, which was a booming suburb of Philadelphia in the 1920s. From 1920 to 1929 Upper Darby grew from nine thousand to forty thousand residents.[7] Gerstner's father was a "[r]estaurant [p]roprietor," and his mother was a homemaker.[8] As a teenager Gerstner sold newspapers on the street corner for the *Philadelphia Evening Bulletin*; this reveals a youthful industriousness that included paid work. During high school Gerstner also developed a romantic relationship that would prove influential in his life. The young woman Gerstner dated was a United Presbyterian (UP) who attended the local Beverly Hills United Presbyterian Church (UPCNA).[9] Because of his relationship with this young woman, Gerstner began attending

2. Gerstner, Interview with Sproul.

3. Gerstner, Interview with Coffin.

4. 1930 United States Census.

5. "Public Education: High Schools."

6. "'4 Presidents' is Distance Runner."

7. Lieber, "U. Darby Chronicle From Farm to Suburb."

8. The occupation of Gerstner's father is listed on Gerstner's undergraduate transcript from Westminster College. The occupation of Gerstner's mother was confirmed in an interview with Gerstner, August 8, 2013.

9. Larsen, Interview with the author; Gerstner, Interview with Coffin, 1–2.

Beverly Hills' worship service and youth group meetings, which provided him with his first experiences within a Christian church.

Gerstner later confessed that during this early period, "I didn't get the Christian message . . . I didn't grasp it at the time; it didn't move me."[10] In 1932 Beverly Hills had a new pastor, Roy Grace, who was solidly evangelical.[11] Even though Gerstner had been attending church, the Christian faith continued to be an incomprehensible abstraction for him. Gerstner recalled, "it was not necessarily the pastor's fault; I may have been thinking more about the girl than the sermons."[12] After Gerstner's high school graduation in 1932, his career plans and religious faith remained uncertain. During the summer, he coincidently ran into one of his former junior high physical education teachers. When Gerstner mentioned that he was not sure what he wanted to do next in his life, his teacher said, "well why don't you go down to the Philadelphia School of the Bible," an institution that was founded in 1914 by Bible teachers C. I. Scofield and William L. Pettengill.[13] Gerstner soon visited the Bible school and asked a school official, "what do you teach here?" One of the institution's officers, J. D. Adams, responded to the youthful inquiry with a thirty-minute lecture on the content and meaning of the Bible, "especially the crimson stream, the Blood of Christ" flowing through Scripture.[14] It was a life-changing conversation between the young student and the administrator.

As Gerstner walked out of the school and down its steps, he perceived that he finally understood the heart of the gospel message. Later he said that his time with Adams was the "[m]ost important half hour of his life."[15] It was a momentous meeting: the inquiring student had discovered a personal faith. What is clear is that Adams did answer Gerstner's question. The extent to which Adams's reply incorporated an apologetic approach is unknown. Perhaps Gerstner's significant meeting with the dean led him to have a high view of apologetics. The young student, eager to learn more, proceeded to take a three-month course at the school, where he developed an enthusiastic attitude towards evangelism. Beverly Hills's pastor, Roy

10. Gerstner, Interview with Coffin, 2.

11. Larsen, Interview with the author.

12. Gerstner, Interview with Coffin, 2.

13. Gerstner, Interview with Sproul.

14. Gerstner told his conversion story on several occasions, but he never identified the school official. Hui, the Cairn University librarian, examined school catalogues to provide me with the identity of the school official and background information on the Philadelphia School of the Bible. Hui, Interview with the author.

15. Gerstner, Interview with Coffin, 2.

Grace, had been a graduate of Philadelphia School of the Bible and later had attended the United Presbyterian's Pittsburgh Seminary before entering the UP ministry.[16] Presumably Grace recognized Gerstner's promise and helped to give guidance on Gerstner's future education. Grace encouraged Gerstner to attend the UPCNA's Westminster College in New Wilmington, Pennsylvania. Westminster provided a Christian liberal arts education and the school seemed a good opportunity for the budding evangelical student. In September 1932 Gerstner, with ten dollars in his pocket, loaded up his "broken-down old Dodge" and set off on the three-hundred-and-forty-mile journey to Westminster.[17] The exuberant, college-bound young man had the goal of becoming a medical missionary because he wanted to help people with their physical and spiritual needs.[18]

At Westminster Gerstner excelled and was actively engaged in the life of the small liberal arts college. He helped to revive two "nearly dead campus organizations, the Non-Fraternity Group and the Gospel Team." The gospel team provided churches with preaching, singing, and young people's meetings. For two years Gerstner headed the Westminster gospel team as the members traveled to United Presbyterian, PCUSA, and Methodist churches in western Pennsylvania and eastern Ohio. In his junior year, he headed the campus Young Men's Christian Association (YMCA) organization. The YMCA had a special role on America's college campuses as a large-scale, nationally prominent fellowship devoted to the practical aspects of the Christian faith.[19] Gerstner was showing signs of leadership. The 1936 *Argo*, the college's yearbook, displays a photograph of the YMCA group that shows Gerstner sitting in the center of the front row; the photograph also shows a Bible professor, John Orr, the organization's faculty adviser, sitting at the end of the front row.[20] During his first two years at Westminster, Gerstner worked in a sanatorium for his room and board. In his last two years he served as "an instructor in Bible study."[21] Gerstner was a serious student, but he was also highly involved in student groups. As a senior, he was the president of the college's nationally affiliated debating fraternity, Tau Kappa Alpha.[22] Gerstner's preparation in this area would have a lasting effect. He

16. "Grace, LeRoy Emerson," 247.

17. Gerstner, Interview with Coffin, 2.

18. Ibid., 2.

19. Ringenberg, *The Christian College*, 148.

20. *Argo*, 1936 Westminster College, 126.

21. "'4 Presidents' is Distance Runner."

22. Ibid.

also ran on the school's cross-country team for a three-year period.[23] He learned the kind of physical discipline and endurance that is necessary for a distance runner. Gerstner was an active participant in campus life and thrived as a student leader.

In his last year at the college he also played the lead role in a dramatic production of Percival Wilde's *The Finger of God* (1915). In December of his senior year the *Philadelphia Evening Bulletin* noted that Gerstner's "hobby is not golf or tennis or picture shows, but philosophy and the study of archeology [sic] of the Old Testament."[24] The newspaper also noted that Gerstner had originally planned to be a "medical missionary but now he plans to become a minister." Gerstner spent his first two years as a science major in order to prepare for medicine, but changed his major to Bible in his junior year. Apparently, a class in "embryology" persuaded him that he was not meant for medicine.[25] The faculty member who influenced Gerstner most profoundly at Westminster was John Orr (1884–1983), the Bible professor. Looking back at this time sixty years later, Gerstner noted that "the influence of Dr. John Orr was absolutely crucial" in his life.[26] Orr was a quiet man of deep learning and the only non-UP Bible professor to teach at a UPCNA college prior to the 1950s.[27] Orr retained his membership in the Presbyterian Church (USA)[hereafter PCUSA] and had graduated from the College of Wooster, Princeton University, and Princeton Seminary before undertaking further studies at the University of Berlin where he listened to Adolf von Harnack (1851–1930), the great German theologian and church historian, lecture.[28] After two years of graduate study in Germany, Orr then had spent eleven years in PCUSA parish ministry. The PCUSA was a much larger northern Presbyterian denomination that was closely tied to

23. Ibid.

24. Ibid.

25. Gerstner, Interview with Coffin, 2.

26. Ibid., 3.

27. Kelly, "The History of Religious Instruction in United Presbyterian Colleges," 131–32.

28. Orr received his BA from the College of Wooster (1907), an MA from Princeton University (1909), a BD from Princeton Theological Seminary (1910), did graduate work at the University of Berlin (1911–1913), and earned a PhD from the University of Pittsburgh (1931). Orr served as the Gelston-Winthrop Fellow in didactic and polemical theology at Princeton Theological Seminary in the 1910–1911 academic year. He also served pastorates at the First Presbyterian Church in Middleport, OH (1913–1919) and at First Presbyterian Church in Howell, MI (1920–1928). At Wooster Orr was a friend with Arthur and Karl Compton. Arthur became a Nobel prize-winning physicist and Karl spent eighteen years as the president of Massachusetts Institute of Technology (1930–1948). On this friendship see John Orr Appreciation Dinner.

the mainstream of American culture and part of the old historic Protestant mainline.[29] The Scotch-Irish influenced UPCNA was also a northern denomination, but had only around 175,000 members in 1930, compared to the PCUSA, which had over 2,000,000 members.[30] Orr, the PCUSA clergyman, had arrived at the UPCNA's Westminster College in 1928 and completed his PhD degree in philosophy from the University of Pittsburgh in 1931. Orr relished learning, but he might have also been required by W. Charles Wallace (1875–1934), Westminster's president, to complete his doctorate. Wallace, a UPCNA minister, worked hard to improve the college's academic standards by hiring faculty with excellent credentials who held the PhD degree.[31] Orr's Pittsburgh dissertation, written under the direction of Mont Robertson Gabbert (1889–1957), a philosopher, analyzed the early phases of English deism.[32] At Westminster, Orr exposed his students to Reformed theology and taught the junior year "Christian Evidences" class. Probably Orr used Floyd E. Hamilton's *Basis of the Christian Faith* (1927) as the course textbook.[33] The Westminster professor sought to defend the faith using a reasoned evidentialist apologetic. Orr was committed to the idea that Christianity needed to be defended on rational grounds. This point will be further explained later.

During one particular lecture Orr stated to his class that "[r]egeneration precedes faith." Orr's words rattled Gerstner. Prior to the lecture, Gerstner believed that he was responsible for his own faith. Orr, however, was teaching that faith was not simply a matter of human choice, but rather the work of God in one's life. For the next few weeks Gerstner agonized over what Orr had said. He prayed about the issue and read Jonathan Edwards, the great eighteenth-century colonial theologian, and Charles Hodge, the famed nineteenth-century Princeton theologian, in an effort to make some sense of the Reformed doctrine of election.[34] Finally, after three weeks of contemplation and study, Gerstner accepted the Calvinist theology that

29. Longfield, *The Presbyterian Controversy*, 4.

30. On the membership statistics of the two denominations, see Luidens, "Numbering the Presbyterian Branches: Membership Trends Since Colonial Times," 39–42.

31. Gamble, *The Westminster Story*, 89.

32. Orr, *English Deism*, 6; Orr, "Eighteenth Century English Deism and Its Sources."

33. Kelly, "The History of Religious Instruction in United Presbyterian Colleges." Kelly notes that in the early 1950s Orr was using a 1946 edition of Hamilton's textbook. The book was originally published in 1927. Hamilton graduated from the College of Wooster (1916), studied at Princeton Seminary from 1916 to 1919 and then received his BD and ThM from Princeton Seminary (1926, 1927).

34. Gerstner, Interview with Coffin, 3.

had initially puzzled him. The young Bible major became close to Orr as Gerstner was charged by his professor with teaching assistant responsibilities that included leading Bible studies and grading papers. Orr was a great encourager to the aspiring student, and Gerstner experienced academic success during his undergraduate years. Gerstner graduated on June 8, 1936 with a Bible degree and finished fifth in a class of one hundred and fourteen students.[35] No professor would exert more influence on Gerstner than Orr.

Gerstner, whose parents did not attend church and were apathetic about faith, had found a spiritual father in Orr. Their relationship would prove to be a lasting one. In order to understand the intellectual and theological environment of Westminster College and the United Presbyterian Church during Gerstner's college years, it is necessary to analyze the UPCNA's key intellectual leaders and institutions and how they related to the wider evangelical world of the first third of the twentieth century. An examination of the UPCNA's evangelical heritage in this period will shed important light on Gerstner and the development of his thought. Moreover, an awareness of this rich background will also allow for a fuller understanding of the subsequent history of the UPCNA and the contentious atmosphere of the seminary Gerstner would later serve for thirty years. It is essential to begin the analysis in 1913, so that the UPCNA's connection to conservative Protestantism and evangelical scholarship can be revealed.

In Xenia, Ohio, during the afternoon of May 6, 1913, the campus of the UP's Xenia Seminary was in a state of celebration. Xenia was one of the UPCNA's two seminaries. At an assembly of gathered guests, students and faculty, James T. McCrory, a UP pastor, rose to celebrate the career of William G. Moorehead (1836–1914), Xenia's distinguished president.[36] McCrory noted that Moorehead's work as a "beloved brother and teacher has wrought itself into the fabric of the United Presbyterian Church." He went on to argue that compared to many other denominations "in this country or in any country . . . the United Presbyterian Church [has] stood firm as adamant against the faith destroying speculations" of "new philosophy," "Darwinian evolution," and "the assaults of Higher Criticism."[37] Moorehead, a spirited defender of the Christian faith, had indeed helped to keep the UPCNA doctrinally conservative in an age of growing religious uncertainty. In the years just prior to his death in 1914, the Xenia Seminary president's work as an apologist had become more visible as he became one of the contributors to *The Fundamentals* (1910–1915), a series of widely

35. Gerstner Undergraduate Transcript, Registrar's Office, Westminster College.
36. McCrory, "A Message From the Past to the Present and the Future," 47–52.
37. Ibid., 49.

circulated paperback volumes devoted to a presentation of Christian truth. Overall, three million copies of the *The Fundamentals* were sent out free of charge to pastors, Christian workers, missionaries, theological students, and others by the Southern California oil tycoon and millionaire Lyman Stewart.[38] Moorehead and another significant UPCNA scholar, Melvin Grove Kyle (1858–1932), both wrote for *The Fundamentals* while serving as professors at Xenia Seminary. Moorehead, who was twenty-two years older than Kyle, had begun teaching New Testament at Xenia in 1873 and had become president of the institution in 1899.[39] He contributed two essays to *The Fundamentals*: one in 1910 and the other in 1912.[40] The staunchly evangelical temperament of the UPCNA was being put on full display in the *Fundamentals*.

By 1913, after teaching at Xenia for forty years, Moorehead had established himself as a leading conservative apologist and had helped to shape the evangelical character of his beloved UPCNA. Moorehead's junior colleague Melvin Grove Kyle had begun his career at Xenia in 1908, serving as lecturer and then professor of biblical archaeology at the seminary. Kyle had earned an international reputation for his pioneering work, publications, and archaeological excavations with William F. Albright (1891–1971), the noted Johns Hopkins University archaeologist. In a 1916 address that Kyle published in *Bibliotheca Sacra*, he noted that Xenia "was the first Theological Seminary in America to give distinct recognition to the new science of biblical archaeology as a separate Department of Seminary work."[41] Kyle firmly established the institution as a world leader in the field of biblical archaeology.[42] Even though Kyle was in the vanguard of archaeological research, he remained firmly committed to conservative evangelical convictions, especially the historical trustworthiness of the Bible. On the basis of Kyle's vast learning, his essay in *The Fundamentals* attempted to show that the "recent testimony of archaeology to Scripture . . . is definitely and uniformly favorable to the Scriptures . . ."[43] In his book *The Deciding*

38. Marsden, *Fundamentalism and American Culture*, 119.

39. Trollinger, "William Gallogly Moorehead," 164.

40. Moorehead's first essay argued that the "moral glory of Jesus" offers "[p]roof of [the Bible's] inspiration." His second short treatise analyzed and refuted the theology of Charles T. Russell, the founder of the Jehovah Witnesses. The Xenia theologian labelled Russell's theology as "counterfeit Christianity." Moorehead, "The Moral Glory of Jesus Christ: A Proof of Inspiration," 61; Moorehead, "Millennial Dawn: A Counterfeit of Christianity," 130.

41. Kyle, "The Bible in the Light of Archaeological Discoveries," 2.

42. Long, *Planting and Reaping Albright*, 21–26.

43. Kyle, "The Recent Testimony of Archaeology," 330.

Voice of the Monuments in Biblical Criticism (1912) Kyle argued that the testimony of the spade could provide evidence of the Bible's truthfulness. "Higher Criticism" of the Bible was guilty in his mind of "circling round and round in its enclosed basin" of the biblical text. Kyle spent great intellectual energies in an effort to show that archaeology has "found nothing that discredits the Book as a narrator of facts."[44] In 1919 Kyle gave the Stone Lectures at Princeton Theological Seminary on the subject of the "Light from Archaeology on Pentateuchal Times."[45] In 1929 he served as the revising editor of the *International Standard Bible Encyclopaedia* and made the reference work more conservative.[46] Gerstner's early interest in Old Testament archaeology can most likely be attributed to Kyle and the UPCNA's emphasis in the new academic field. It should also be noted that Robert C. McQuilkin (1886–1952) studied privately under Kyle, was ordained in the UPCNA (1917) and subsequently founded Columbia Bible College (SC) in 1923. McQuilkin played a key role in spawning fundamentalism in the American south.[47] The scholarly contributions and careers of Moorehead and Kyle demonstrate the UPCNA's conservative theological orientation in the first third of the twentieth century.

In 1920 Xenia Seminary moved to St Louis, Missouri, in order to secure a more promising financial future, but also to place the seminary in a more cosmopolitan environment. The seminary was now located in close proximity to Washington University, the famed research institution, and the two schools maintained a cordial relationship. While the six UPCNA liberal arts colleges were located in rural areas, both of the UP's seminaries, Pittsburgh and Xenia, were by the 1920s in large cities.[48] In 1922 Kyle became Xenia's president. Despite the school's urbane new surroundings, Xenia remained devoted to its conservative brand of evangelical scholarship. During the 1920s other UPCNA schools also appeared to adhere to an evangelical position, but the intellectual currents of early twentieth-century America

44. Kyle, *The Deciding Voice of the Monuments in Biblical Criticism*, 295.

45. *Minutes of the General Assembly of the Presbyterian Church in the United States of America, 1920*, 300.

46. Kyle did this by dropping some less conservative articles and adding more fundamentalist ones. On this point, see Scorgie, *A Call for Continuity*, 154; and *International Standard Bible Encyclopaedia*, 1:xiii.

47. McQuilkin, *Always in Triumph*, 85–86; Bundy, "McQuilkin, Robert Crawford," 157–58; Glass, *Strangers in Zion*, 226–82.

48. The six UP liberal arts colleges were Knoxville College (Knoxville, TN), Monmouth College (Monmouth, IL), Muskingum College (New Concord, OH), Sterling College (Sterling, KS), Tarkio College (Tarkio, MO), and Westminster College (New Wilmington, OH). Knoxville was an African-American institution of higher learning.

were causing some anxiety among United Presbyterians. In 1925 W. E. McCulloch, a Los Angeles UP pastor, maintained that "we are suffering from what has been termed the secularization of education," and that this "constitutes what is, in some respects, the most serious problem that confronts us today."[49] In order to combat secularization, higher criticism, and religious modernism, courses in Christian evidences remained prevalent on UP campuses.[50] Conservatives also expressed criticism over particular Bible professors who drifted away from strict orthodoxy. United Presbyterian concern was manifest at the UP's Sterling College in Kansas in 1921 when J. L. Graham, a Bible professor, left the school after alumni and supporters of the college complained about Graham's modern methods of Bible instruction.[51] In 1929 G. Reid Johnson, another Bible professor, departed from Muskingum under similar circumstances.[52] At Xenia, Kyle sought to strengthen the school's conservatism by developing close ties to scholars from Princeton Seminary. In the mid-1920s J. Gresham Machen and Robert Dick Wilson, two conservative Princeton Seminary Bible professors, both gave multiple lectures at Xenia.[53] Machen had established himself as the most outstanding conservative New Testament scholar of his era and was working vigorously to defend the Bible's historical trustworthiness. By the 1920s Machen had also become increasingly known as a church leader opposed to modernism within the PCUSA. UP colleges were also influenced by the wider fundamentalist movement, which was responding in its own way to the new challenges. In 1920 the faculty of the UPCNA's Muskingum College in New Concord, Ohio, voted to give an honorary doctorate to Bob Jones, the fundamentalist evangelist, who had given some popular chapel sermons at the school.[54] A generally conservative orientation pervaded UP institutions during the period.

Kyle, who was perhaps the UP's most famous scholar in the first third of the twentieth century, was a nationally known evangelical leader; in 1926

49. McCulloch, *The United Presbyterian Church and Its Work in America*, 141.

50. Kelly, "The History of Religious Instruction in United Presbyterian Colleges." Even after 1950 Sterling and Westminster still offered courses in Christian evidences.

51. Ibid., 116.

52. Kelsey claims that Montgomery, Muskingkum's president, asked "Dr. Johnson to seek work elsewhere at the close of the college term in 1929." See Kelsey, *The Life Story of a Garden Variety Preacher*, 45–46. In 1929 Kelsey served as Muskingkum's vice president and professor of Bible.

53. It is interesting to note that Kyle gave a series of lectures in Princeton in February 1928; see his comments in "Says Bible Unhurt by Archaeologists," 1, 5.

54. Fisk, *A History of Muskingum College*, 166. Later, Muskingum used the name Robert Jones on its list of honorary doctorate holders in order to avoid embarrassment.

he helped Machen to form the League of Evangelical Students.[55] Princeton Seminary students and Machen had decided to start a new evangelical student organization after an inter-seminary group, of which they were a part allowed a Unitarian school to join. The newly created League stated in 1928 that it was committed to "promoting the intellectual defense of the evangelical faith" and to "exalt[ing] our Lord Jesus Christ . . . as presented in the inerrant Word of God."[56] Kyle served on the advisory board for the League and wrote several articles for its publication *The Evangelical Student*. He also spoke on various archaeological topics at the League's 1926, 1927, and 1932 national conventions. As president of Xenia he considered his entire student body to be a part of the League. His enthusiasm for the League's scholarly and spiritual program is reflected by the fact that Xenia hosted the League's second annual convention in St Louis, Missouri, in 1927. Moreover, the League's first treasurer, Wallace L. Kennedy, was a Wheaton College graduate and a Xenia student. Xenia was clearly a strong outpost of evangelical learning, but there were other signs of evangelical academic leadership in the UPCNA as well.

Muskingkum's professor of Bible since 1919 and vice-president since 1921, Hugh A. Kelsey (1872–1958), served as the faculty adviser to the League at his school and wrote a January 1931 article in *The Evangelical Student*. After citing a Congregational pastor's fears about where liberalism could lead spiritually, Kelsey noted that the "disposition to neglect the Word of God, to repudiate its great doctrine of sin and salvation, and to deride its authority to teach things spiritual, is ever tending to spiritual starvation and suicide."[57] In 1933 Kelsey became the president of the UP's Sterling College in central Kansas and successfully built the school into a solid evangelical UPCNA liberal arts institution.[58] On several occasions Gerstner later lectured at the college and once even led the Kansas school's spiritual emphasis week.[59]

Another influential scholar who was teaching within a UPCNA institution and who participated in the League was Gerstner's mentor John

55. Kyle is listed on the advisory board of the League's first publication, *The Evangelical Student* 1, no. 1, p. 2.

56. *The Evangelical Student* 3, no. 1, inside cover.

57. Kelsey, "Enrichment of the Spiritual Life," 7–8. On Kelsey's career, see his autobiography recently republished as *The Life Story of a Garden Variety Preacher*.

58. Sterling would be the only UPCNA college in the second half of the twentieth century to retain its evangelical commitment. The Kansas institution is the only former UPCNA college to become a member of the evangelical Council of Christian Colleges and Universities.

59. On this point, see chapter 3.

Orr. In Orr, the evangelical UPCNA intelligentsia had a direct link to the Old Princeton tradition. Old Princeton refers to the conservative Calvinist doctrinal tradition that existed at Princeton Theological Seminary from 1812–1929.[60] Orr, a student of Warfield and Machen, was disseminating the Old Princeton theology in the UPCNA via one of the UPCNA's most significant colleges—Westminster. In 1934, halfway through Gerstner's time at Westminster, Orr had produced an important study entitled *English Deism: Its Roots and Fruits*.[61] Orr's book, which became a standard work in the field, offered readers meticulous research and exhaustive analysis.[62] His definition of deism, which relied on the work of Robert Flint (1838–1910), a Scottish divine, held that it was a belief that "maintained that God endowed the world at creation with self-sustaining and self-acting powers and then abandoned it to the operation of these powers acting as second causes."[63] Perhaps the most important aspect of Orr's *English Deism* was the "*Fruits*" part of the book's subtitle. Orr linked deism to the theological modernism of the twentieth century and to the "leading modernist" of the period, Harry Emerson Fosdick. Orr noted that there was "undoubtedly a direct line of influence of the deists themselves upon at least some prominent Modernist leaders."[64] While this claim might appear implausible, Orr carefully showed the various connections, but simultaneously insisted that there were real differences between the two movements.[65] Yet he argued that theological modernism was "in a large measure a continuation" of the earlier Deism. Nowhere was this more evident than in the modernist's rejection of the supernatural and the miraculous. The book represented a high level of serious academic research that pushed Orr to the front rank of evangelical scholarship. On February 23, 1935 Orr addressed the League of Evangelical Students' national convention, which was held in Philadelphia.[66] Perhaps

60. For more discussion of Old Princeton, see chapter 6.

61. Orr, *English Deism*. Parts I and II constituted Orr's dissertation, but Part III was work added later.

62. Virtually every significant book consulted on the history of English deism mentions Orr's study. Talbot, a Hume scholar and Wheaton College philosophy professor, noted in an interview that in his decades of research on deism "Orr's book kept popping up" and that he considers "Orr's book a standard work in the study of deism." Interview with Talbot. See also Hurlbutt, *Hume, Newton and the Design Argument*, vii, 65–78.

63. Orr, *English Deism*, 13. On Flint, see Sell, *Defending and Declaring the Faith*, 39–63.

64. Ibid., 260.

65. Ibid., 250–64.

66. *The Evangelical Student* 9 and 10, no. 1 (1935) inside cover.

Gerstner attended the event with his mentor. While Gerstner's presence is unknown, Orr's contribution was recognized by convention organizers and the wider evangelical movement.

In 1934 Cornelius Van Til (1895–1987), the Westminster Seminary professor of apologetics, argued in *Christianity Today* that Orr had "succeeded admirably" in giving a 'careful study of the writings of the Deists' and noted that " [t]he critics of Christianity at the present time are making much the same objections that the deists made."[67] In the same year, Alexander Ross, a Free Church of Scotland pastor, wrote an extensive review of *English Deism* in the pages of the *Evangelical Quarterly*. Ross noted that Orr "proves by citations from Fosdick's *Modern Use of the Bible* [1924] that this shallow pulpit orator is merely echoing ancient and musty deistic heresies, or heresies that are much more venerable, in as much as they go back to Celsus, and others like him."[68] A few years later, in the July 1937 issue of *Moody Monthly*, P. B. Fitzwater, professor of theology at Moody Bible Institute, wrote that Orr's 289-page book on Deism was significant for the evangelical movement because Orr "traces English Deism" down through the centuries and links it to the "literature of infidelity" and "present day Modernism."[69] In laudatory tones Fitzwater wrote, " [e]very Christian leader should become acquainted with this [Orr's] book." Unfortunately for conservative Protestants, Orr's scholarship was not sustained, and *English Deism* remained the only book he ever produced. The Westminster College professor later turned away from published scholarship and put his energies into teaching, mentoring, and administration. Orr served as acting dean of the college three times and for almost two years served as acting president of the college. Another explanation of Orr's discontinuation of academic writing was his generosity; he wanted to give students his all.[70] He served as chairman of the Westminster College Bible department until 1954. H. Dewey Dewitt, the long-time professor of chemistry at Westminster, later recalled that Orr had a "gentle kindness," but that he had "high academic standards" and was indeed "a true intellectual."[71] Overall, Orr provided Ger-

---

67. Van Til, Review of *English Deism*, 73.

68. Ross, Review of *English Deism*, 441. Ross received his MA and BD from the University of Aberdeen and a DD from the Presbyterian College of Montreal. He served as minister and later as professor of New Testament at the Free Church College in Edinburgh.

69. Fitzwater, Review of *English Deism*, 598.

70. This explanation was provided in an interview the author had with Dennison June 19, 2013. Dennison was conveying what he remembered Gerstner saying about the subject.

71. DeWitt, Interview with the author, July 6, 2010.

stner with a model of evangelical scholarship that took seriously the history of thought.

After Gerstner's graduation from Westminster in 1936, he decided to prepare for the UPCNA ministry at the newly consolidated Pittsburgh-Xenia Theological Seminary in Pittsburgh, Pennsylvania. In 1930 Melvin Grove Kyle had retired and Xenia had shut its doors in St Louis because of financial problems related to the stock market crash of 1929.[72] Xenia quickly joined together with the other UP seminary, Pittsburgh Theological Seminary. Xenia's conservative evangelical stance was now diluted by the more moderate evangelical approach of William McNaugher (1857–1947), Pittsburgh Seminary's president. On July 17, 1930 McNaugher, who had begun teaching New Testament at Pittsburgh Seminary in 1887, stated that that new Pitt-Xenia "will remain in irreducible antagonism to all modernistic, free-lance dogmas." Nonetheless, McNaugher did not believe in what he called the "lethargic acceptance of any narrow hide-bound traditionalism."[73] In 1925 McNaugher had taken the leading role in modernizing the UPCNA's theological standards by creating the Confessional Statement of 1925. The statement removed or softened some of the language and positions of the *Westminster Confession*, which McNaugher labeled "scholastic and antique" and "ultra theological."[74] He was especially uncomfortable with Westminster's positions on the atonement, election, and irresistible grace.[75] McNaugher was a key denominational leader; he was often referred to within the UP as "Mister United Presbyterian" or "the Pope."[76] As a seminary president and churchman he opposed "obstinate, obscurant conservatism" in favor of a more restrained and tolerant evangelical stance. Kyle had pursued erudition and scholarly research whereas McNaugher was content with practical academic work that he considered beneficial to the church.[77] McNaugher's moderate stance represented a stark difference from that of Kyle and the UP scholars who were associated with the League of Evangelical Students.

In the fall of 1936 Gerstner entered the combined Pitt-Xenia that McNaugher had tried to create. Gerstner's studies at Pitt-Xenia, however, did

72. Jamison, "The United Presbyterian Seminaries," 113.

73. McNaugher quoted by Coleman, "The Life and Works of John McNaugher," 119.

74. McNaugher quoted by Dennison, "John McNaugher and the Confessional Revision of 1925," 224.

75. Coleman, "The Life and Works of John McNaugher," 315.

76. Ibid., 317.

77. Jamison, *The United Presbyterian Story*, 137.

not go well.[78] He was deeply disappointed in the seminary's inability to offer what he later called "a serious Reformed education."[79] In retrospect Gerstner commented that the Pitt-Xenia professors were either "apathetic" about Reformed theology or simply "not very knowledgeable." Gerstner, who had been in awe of John Orr and his Reformed teaching, found no comparable figure at Pitt-Xenia. He was uninspired by what he considered to be school's lax theological atmosphere and abruptly withdrew from the seminary after one semester. It was a difficult period for the young theological student. Despite this setback during his first semester in seminary, the young scholar sought to broaden his intellectual horizons by taking additional coursework at the University of Pittsburgh (Pitt). According to Gerstner's university transcript, he took one course in education and two in religion at Pitt.[80] He earned three Bs in his Pitt coursework; this indicates Gerstner's competence to complete graduate-level coursework at a large secular university.[81] During the 1936–1937 academic year, Gerstner had been exposed to secular learning at the University of Pittsburgh and had experienced disappointment at his denominational seminary Pitt-Xenia. Despite his negative experience at Pitt-Xenia, Gerstner decided to press on with his seminary education in another institution.

In the fall of 1937 Gerstner arrived on the campus of Westminster Theological Seminary in suburban Philadelphia. He had learned about the seminary as a college student and followed the press reports of J. Gresham Machen's ongoing disputes with the mainline PCUSA. Machen had founded Westminster in 1929 when he and three other Princeton Seminary professors had left the institution because of what they had considered to be the liberalization of the school's board.[82] The seminary's board was re-organized by the 1929 General Assembly and placed two signers of the Auburn Affirmation (1924), the famed modernist theological statement, on the seminary's board.[83] Machen could not fathom the denomination's re-organization of his much beloved seminary. Westminster Seminary had been founded as the chief institutional product of the theological controversies that had raged within the PCUSA in the 1920s and 1930s. In 1933, in an effort to counter what he had perceived to be liberal trends among PCUSA missionaries, Machen and several associates, including J. Oliver

78. Gerstner, University of Pittsburgh Transcript.

79. Gerstner,, Interview with Coffin, 4.

80. Gerstner, University of Pittsburgh Transcript.

81. Ibid.

82. Longfield, *The Presbyterian Controversy*, 162–80.

83. Stonehouse, *J. Gresham Machen*, 441.

Buswell (1895–1977), president of Wheaton College (IL), had established the Independent Presbyterian Board of Foreign Missions. The PCUSA judicatories had been extremely hostile to this action, and in 1936 Machen had been suspended from the ministry for creating a rival mission agency to the PCUSA's mission board.[84] In response, Machen had founded the Presbyterian Church of America in the summer of 1936. In 1939 Machen's denomination changed its name to the Orthodox Presbyterian Church. As a college student, Gerstner agreed with Machen and other conservatives who had been involved in the controversies. Years later he recounted the episode by saying, "I did feel that Machen had been a little precipitate himself, but that fundamentally—I'd been reading the literature of it—he had been making proper protests against the developments at home and abroad in the USA denomination."[85]

Gerstner largely agreed with Machen's arguments, but not necessarily with separatism. At Westminster, Gerstner encountered Presbyterian separatism, but also what he later described as "a real Reformed education."[86] He excelled in his coursework at Westminster, achieving "honors standing."[87] His seminary transcript reveals that he received a comprehensive education in biblical and theological studies. Thirteen of his forty classes were in Old and New Testament studies. Four classes were in Hebrew and Greek. Nine courses were in various areas of theology including the "Theology of Calvin" and the "Theology of Crisis." He took nine classes in practical areas such as "Church Government" and "Homiletics." However, his transcript shows that he took only three church history courses and two classes in "Apologetics" and "Evidences" respectively.[88] Gerstner was receiving a comprehensive theological education in an institution known both for its academic rigor and its conservative Calvinist character.

As a student Gerstner disagreed with the presuppositional apologetics of Westminster professor Cornelius Van Til (1895–1987), but he later recounted that Van Til was "one of the two best pedagogues I've ever had from the standpoint of stimulating thought."[89] Van Til's presuppositionalism did not seek to prove various Christian assertions, but rather sought to examine the foundational presuppositions of belief systems.[90] Van Til held

84. Longfield, *The Presbyterian Controversy*, 209–12.

85. Gerstner, Interview with David Coffin, June 15, 1992, 5.

86. Ibid., 5.

87. Gerstner, Westminster Theological Seminary transcript.

88. Ibid.

89. Gerstner, Interview with Coffin, 6.

90. On Van Til's thought, see Frame, *Cornelius Van Til*; and Muether, *Cornelius*

that the presuppositions of the Christian faith make the most sense when compared to alternative positions. Gerstner recalled that he was not swayed by Van Til's approach to apologetics and held firm to the evidentialism he had imbibed from Orr.[91] From the evidentialist perspective, the Christian faith was best defended not by presupposing God, but by demonstrating the truthfulness of Christian claims. On the assumption of common sense, the truth of the Christian faith could be established reasonably to other people. The Westminster professor whom Gerstner found to be the most inspiring was John Murray (1898–1975), a Scottish theologian who had studied and served as an instructor at Princeton Seminary before coming to Westminster.[92] Gerstner noted that Murray's lectures were simple and that Murray included little discussion in class sessions. Yet he discovered that Murray had the ability to provide "beautiful theological articulation."[93] Westminster provided Gerstner with the opportunity to study under solid scholars who had a firm grasp of differing viewpoints and theological orientations.

At Westminster Gerstner thrived intellectually and embraced the school's emphasis on academic achievement. Significantly, it was during his time at Westminster that he began to think of an academic career.[94] On one memorable day Gerstner ran into Paul Woolley (1902–1984), his church history professor, as Woolley was coming into a building.[95] Gerstner, who was near the doorway, straightforwardly asked Woolley, " [w]here do you think I ought to continue?" Woolley, who encouraged academic excellence, responded by saying, "[w]ell, I would advise Harvard."[96] Even though Gerstner had considered programs at the University of Chicago and at Princeton Theological Seminary, he settled on Harvard because of his respect for

---

Van Til.

91. Gerstner, Interview with Coffin, 6.

92. On Murray, see Murray, *The Life of John Murray.*

93. Gerstner, Interview with Coffin, 7.

94. Ibid., 5.

95. On Woolley, see Muether "The Significance of Paul Woolley Today," 7–23. Woolley earned his BA from Princeton University (1923) and a BD and ThM from Princeton Theological Seminary (1925, 1928). Woolley was ordained by the Moody Church in Chicago in 1926 and served as the secretary of the League of Evangelical Students from 1928 to 1929. In 1929 he became registrar and professor of church history at the newly founded Westminster Theological Seminary in Philadelphia. Wooley was ordained by the PCUSA in 1932 and suspended from the ministry of the PCUSA in 1936.

96. Gerstner, Interview with Coffin, 9.

Woolley.[97] In 1940 Gerstner graduated with a BD and a ThM degree from Westminster.

While he attended seminary, however, Gerstner had pursued other interests besides academics. During his time in seminary, Gerstner developed a romantic relationship with Edna Suckau (1914–1999) that would prove to be lasting. The two met one Sunday at Calvary Orthodox Presbyterian Church in Middletown, Pennsylvania, where Gerstner was guest preaching. When Edna arrived at the church, she was upset because the church's pastor Edward Kellog was not preaching.[98] After the service the pastor's wife, Eleanor Kellog, invited Gerstner and Suckau to lunch. For Edna Suckau, it was not love at first sight. Nonetheless, the two started courting, and Edna found Gerstner's possible missionary plans congruent with her own ambitions.[99] From 1909 to 1920 Edna's family had served as missionaries in Chandkuri, Champa, and then Korba, India. After a one-year furlough the family had returned to Korba as missionaries, but illness and fatigue had forced the Suckaus to leave the country and return to the United States in 1928.[100] Her father, Cornelius (1881–1951), had built the reputation of a well-known conservative General Conference Mennonite missionary and church leader. He had taken a temporary position that had turned into a permanent one as pastor of the First Mennonite Church in Berne, Indiana, the largest Mennonite church in the United States at the time. At Berne, Suckau had become involved in the transdenominational evangelical movement as evidenced by his giving the 1938 commencement address at the strongly evangelical Wheaton College (IL), which also awarded him an honorary DD. Suckau had criticized liberal trends in the Mennonite General Conference and its colleges, especially Blufton.[101] As a missionary returning home he had become deeply disturbed by the rise of modernism within American churches; he had corresponded with J. Gresham Machen, about the issue.[102] In an effort to counter perceived modernism in Mennonite colleges and to promote a distinctively evangelical Mennonite institution, Suckau was instrumental in founding Grace Bible Institute in Omaha, Nebraska, in 1943. Suckau served as the president of Grace from 1944 to 1951.

97. Ibid., 9.

98. Gerstner, Interview with the author, June 15, 2010.

99. Ibid.

100. Steely, "Cornelius Herman Suckau," 15.

101. Ibid., 17.

102. Kuhlman, *The Story of Grace*, 70.

His daughter, Edna, had graduated from Wheaton College with "High Honor" in 1934.[103] After college Edna had moved to Philadelphia and had completed the University of Pennsylvania's M.A. program in literature. At Wheaton she had encountered conservative Presbyterians and "embraced Calvinism through OPC church work."[104] Edna had served for a time as a secretary of an Orthodox Presbyterian Church in Portland, Maine. She also had taught German and English for a short period at the Berne High School. Her evangelical and Reformed background in combination with her intellectual achievements undoubtedly impressed Gerstner. The two were married in the First Mennonite Church in Berne on September 7, 1940. Edna's father conducted the ceremony "against the pleasing background of ferns given dignity by a simple white bridal bouquet overhanging the pulpit railing." The *Berne Witness* newspaper reported that the sanctuary was "the scene of the season's most interesting and outstanding wedding."[105] After the wedding, the couple set off for Cambridge, Massachusetts, and honeymooned along the way.

Gerstner and his bride arrived at Harvard in September 1940. In retrospect Gerstner claimed that he was attracted to Harvard because of its high academic standing and because it was an institution that was "thoroughly liberal; and yet, able to live and let live."[106] Gerstner believed that the members of the Harvard Divinity School faculty were not antagonistic towards theologically conservative students as long as they excelled academically.[107] Indeed, during the 1940s Harvard attracted approximately a dozen evangelical students.[108] During the 1930s and early 1940s, Harvard admitted these theologically conservative students, apparently in an effort to boost enrolment.[109] Gerstner entered a university that represented the pinnacle of academic achievement and that was also a haven for secular modes of thought. Even though he was a fledgling scholar with deeply held religious beliefs, he was not intimidated by Harvard. Gerstner noted, "I went there because it was ultraliberal and academically competent, desiring my conservatism to be put to its tests."[110] Even though Gerstner later recounted that

---

103. Suckau, Wheaton College Transcript, Gerstner Papers, Chandler, AZ.

104. Gerstner, Interview with the author, June 15, 2010.

105. "Edna Suckau Wed to John Gerstner in Local Church," 1.

106. Gerstner, Interview with Coffin, 9.

107. Nelson, *The Making and Unmaking of an Evangelical Mind*, 58–59.

108. Ibid., 54.

109. Ibid., 57.

110. Gerstner quoted by Nelson, *The Making and Unmaking of an Evangelical Mind*, 58.

he was treated relatively fairly by his Harvard professors, he also recalled that "my head was bloody all the time." He claimed that "they raised some issues, you know, [that] made me think hard."[111] One of Gerstner's qualities as a scholar was his ability to entertain a wide diversity of thought. Indeed, the young evangelical scholar was experiencing life in a school known for its Unitarianism, its embrace of the philosophy of William James (1842–1910), and its progressive thinking.

Gerstner later expressed his open-mindedness and claimed that "I was open to it [their thinking]; I wanted to [be open-minded], if there was any validity in it . . ." even if meant "I had to give up my ministry."[112] In retrospect he held that "it was a good experience that way, and I bear tribute to Harvard that it was a very humane treatment that they gave us, even though it was a sort of condescending and pitying one in a sense." From his perspective the Harvard professors were "sophisticated"; Gerstner argued that they "weren't condescending directly" but rather "condescending through the whole pattern of thought."[113] Apparently this meant that Harvard's educational philosophy and theological coursework were designed from a liberal perspective and therefore contrary to evangelical beliefs. Despite the ideological differences, Gerstner quickly proved that he could achieve in his new avant-garde environment. During the 1940–1941 academic year, his first year at Harvard, Gerstner did well: he earned two A grades in theology, one B+ in theology, one A and one A- in the history of religion, a B+ in Old Testament and a B+ in Philosophy.[114] The official title of Gerstner's PhD program, which Harvard had initiated in 1934, was "The History and Philosophy of Religion." It was a promising start for the new Harvard Divinity School student.

The stated goal of Gerstner's degree was to help the student "lay a broad and sufficient foundation for teaching and study within the field of religion" and to enable students to do "research."[115] Even though history was expected to be an important dimension of Gerstner's course of study, his Harvard transcript reveals that he did not take a single course from the Church History department. Instead, Gerstner focused on the study of philosophy. He even completed additional philosophy coursework at Boston

111. Gerstner, Interview with Coffin, 13.

112. Ibid., 13.

113. Ibid., 13.

114. Gerstner Report Card, Gerstner Student File.

115. "History of the Harvard PhD program in the History and Philosophy of Religion."

University.[116] It seems that the young evangelical student was less interested in historical context and more focused on ideas themselves. This preference would continue to be a theme throughout Gerstner's career. Gerstner later noted that he was "all over the [Harvard] campus," sitting in on "economics classes and art and literature, and all that type of thing, but more in philosophy than anything else."[117] One syllabus Gerstner kept from a 1941–1942 Harvard philosophy class included readings from Durant Drake's *Invitation to Philosophy* (1933), Edwin Burtt's *The English Philosophers from Bacon to Mill* (1933), Immanuel Kant's *Fundamental Principles of the Metaphysics of Ethics* (1785), and a 1939 Charles Darwin reader produced by Julian Huxley.[118] Gerstner was receiving a solid grounding in the great minds of Western philosophy.

At Harvard, where Unitarianism had reigned for several generations, Gerstner studied under an accomplished cadre of professors. Henry Joel Cadbury (1883–1974) served as professor of New Testament and had an outstanding reputation as a scholar and as a fair-minded teacher. Cadbury was a pacifist Quaker with vast knowledge of his field and modernist leanings towards the Bible. He was an authority on the origins of the biblical Luke-Acts.[119] Gerstner considered Cadbury to be "stimulating and an intellectual provoker of serious thought."[120] To Gerstner's surprise Cadbury was familiar with conservative New Testament scholarship and used Machen's *The Origin of Paul's Religion* (1921) in his Hellenism course. While Cadbury did not share Machen's perspective, he told Gerstner that Machen's book was the "best statement and critique of the various interpretations of Paul which I know."[121] Gerstner also studied theology with Julius Bixler (1894–1985). Bixler was an authority on William James and Gerstner claimed that Bixler lectured too extensively on James while giving little attention to what he considered to be important theologians of the past

116. It appears that Gerstner took two philosophy courses at Boston University earning a B+ and an A-. Gerstner Report Card, Gerstner Student File, Harvard University Archives.

117. Gerstner, Interview with Coffin, June 15, 1992, 12.

118. Philosophy B1hf 1941–1942, Harvard University Reading Assignments, Gerstner Papers, Chandler, Arizona.

119. D'Elia, *A Place at the Table*, 24–25.

120. Gerstner, Interview with Coffin, June 15, 1992, 10.

121. Gerstner, "Harvard," 108. Gerstner's statement about Cadbury's use of Machen's book contradicts Dorrien's assertion that "nobody at Harvard or Boston bothered to read the Hodges, Warfield, or Machen." See Dorrien, *The Remaking of Evangelical Theology*, 68.

such as Thomas Aquinas.[122] James' pragmatism reconceptualized religion as relative to experience (subjective) and not found in revelation or timeless doctrinal truth.[123] John Orr pointed out that James "was radically empirical" and "hostile to metaphysics" and therefore to traditional Christian theology.[124] In retrospect Gerstner recounted that Bixler "lectured on systematics as Karl Barth lectured on natural theology—to show that the subject had no right to exist."[125] Gerstner recalled that Bixler was "very friendly with me, but he said: abominable theology, Gerstner. How can I even like you, you see?"[126] In 1942 Bixler left Harvard to serve as president of Colby College in Maine.

Gerstner also worked closely with John D. Wild (1902–1972), an Episcopalian layman and philosophy professor.[127] Wild had arrived in the Harvard philosophy department in 1927 and had written important works on realistic philosophy and on the life and thought of George Berkeley (1685–1753), the Irish philosopher. Indeed, Wild was known at the time as a proponent of critical realism.[128] Gerstner remembered that Wild's "strong Platonic and Thomistic strain made him congenial to orthodoxy."[129] During the 1942–1943 academic school year Gerstner served as a tutor for Wild's students in the philosophy department.[130] Another Harvard philosophy professor under whom Gerstner studied was Ralph Barton Perry (1876–1957). After earning his PhD at Harvard under William James in 1899, Perry had begun his tenure as a Harvard philosophy professor in 1902. He too was a faithful disciple of James and in 1936 had won a Pulitzer Prize for a two-volume work on his mentor's thought.[131] Perry would prove helpful to the young evangelical doctoral student when Gerstner entered the dissertation phase of his program. Perry, who had once considered the Presbyterian ministry just after graduating from Princeton, appears to have

122. On Bixler, see Taylor, "Bixler, Julius Seelye (1894–1985)," in Shook, ed., *Dictionary of Modern American Philosophers*, 1:233–44.

123. Wilkens and Padgett, *Christianity and Western Thought*, 2:236.

124. Orr, *English Deism*, 232.

125. Gerstner, "Harvard," 108.

126. Gerstner, Interview with David Coffin, June 15, 1992, 13.

127. Williams, *The "Augustan Age,"* 321. This book is part of the three volume: Religion at Harvard series.

128. Trippert, "Wild, John Daniel, Jr. (1902–1972)," in Shook ed, *Dictionary of Modern American Philosophers*, vol. 1, 2596–2600. See also Kaufman, *John Wild*.

129. Gerstner, "Harvard," 109.

130. Gerstner Report Card, Gerstner Student File, Harvard University Archives.

131. Lemos, "Perry, Ralph Barton," 660.

had some sympathy with the budding Christian scholar. Perry might even have wanted to attend Princeton Seminary.[132] The Harvard philosopher told Gerstner that he turned away from the pastorate because some ministers with whom he had consulted had avoided some questions he had about the faith.[133] Perhaps Perry's own story reinforced in Gerstner's mind the need for Christians to adopt an apologetic approach to questions about faith and philosophy. Gerstner would not confine himself to the Divinity School walls and, in fact, found a home in a place where he could explore the varied dimensions of Western thought, the Harvard philosophy department.

While Gerstner was not a formal student of Perry Miller (1905–1963) at Harvard, it seems likely that Gerstner had at least some acquaintance with him. Miller was an authority on Puritanism, but from 1942 to 1945 he was absent from Harvard, serving in the U.S. Army's Office of Strategic Services.[134] Other Harvard professors under whom Gerstner studied included: William E. Hocking (1873–1966) and Robert H. Pfeiffer (1892–1958). Hocking was an idealist philosopher and a liberal Congregationalist who argued for a modernist missionary program in *Re-Thinking Missions* (1932).[135] Hocking's work on missions in the 1930s had sparked the final phase of the "Presbyterian Controversy" that involved Machen and his suspension from the ministry in 1936.[136] Gerstner later commented that Hocking's "theology was as relativistic as his philosophy was absolutistic."[137] Gerstner rejected an offer by Hocking to supervise a dissertation "comparing the doctrine of God" in "Christianity and Islam and Hinduism." Afterwards he remembered "I begged off that one, because I didn't know Sanskrit, and I wasn't familiar with Arabic, and I'm never much interested in language."[138] The emphasis Gerstner put on ideas and his lack of interest in language would later prove problematic for the scholar. Pfeiffer was an accomplished Old Testament scholar who Gerstner thought was an "integral part of old Harvard liberalism and radicalism." Apparently, Gerstner became uncomfortable during one class when Pfeiffer declared to his students that "I dismiss it [an Old Testament miracle] as nonhistorical."[139] Evangelical students trained in conservative Protestant institutions would have been taught about liberal

132. Simon, *William James Remembered*, 199.

133. Gerstner, "Harvard," 110.

134. Middlekauff, "Perry Miller," 168.

135. Hocking et al., *Re-Thinking Missions*.

136. Longfield, *The Presbyterian Controversy*, 200.

137. Gerstner, "Harvard," 109.

138. Gerstner, Interview with Coffin, 12.

139. Gerstner, "Harvard," 109.

naturalistic *a priori* bias and yet it appears that when the young student actually heard it being presented the experience was a little unsettling.

While Gerstner's Harvard professors did not share the same religious commitments, the institution did provide Gerstner with the opportunity to study, learn, and work with advanced scholars. His Harvard education broadened his learning and deepened his grasp of this philosophical tradition. Yet it does not appear that Gerstner's evangelical mind was changed very much by his Harvard professors.[140] He found some of their teaching to be quite challenging to his conservative conception of the Christian faith, but he does not seem to have become too enamored with it or overly troubled by it. Perhaps the best explanation for this resilience is that Gerstner's apologetic views were largely developed by the time he arrived at Harvard. At Westminster Seminary, Gerstner had already clung to his evidentialist apologetic against the presuppositional teaching of Cornelius Van Til. As a doctoral student at Harvard, Gerstner continued to stick to his apologetic guns while simultaneously deepening his grasp of philosophy. Just as Gerstner's mentor and scholarly model, John Orr, had withstood his liberal theological education in Germany in the 1910s, so too it seems that Gerstner sought to persevere through the perceived intellectual challenge he faced at Harvard. Yet Gerstner's decision not to take a single church history course indicates that he was more concerned with right ideas, rather than gaining an understanding of the context in which a thinker's ideas emerged.

The theological climate and largely secular atmosphere of Harvard were not completely suffocating for the young evangelical scholar. Gerstner found emotional and intellectual empathy from other evangelical students who also were studying at the Divinity School in the early 1940s. Paul Jewett (who later taught at Fuller Seminary) and Kenneth Kantzer (who later taught at Wheaton College and Trinity Evangelical Divinity School) became two of Gerstner's evangelical friends at Harvard.[141] Overall, the young doctoral student thrived. He excelled in his coursework, studied under well-known scholars and was able to do serious research into a topic that had significance for his own intellectual and religious tradition. Evangelicals were benefiting from a truly liberal perspective that made space for a wide diversity of viewpoints. Gerstner later recalled an anecdote about an encounter he once had as a student in the Harvard Yard with Arthur Darby Nock (1902–1963), who was his adviser. Gerstner claimed that Nock, the celebrated Harvard histo-

140. Nelson points out that some of the Harvard evangelicals of the 1940s started their programs late in their careers and "had less time for the struggle with conceptual problems" as they related to Christian faith. On this idea, see Nelson, *The Making and Unmaking of an Evangelical Mind*, 60.

141. Gerstner, Interview with Coffin, 9.

rian, "teased" him "because I rested my faith on history rather than doing as he did—totally separating the two."[142] While Nock may not have agreed with Gerstner's viewpoint the evidence clearly indicates that Nock helped the young student in a major way. Gerstner's Harvard student file contains a letter from L. S. Mayo, the Divinity School Dean, to Arthur Darby Nock in which Mayo asked Nock whether he would recommend that Gerstner should "receive credit for three fourths of a year of graduate work on the basis of study at Westminster Theological Seminary."[143] Nock responded to Mayo that he did recommend that Gerstner should receive the credit. Gerstner greatly benefited from not having to take the additional coursework. By 1943 he could focus solely on the research and writing that he needed to complete his dissertation. The Mayo and Nock correspondence indicates that the Harvard Divinity School chose not to penalize Gerstner for work he had done at a conservative theological institution. Other evangelical students at Harvard during this period commented on the challenging yet supportive environment that Harvard provided for evangelical students in the 1940s.[144] George Eldon Ladd noted that his Harvard professors "didn't care what he [Ladd] believed as long as he produced good work."[145] The evidence seems clear that Gerstner and his fellow evangelicals were treated reasonably well by their Harvard professors.

While working on his degree, Gerstner simultaneously served as the stated supply pastor of the United Presbyterian congregation in Brockton, Massachusetts, from 1941 to 1943.[146] Gerstner missed military service because of his ministry duties. When Gerstner completed his doctoral coursework in 1943, he and Edna moved to Sunset Hills Presbyterian Church in the Pittsburgh suburb of Mt Lebanon, Pennsylvania.[147] As stated supply pastor of Sunset Hills, Gerstner helped the small church to transition from a UPCNA-funded mission church to a self-supporting congregation. In addition, he provided leadership as the church began a building campaign for a new church structure.[148] While serving at Sunset Hills, Gerstner performed his pastoral duties of preaching, leading youth group meetings, and visiting

142. Gerstner, "The Contributions of Charles Hodge, B. B. Warfield, and J. Gresham Machen to the Doctrine of Inspiration," 377.

143. Mayo, Letter to Nock, Gerstner Student File.

144. Nelson, *The Making and Unmaking of an Evangelical Mind*, 58.

145. Ladd quoted in D'Elia, *A Place at the Table*, 23.

146. Gilliland Jr., "Gerstner, John H.," in Gilliland Jr., ed., *Truth and Love*, 239.

147. Gerstner, Interview with David Coffin, 14.

148. Gracey, Interview with the author, November 6, 2013. I have been able to find only a small amount of information on the Sunset Hills and Brockton churches.

parishioners. Under Gerstner's leadership the church "reached about 160 members."[149] While pastoring there, he also began his research and writing for his dissertation. It was a busy time for the aspiring scholar.

Gerstner first approached Henry Joel Cadbury, the Harvard New Testament scholar, about writing a dissertation on how form criticism demonstrates the reliability of the gospels. Cadbury was held in esteem by many of the Harvard evangelicals of the period and apparently was a logical choice for Gerstner.[150] Cadbury was happy to undertake the project with Gerstner, but told him that the rest of the faculty would not be too keen on passing the project.[151] Upon being rebuffed, Gerstner then "moved over to the area I really preferred," which was philosophy. In his search for a dissertation supervisor, Gerstner enquired of Ralph Barton Perry, a scholar from outside the Divinity School walls. The Harvard philosopher was a founder of the school of new realism within American pragmatic philosophy.[152] New realism—a refutation of idealism—argued that things known are not the result of the knowing relation, but have separate knowable existence.[153] Perry, who was nearing the end of a legendary philosophical career, agreed to be Gerstner's supervisor, and Gerstner recalled that they "worked well together."[154] Gerstner's dissertation analysed the influence of "Scotch Realism, Kant and Darwin" on the thought of Princeton's philosopher president James McCosh (1811–1894).[155] McCosh was a Calvinist philosopher who had an extensive knowledge of his field and marshalled his learning in an effort to combat or reconcile intellectual currents that posed a threat to traditional Christian faith.[156] Gerstner noted that his dissertation was primarily "concerned to present his [McCosh's] Realistic criticism of the great German [Kant]."[157] The topic appealed to Gerstner because McCosh offered "careful comparisons and shrewd criticisms" of Kant. McCosh criticised Kant's skeptical,

149. Gerstner, Interview with Coffin, 14.

150. Nelson, *The Making and Unmaking of an Evangelical Mind*, 58–59.

151. Gerstner, Interview with Coffin, 10.

152. "Ralph Barton Perry."

153. Delaney, "New Realism," 610.

154. Gerstner, Interview with Coffin, 10.

155. Gerstner, "Scotch Realism, Kant and Darwin in the Philosophy of James McCosh."

156. On McCosh, see Hoeveler, *James McCosh and the Scottish Intellectual Tradition*; Moore, *The Post-Darwinian Controversies*; Gundlach, *Process and Providence*; Livingstone, *Darwin's Forgotten Defenders*; Roberts, *Darwinism and the Divine in America*.

157. Gerstner, "Scotch Realism, Kant and Darwin in the Philosophy of James McCosh," 1–2.

anti-inductive method in metaphysics, which sought to come "between us and things."[158] McCosh rejected Kant's " [i]mpressionism," which limited the reality of thought and left people "without knowledge of the external world."[159] For Gerstner, McCosh's critique of Kant demonstrated that actually knowing things was possible, however imperfect. A dissertation on the Scottish-born Princeton president helped Gerstner to grasp the significant intellectual challenges facing the Christian faith and to analyze the way in which McCosh responded to them.

Kant held that knowledge of God was beyond people's sense experience and reason. On the other hand, Darwinian evolution attempted to show something different by arguing that the natural world and its processes had adequate explanatory power and that God was no longer needed. McCosh, according to Gerstner, was a helpful theistic thinker because he demonstrated that Darwinian evolution "[r]ather than being a substitute for a teleological explanation of the universe" showed that the theory "requires such an explanation itself."[160] Gerstner noted that "McCosh finds Evolution to be but a tutor to bring us to God." Evolution from McCosh's perspective was question begging. Gerstner summed up McCosh's thought by noting that, according to the Scottish philosopher, the "traditional arguments [for the existence of God] remain and are strengthened." He noted that the "most interesting, if not the most important, of McCosh's arguments for the existence of God in this evolving universe is his contention that there is design in Development itself."[161] Darwin's contention that evolution removed God from the picture was denied by McCosh. McCosh's arguments against mistaken inferences from Darwin, Gerstner argued, showed that

> [t]he causal, teleological and moral facts of this evolving world require God even more than did those same facts formerly thought of as existing in a world of more or less fixed species.[162]

In McCosh, Gerstner found a scholar who could offer "acute analysis" and a reasoned rebuttal to Kant *and* a harmonization with Darwin. Kant's assault on religious reason and Darwin's evolutionary thought were not insurmountable challenges for Christian scholars.

McCosh's deep learning in combination with clever argumentation provided the aspiring scholar with a model for Christian scholarship.

158. Ibid., 73.
159. Ibid., 76.
160. Ibid., 190.
161. Ibid., 181.
162. Ibid., 190.

Gerstner noted that "after the [philosophical] fight the banner of [Thomas] Reid was planted and the land again belonged to God who was, after all, the omega if not the alpha of all of McCosh's thinking." Reid (1710–1796), a Scottish philosopher, argued against David Hume's skepticism and asserted a common sense philosophy that the mind can know the external world.[163] McCosh's thought was able to "regain the world for God" by removing the "camouflage [that] was Kant" and by overcoming Darwin through "hard fighting."[164] After two years of work on his dissertation, Gerstner's project was approved and in June 1945 Gerstner received his PhD from Harvard.

Significantly, McCosh's philosophical perspective had been bequeathed to many of his former students, most notably to Benjamin B. Warfield (1851–1921), the renowned Princeton Seminary theologian. In his subsequent career Gerstner wrote little on McCosh and instead turned his attention to Warfield. Gerstner's study of McCosh helped him to grasp the intellectual background to Warfield's thought, but Warfield provided Gerstner with a more potent response to liberal biblical critics who had attempted—for several generations—to undermine the Bible's trustworthiness. Nevertheless, McCosh influenced Gerstner to believe that there did not necessarily have to be conflict between science and evolution on the one hand and religion on the other—reconciliation was possible.[165]

In the same year that Gerstner finished his PhD program at Harvard, he accepted a call to the nine-hundred-and-three-member Second United Presbyterian Church in Wilkinsburg, Pennsylvania.[166] Second United was an established urban church near Pittsburgh and Gerstner continued his pastoral ministry there. Gerstner faithfully carried out pastoral duties, but he had no intention of restricting himself to the conventional routine of a pastor.

During this period Gerstner began to write regularly for the *United Presbyterian* magazine. His recently completed Harvard PhD and his writing for a denominational periodical raised Gerstner's profile within the United Presbyterian Church. His essays in the *United Presbyterian* addressed a wide variety of topics. Gerstner expressed concern over racial issues after hearing Mordecai Johnson (1890–1976) lecture on the injustice of segregation. Johnson served as president of Howard University, a leading

163. Lehrer, "Reid, Thomas," 783–87.

164. Gerstner, "Scotch Realism, Kant and Darwin in the Philosophy of James McCosh," 191.

165. See, Gerstner, *Reasons for Faith*, 189–96; Gerstner, "The Science-Religion Conflict: Its True Locus," 61–73.

166. Gerstner, Interview with Coffin, 15; Kirk, Interview with the author.

African-American school, and the cogency of Johnson's remarks spurred Gerstner to action.[167] In January 1945 Gerstner took up his pen and criticised segregation within the pages of the *United Presbyterian*. Gerstner was aggressively opposed to those who claimed that desegregation should occur slowly. He wrote, " [a]s for the method itself we are inclined to believe that only the radical alternative is thoroughly Christian." "Since the Negro is our brother now, he should be treated as such—now," Gerstner argued.[168] He was especially upset by Southerners who claimed to want racial equality, but who, in fact, kept perpetrating inequality.

He did not approve of the way Christians in the American South were justifying segregation. Their arguments were highly lamentable. Gerstner noted that full integration was needed immediately and that any other plan could not be "entertained when the Word of God teaches so emphatically the unity of the human race, its origin from a common Creator and its union in the Savior of the world . . ." To "presume racial superiority" or "restrict our fellowship" with other races is "grossest hypocrisy."[169] While Gerstner agreed with the more progressive intellectual forces on the issue of race, he disagreed sharply with those pushing for a secularized American academy. In a February 1945 article entitled "Is Our Civilization Worth Keeping?" Gerstner analyzed the decline of Christian faith among the "scholars," but noted that "multitudes still believe."[170] Gerstner was progressive on the race issue, but clearly worried about the state academy.

The majority of Gerstner's writings in the *United Presbyterian* dealt with social questions or practical issues facing Christians. He did, however, also write some book reviews. He wrote an extensive review of Wilbur Smith's (a Moody Bible Institute professor) *Therefore Stand* (1945). Gerstner noted that Smith's apologetics book was "significant and valuable." In the first part of his book Smith had traced the "attacks on Christianity and the retreat of the churches." Smith, in Gerstner's mind, had correctly analyzed the intellectual challenges facing the Christian faith and Gerstner was in agreement with Smith's call for a rigorous apologetic defence of the Christian faith. While Gerstner criticized the length of the book, he noted that the book was "very, very good." He wrote that the book was special "because it

---

167. Johnson was Howard's first African American president. On Johnson' life and thought, see McKinney, *Mordecai, the Man and His Message*.

168. Gerstner, "The Relation of White To Colored People," 20.

169. Ibid.

170. Gerstner, "Is Our Civilization Worth Keeping?," 25.

is the first substantial and fairly comprehensive treatise of its kind to appear for quite awhile."[171]

In another review, he analyzed Cornelius Van Til's *The New Modernism* (1946). Beginning with his provocative title, Van Til had attempted to show that the theology of Swiss Reformed theologian Karl Barth (1886–1968) was the new theological modernism. Gerstner noted that some criticisms in Van Til's book were the result of what he considered to be Van Til's "complete disparagement of Karl Barth." Gerstner argued that Van Til had been "too violent in his iconoclasm and shows virtually no appreciation of Barth's merits."[172] Despite this criticism Gerstner held that the book is "far and away the most searching examination we have seen Barth thus far receive." He agreed with Van Til's argument that Barth "is in the line of Kant" (suppressing reason in theology) and he emphasized Van Til's argument that Barth rejected God's transcendence. Gerstner kept his UP readers informed of the latest literature and addressed practical issues facing believers. His experience as a pastor and as a writer for a denominational magazine led him to have concern for the common person. Later, he would refuse to be restricted to the scholarly arena.

The early years of Gerstner's life were highly transformative. In high school he was involved in numerous activities and did well academically. His relationship with his high school girlfriend provided him with his first contact with a church and introduced him to the world of the United Presbyterians. Even though he did not come to faith in this early church experience, his participation in the Beverly Hills congregation at least led him to begin thinking about faith issues. Gerstner's conversion occurred during his visit to the Philadelphia School of the Bible. Remarkably, Gerstner came to faith when a school official explained to him the meaning and content of the Bible. Perhaps this acute experience led Gerstner to believe that faith could be reasonably demonstrated and that an apologetic approach might have a lasting impact in evangelism. If human explanation could play such a powerful role in own his coming to faith, then defending the faith using argument had to be a valid practice for Christians. And yet the event always seemed to remind him of the importance of experience in the Christian life and faith. At Westminster, Professor John Orr further reinforced Gerstner's apologetic viewpoint by exposing him to "Christian Evidences." In college Gerstner was very active socially and thrived intellectually.

Gerstner had found in Orr a trusted mentor and guide through the thickets of both historic and modern thought. His acceptance of Calvinism

171. Gerstner, Review of Smith's *Therefore Stand*, 9.

172. Gerstner, Review of Cornelius Van Til's *The New Modernism*, 2.

changed his thinking about his own conversion and connected him to the Calvinist tradition (and Old Princeton). While faith could be rationally demonstrated, it was ultimately God who brought people to himself. This view, which was mediated to Gerstner by Orr, initially traumatized Gerstner, but after some study he affirmed what Orr had told his class, "regeneration precedes faith." Orr's Calvinist tutoring and evangelicalism affected Gerstner deeply. Gerstner's challenges as a student later at Pitt-Xenia were an indication of how devoted Gerstner was to Orr and to his mentor's evangelical Calvinism. Westminster College had molded Gerstner in the stream of evangelical United Presbyterianism, a tradition which, in the 1920s and 1930s, had aligned itself in various ways with Machen's League of Evangelical Students. His experience at Westminster Seminary expanded Gerstner's Calvinist perspective, but also reinforced the peril of liberal theology. Gerstner excelled in seminary and came away from Westminster with an intelligent wife who shared his evangelical faith. Gerstner's choice of Harvard for a PhD offered both a challenge and prestige to this accomplished Christian student. Gerstner's understanding of theology and philosophy were aided by his post-graduate studies, but it does seem clear that it was Gerstner's undergraduate work with Orr that cemented his mind to Old Princeton, rational apologetics, and evangelical Calvinism. The completion of his Harvard doctorate did not immediately lead to a teaching position. Nonetheless, Gerstner gained valuable pastoral experience and an opportunity to write in a denominational periodical that gave his ideas exposure. An evangelical scholar was born and his future looked bright.

3

The Emergence of a Reformed Professor (1950–1959)

JOHN GERSTNER BEGAN HIS TEACHING CAREER AT PITTSBURGH-XENIA Theological Seminary in September 1950. The school was the only seminary of the United Presbyterian Church of North America and had a rich history of evangelical theological education. In 1950 Pitt-Xenia emphasized "Christian service," "knowledge of the doctrine of the Scriptures," and the theological "standards" of the UPCNA.[1] Prior to its 1930 merger with Pittsburgh Seminary, Xenia had been a solidly conservative seminary aligned with the League of Evangelical Students and the sole publisher of the evangelical periodical *Bibliotheca Sacra*.[2] Pittsburgh, however, held to a more moderate evangelical position. Yet when Gerstner arrived, Pitt-Xenia was changing and taking steps to strengthen its evangelical and Calvinistic doctrinal character. This evangelical effort was implemented by the seminary's dean, who sought to improve academic standards and the school's commitment to Reformed evangelicalism. During the 1950s, Gerstner played a leading role in helping the seminary embrace a more conservative theological orientation. As Pitt-Xenia moved forward, the seminary was faced with a historic denominational merger in 1958. These events, when combined with the influence of the broader evangelical movement, shaped Gerstner in powerful ways. During the 1950s, Gerstner was one of only a few evangelicals teaching in any mainline Protestant seminary.

---

1. *Pittsburgh-Xenia Theological Seminary: Annual Catalogue 1950–1951*, 12.

2. Hannah, *An Uncommon Union*, 107; McNaugher, *Theological Education in the United Presbyterian Church and its Ancestries*, 76–77. Kyle served as the editor of *Bibliotheca Sacra* until his death in 1933. In 1931 McNaugher does note that the journal was published under the auspices of the combined Pitt-Xenia. After Kyle's death, however, Pitt-Xenia sold *Bibliotheca Sacra* to Dallas Theological Seminary.

Xenia Seminary traces its founding to 1794 when the Associate Synod founded a seminary in Service, Pennsylvania. The Pittsburgh Seminary was founded by the Associate Reformed Presbyterian Church and dates from 1825. In 1931 John McNaugher, president of Pitt-Xenia, surveyed the long history of UPCNA theological education and noted that "Pittsburgh and Xenia [and their predecessors] never lost their way doctrinally" and that the two schools "remained anchored in that evangelicalism which is witnessed in the unshakable Creeds of the Church, especially in the Westminster documents."[3] He insisted that Pitt-Xenia's aim "will ever be to shun doctrinal vagueness and an uncertain, precarious orthodoxy." What is distinctive about the UPCNA seminaries is that they held firm to their evangelical Calvinism, participated in some parts of the American evangelical and fundamentalist movements, and were not significantly affected by Protestant modernism or by liberal European scholarship. As already said Xenia was especially innovative in its use of biblical archaeology as a tool to defend the Bible's historical trustworthiness and ward off the encroachments of liberal biblical criticism. Even though Gerstner had found the more general evangelicalism of Pitt-Xenia to be distressing as a student, he now had an opportunity, as a professor, to stiffen the institution's Reformed evangelical theological stance.

Gerstner's inauguration as professor of church history and government took place on November 16, 1950 at the First United Presbyterian Church, Pittsburgh. Numerous academic dignitaries attended the event and processed into the church singing "The Church's One Foundation."[4] The seminary choir sang, and the charge to the young professor was delivered by J. Lowrie Anderson (1902–1980), the moderator of the UPCNA. Anderson, who had served for twenty-five years as a missionary to South Sudan, could not tell Gerstner "how to teach church history," but added there were some things "the church expects your students to learn."[5] From the pulpit the moderator implored Gerstner to explain to his students why Islam swept across formerly Christian lands and how Roman Catholicism was able to win back whole peoples that had been Protestants. In his charge, he also asked Gerstner to explain to his students how so many "strange sects arose out of the heart of Protestantism." Anderson appeared to be concerned with challenges facing Protestants and expressed hope that Gerstner could supply some remedies. Gerstner apparently took Anderson's words to heart be-

---

3. McNaugher, *Theological Education in the United Presbyterian Church and Its Ancestries*, 78.

4. *Inauguration Bulletin of the Reverend Dr. John Gerstner, Jr., PhD.*

5. "Pittsburgh-Xenia Seminary Holds Inauguration Service," 7.

cause some of his later research would focus on Roman Catholicism and the vast array of cults. After Anderson completed his charge, the congregation sang from the Psalter hymnal. Gerstner then rose to give his inaugural address entitled "Why Did Presbyterianism Not Win England 1640–1660?" In his address, Gerstner discussed the "popular," "political," and "religious" reasons why Presbyterianism did not succeed in England. He maintained that the "most potent" cause of Presbyterian failure was Oliver Cromwell, who was most "sympathetic" to the Independents.[6] The December 4 report of the event in *The United Presbyterian* magazine featured John Orr's picture in the top center of the article with Gerstner on Orr's left and Anderson on Orr's right. The centrality of Orr to the festivities is evident in the fact that the sixty-six-year-old Orr served as the main speaker for the inauguration banquet.[7] While Orr's topic remains unknown, he continued to influence his former student.

When Gerstner arrived at Pitt-Xenia in 1950, the school was led by George A. Long (1884–1969), who had succeeded John McNaugher as president in 1943. Long, a graduate of Westminster College (Pennsylvania) and Pittsburgh Seminary, had returned to the school in 1943 after serving thirty-one years in pastoral ministry.[8] As an administrator, he reinitiated the school's ThM degree program, implemented new summer institutes of theology, and hired the school's first female professor, Florence M. Lewis (1918–2013), who was charged with creating a department of religious education.[9] Officially Pitt-Xenia's faculty members were elected by synods, which reveal that Pitt-Xenia was an institution orientated to the church rather than to the academy.[10] Theophilus Mills Taylor (1909–1989), who had also arrived in 1943, served as professor of New Testament and was highly involved in denominational and ecumenical affairs.[11] H. Ray Shear (1889–1961) had been a pastor for many years before becoming professor of practical theology in 1947.[12] The anchor and most senior member of the

6. Gerstner, "Why Did Presbyterianism Not Win in England Between 1640 and 1660?," 105.

7. "Pittsburgh-Xenia Seminary Holds Inauguration Service," 8.

8. Long served as president from 1943 to 1955.

9. Kelley Jr., "Pittsburgh-Xenia Seminary," 124. Lewis taught at Pitt-Xenia from 1946 to 1952. Lewis held a BA from Carnegie Institute of Technology (1939); MA McCormick Theological Seminary (1946).

10. Smith, *The Presbyterian Ministry in American Culture*, 199.

11. Taylor earned a BArch University of Pennsylvania (1935), a ThB Pittsburgh-Xenia 1941) and PhD Yale University (1956). He served as moderator of the UPCUSA in 1959–1960. Taylor taught at Pitt-Xenia from 1942 to 1962.

12. BA Westminster College (1911), Princeton Theological Seminary (1912–15),

faculty in 1950 was James L. Kelso (1892–1978), who held the professorship in semitics and biblical archaeology.[13] Kelso had started his teaching career at the old Xenia Seminary in 1923 and was the only surviving Xenia professor still teaching at the new Pitt-Xenia. The Xenia tradition lived on in Kelso. As a veteran of many excavations in ancient Palestine, Kelso brought back numerous antiquities to the school and created a widely-known Bible Lands Museum. Kelso was a protégé and colleague of Melvin Grove Kyle, the famed UP archaeologist, and kept the seminary in the vanguard of biblical archeology.[14] The 1950 *Pittsburgh-Xenia Theological Seminary Annual Catalogue* noted that the Bible Lands Museum's "objects all illustrate in the most striking way the life of the people of the Bible Lands, and so become of great value for interpretation as well as for apologetics." The catalogue also notes that the museum's artifacts "illumine and corroborate the Biblical narratives." The "objects of the Museum are used constantly in the classes" and "an ineffaceable impression is made upon the student of the trustworthiness of the Biblical record."[15] Even though the seminary made solid contributions to the discipline of biblical archaeology and while many of the seminary's professors were competent, Pitt-Xenia was not widely known in the academic world for its penetrating scholarship.[16] From the consolidation of Pittsburgh and Xenia seminaries in 1930 to the end of John McNaugher's presidency in 1943, Pitt-Xenia's ethos could be described as moderately Reformed and evangelical.[17]

In 1946, Addison H. Leitch (1909–1973) was appointed to teach philosophy of religion and religious education.[18] Leitch grew up in the UPCNA and graduated from the UP's Muskingkum College (Ohio) in 1931 and from Pitt-Xenia in 1936. Later, he completed his PhD from Cambridge University in 1941. His dissertation was entitled "The Relevancy of Calvin to Modern Issues Within Protestantism."[19] At Cambridge Leitch was influenced by J.S. Whale, who served as president of Cheshunt College, Cam-

---

MA Princeton University (1914). Shear taught at Pitt-Xenia from 1947 to 1959.

13. AB Monmouth College (1916), AM Indiana University, BD Xenia (1918), ThD Xenia. Kelso taught at Xenia from 1923 to 1930 and at Pitt-Xenia from 1930 to 1960 and at PTS from 1960 to 1963. On Kelso's career, see Coughenour, ed., *For Me To Live*.

14. On Kyle, see chapter 2.

15. *Pittsburgh-Xenia Theological Seminary: Annual Catalogue 1950–1951*, 32.

16. Pitt-Xenia receives no mention in Miller's comprehensive history of American Protestant theological education, *Piety and Profession*.

17. Gerster, interviewed by Coffin Jr. July 15, 1992, PCA Historical Center, 18–19.

18. BA Muskingkum College (1931), BD & ThM Pitt-Xenia (1936), PhD Cambridge University (1938).

19. Leitch, "The Relevancy of Calvin to Modern Issues within Protestantism."

bridge, a Congregational theologian who opposed modernism and sought to help strengthen his denomination's commitment to Calvinist doctrine and churchmanship.[20] Whale was not interested in a rigid fundamentalism, but was rather concerned with helping Protestantism maintain continuity with classical Christian faith.[21] The mild-mannered Leitch hoped to do the same in the UPCNA. Leitch became a seasoned professor and administrator, having previously served at Assuit College in Egypt, at Pikeville College (Kentucky) and at Grove City College (Pennsylvania).[22] His intellectual gifts were recognized from his arrival in 1946, and in 1949 he was installed in the chair of systematic theology.[23] Leitch was a committed Reformed evangelical theologian, and his appointment within the seminary represented a shift in a more distinctly evangelical direction. In 1949 Leitch also became the dean of the seminary and in 1955 its president. One observer of Leitch's career, William L. Fisk, who served as the longtime professor of history at Muskingum College, noted that Leitch was the first Pitt-Xenia president with an "earned rather than honorary doctorate . . . who directed the seminary more forcefully than ever before into the world of university education."[24] Nonetheless, Leitch also wanted to reinforce the school's Reformed and evangelical theological stance. Unlike most other mainline Presbyterian seminary theologians of his era, he eschewed liberal theology and had deep reservations about the neo-orthodox theology of both Karl Barth and Emil Brunner. Leitch was intent on taking Pitt-Xenia down a more conservative Reformed theological path. An example of his perspective is seen in his preference for who he thought should receive the Pitt-Xenia chair in systematic theology. The scholar Leitch thought most capable for this task was John Gerstner, a young local Pittsburgh pastor.

In 1949 Leitch decided that Gerstner should be the school's main professor of theology. According to Gerstner, "Leitch wanted me to take the chair of theology, but see, there was a real log-rolling thing there."[25] The "log rolling" that Gerstner referred to dealt with negotiations surrounding his nomination and the appointment of Gordon E. Jackson (1918–2000) to the faculty. Jackson was a more progressive-minded Christian education

20. Morgan, *Barth Reception in Britain*, 79–81; "Whale, John Seldon," 1171.

21. See Whale, *Christian Doctrine*.

22. Leitch also served as an assistant football coach and briefly as the head football coach at Grove City College.

23. Leitch taught at Pitt-Xenia from 1946 to 1960 and from 1960 to 1961 at PTS.

24. Fisk, "Addison H. Leitch," 142.

25. Gerstner interviewed by David Coffin, 18.

scholar who was pursing his PhD at the University of Chicago.[26] During the selection process, the different parties agreed that if one of the scholars was selected, the other scholar would join the faculty as well.[27] This process was done to satisfy the various groups and most probably to keep the peace. In the end Jackson was hired, Leitch stayed in his chair, and Gerstner was appointed as professor of church history.[28] Gerstner then set about teaching the basic church history courses: "Apostolic and Ancient," "Medieval," "Modern," and "History of Doctrine."[29] From the very beginning of Gerstner's career at Pitt-Xenia his elective courses included: "Jonathan Edwards and the New England Church," "Augustine," "The History of the Doctrine of the Inspiration of the Bible," "The History of Dispensationalism," and "Major Sects."[30] This shows Gerstner's early interest in Edwards and his aim of introducing the colonial theologian to his students. It appears that Gerstner believed that Edwards was a potent evangelical theologian whose theology needed to be communicated to a modern audience.

By the middle part of the twentieth century there was a revival of interest in Edwards. Two neo-orthodox scholars who helped draw attention to Edwards and his legacy were Joseph Haroutunian (1904–1968) and H. Richard Niebuhr (1894–1962). Haroutunian's *Piety versus Moralism* (1932) and Niebuhr's *The Kingdom of God in America* (1937) helped recover Edwards's legacy as a great American theological mind.[31] Ola Winslow's 1940 biography provided a solid study of Edwards's life. However, the person most responsible for resurrecting Edwards was Perry Miller (1905–1963)—a Harvard University literary scholar. Miller promoted writing and research on Edwards and in 1949 published a landmark study of Edwards's thought.[32] Miller's efforts sparked the sustained rise of Edwards studies and by 1954 a

26. A 1953 evangelical graduate of Pitt-Xenia, Wilson, wrote in a letter to Henry that "Jackson plays footsie with Ferre and the agape boys." Wilson told Henry "that one doesn't mind disagreeing with him [T. M. Taylor], as it is bound to be stimulating. This is hardly true of Dr. Jackson." Wilson to Henry, 2 March 1956, Graham Center Archives, Wheaton College, IL. In an interview later in life Gerstner argued that Jackson had been a "core liberal" all along and that Jackson was a "process theologian." Gerstner, Interview with Coffin, PCA Historical Center, 19.

27. Gerstner, Interview with David Coffin, 18.

28. Jackson taught at Pitt-Xenia from 1949 to 1960 and 1960 to 1983 at PTS. BA Monmouth College (1940), BD and ThM Pitt-Xenia (1943), PhD University of Chicago (1954).

29. *Pittsburgh-Xenia Theological Seminary: Annual Catalogue 1950–1951*, 30–31.

30. Ibid., 31.

31. Crocco, "Edwards Intellectual Legacy," 310–13.

32. Miller, *Jonathan Edwards.*

grant was received by Miller to launch the Yale edition of Edwards's works.[33] This renewed vitality in Edwards studies would continue to develop and expand.

Gerstner would play a key role in the rise of Edwards studies, but he also blossomed in the classroom. As a teacher, one student recalled that Gerstner was "dynamic and demanding." Joe Barr (1929–2014), who arrived as a student in 1953, remembers Gerstner as an "enthusiastic" and "scholarly" professor who was "highly thought of in the seminary."[34] Another student, Jack B. Rogers (1934–), found Gerstner to be an "engaging" instructor and noted that it was "fascinating to watch him work [lecture]" in the classroom. The young professor rapidly grew as a teacher and scholar, and by most accounts he was handling his work with self-confidence.

Gerstner's family during the early 1950s was also growing. In 1951 John and Edna welcomed into their home an eight-year-old foster daughter named Judy who hailed from the mountains of Appalachia.[35] As foster parents John and Edna seemed to excel, and their relationship with Judy developed into a long-term arrangement. Later, in 1953, Edna gave birth to a baby girl named Rachel. The Gerstner household was expanding and busy. The family drove back and forth from Ligonier to Pittsburgh and traveled regularly halfway across the country to visit Edna's parents in Omaha, Nebraska. As a three year old, Rachel would talk "a great deal about going to Omaha," which might have seemed like an exotic location for this Pennsylvania family.[36] In a letter dated April 16, 1956, Edna told her mother that "We are all well and happy," but there were also fears. Like other parents in this era, Edna worried about polio, writing that she would be able to "rest easier" when her daughter received the "Salk vaccine," which was developed in Pittsburgh.[37] The young professor's life was changing rapidly, but he seemed happy, telling his wife "The Lord has been most gracious to me and has blessed me greatly in my family."[38]

As a seminary teacher Gerstner faced new responsibilities and challenges at work. By the early 1950s, most of the faculty was new to the school. Even though a minor debate occurred in the church over the Jackson and Gerstner appointments, the faculty itself was mostly unified and congenial. While Jackson held more moderate theological views and some leadership

---

33. Crocco, "Edwards Intellectual Legacy," 314.

34. Barr, Interview with the author.

35. Gerstner, Interview with the author.

36. Gerstner, Letter to Suckau.

37. Gerstner, Letter to Suckau.

38. Gerstner, Letter to Gerstner.

skills, he did not really have the necessary power to change what was by all accounts a largely evangelical faculty. According to Gerstner, the rest of the faculty were "definitely sympathetic" to the evangelical Calvinist theology that Leitch and Gerstner were promoting. They were not as "aware" or "knowledgeable" about it "as Leitch and I were," but they "came along" with it. He later said he worked "under Leitch's leadership" and "sort of assisted" Leitch, noting that Leitch "carried the ball and I ran interference for him."[39] The pair was able to pursue their goal of making the school a notable center of evangelical Reformed theology.[40] From Gerstner's perspective, Pitt-Xenia during the early and mid-1950s "was moving, definitely, in a conservative direction." During this period, evangelical luminaries such as Clarence E. Macartney (1879–1957), the famed conservative Pittsburgh PCUSA pastor, and Billy Graham (1918–), the celebrated evangelist, served as special speakers.[41] During the 1950s, evidence suggests that Pitt-Xenia was becoming a more distinctively evangelical seminary.

In retrospect Gerstner speculated that these developments at the seminary were "alarming the [PC] USA people."[42] He thought that if the seminary became too conservative a proposed merger between the PCUSA and the UPCNA might not happen or at least it would make it more difficult. During the 1950s, Leitch and Gerstner and their allies were "rejoicing" in the seminary's more prominent evangelical stance.[43] One "evangelical" student who arrived in 1955 and "loved" his time of study at Pitt-Xenia was Jack B. Rogers. During his doctoral studies, however, Rogers came to the belief that the seminary "was not a good academic school" and claimed that "Pitt-Xenia had no consistent theology."[44] Rogers noted that "we didn't study Karl Barth or even B. B. Warfield," for we just "read whatever our theology profs were interested in." Yet Rogers appears to confirm the view that the seminary became more conservative when he observes that "Gerstner's view was right wing on a right wing faculty."[45] During the 1950s,

39. Gerstner, Interview with Coffin, 18–19.

40. Ibid., 19.

41. Macartney is listed as a special lecturer in the *Pittsburgh-Xenia Theological Seminary, Annual Catalogue 1949–1950*, 73. Graham is listed in the *Pittsburgh-Xenia Theological Seminary, Annual Catalogue 1952–1953*, 79.

42. Gerstner, Interview with Coffin, 19.

43. Ibid., 20.

44. Rogers, Interview with the author. Rogers received his ThD from the Free University of Amsterdam and then taught theology at Westminster College (PA), Fuller Seminary (CA) and San Francisco Theological Seminary (CA). He served as moderator of the PCUSA in 2001–2002.

45. Ibid.

Pitt-Xenia and Gerstner may have had critics on the outside, but inside the school, the faculty fostered a more harmonious culture. As a teenager Bob Kelley (1927–) heard Gerstner speak, graduated from the seminary in 1951, pursued graduate work at Princeton Seminary and finally returned to the school in 1955 to teach biblical languages.[46] Kelley would recall that during the 1950s Gerstner was "well respected" and "very popular" within the UPCNA.[47] He noted the unity inside the seminary, commenting that "Gerstner related very well with other faculty" and that they were a "congenial group." Importantly, Kelly held that "Gerstner symbolized UP identity." The evangelical UPCNA tradition was alive and well at Pitt-Xenia during the 1950s, and Gerstner was doing what he could to continue the legacy.

Other important American church leaders were taking notice and recognizing the developments at Pitt-Xenia as well. On March 16, 1956, Carl F.H. Henry (1913–2003), a Fuller Seminary theologian and the new editor-in-chief of *Christianity Today*, wrote a confidential letter to Gerstner inviting him to become a contributing editor. *Christianity Today*, according to Henry, was a "strategic project" that could provide "evangelical impact" upon the church and nation. Henry apparently had been told about the circumstances at Pitt-Xenia by Edward Carnell, Fuller's president and professor of apologetics, who had attended Leitch's October 1955 presidential inauguration.[48] Also, an analysis of Gerstner and the rest of the Pitt-Xenia faculty had been provided to Henry in a March 2, 1956 letter written by Talmage Wilson (1926–2006), who had studied at Fuller before completing his seminary education at Pitt-Xenia in 1953.[49] Wilson explained to Henry, his former professor, that the "real conservative power behind the throne at Pitt-Xenia has been Dr. John H. Gerstner."[50] He added that at Pitt-Xenia we "have a fine group" that "has been greatly strengthened by recent developments." Henry quickly reached out to Gerstner. In Henry's letter to Gerstner he wrote that the periodical's strategy and list of contributing editors were being shared in "high confidence."[51] A week later, Gerstner responded to the invitation, saying that it was an "honor" to be selected and that he

---

46. Kelley, Interview with the author. Kelley earned his BA at the University of Pittsburgh, his BD at Pitt-Xenia, a ThM at Princeton Seminary and a PhD at Princeton University. Kelley taught at Pitt-Xenia from 1955 to 1960 and at PTS from 1960 to 1995.

47. Kelley, Interview with the author.

48. Wilson, Letter to Henry.

49. Ibid.

50. Ibid.

51. Henry, Letter to Gerstner.

should "be happy to render what service I can to this important cause."[52] Gerstner mentioned to Henry that he had had a conversation with Leitch about the new magazine. Even though Leitch declined an offer by Henry to become a contributing editor, he did write an article for the inaugural issue and urged Gerstner to become a contributing editor.

Gerstner and Cary N. Weisiger III, pastor of the large Mt Lebanon United Presbyterian Church in Pittsburgh were the two UPCNA clergy listed as contributing editors on the *Christianity Today* masthead.[53] The magazine quickly became a boon for the evangelical movement because, unlike many other evangelical periodicals, it was more forward-looking, culturally aware, and devoted to interaction with mainstream culture and churches. The periodical's goals were probably one of the reasons why Gerstner and Leitch were selected: they were scholars within a mainline Protestant denomination. The well-funded periodical, which was housed across the street from the White House in the District of Columbia, provided evangelicalism with an important alternative to more separatist and culturally narrow fundamentalist magazines.[54] Gerstner recognized the opportunity that *Christianity Today* represented, and told Henry, "I am doing what I can to publicize Christianity Today and its significance."[55] Gerstner's relationship with *Christianity Today* as a contributing editor aligned him with the broader evangelical community and helped to introduce his ideas to people across the theological and denominational spectrum.

By the mid-1950s, Gerstner was simultaneously developing key relationships with non-mainline Presbyterians such as the Reformed Presbyterians. In the fall of 1954, Gerstner gave a series of lectures at College Hill Reformed Presbyterian Church in Beaver Falls, Pennsylvania. College Hill was adjacent to the campus of Geneva College, and both institutions were affiliated with the Reformed Presbyterian Church of North America (RPCNA). The RPCNA was a small denomination that traced its origins back to the seventeenth-century Scottish Covenanters. They held to classical Reformed doctrine, the inerrancy of the Bible, and exclusive psalm singing.[56] One Geneva freshman who attended Gerstner's lectures at Beaver Falls, John H. White (1936–), later said his "life was changed" by the experience.[57]

---

52. Gerstner, Letter to Henry.

53. Masthead, *Christianity Today*, 2.

54. Marsden, *Reforming Fundamentalism*, 158.

55. Gerstner, Letter to Henry.

56. Weir, "Reformed Presbyterian Church of North America, Covenanter Synod," 211–12.

57. White, Interview with the author, May 15, 2012. White served as pastor of

White remembers the young professor's "incredible energy" and how he himself "was kind of like converted under Gerstner's preaching."[58] Partly because of his forceful speaking style, Gerstner "packed" the church with laypeople, students, and faculty. According to Wayne Spear (1935–), a Reformed Presbyterian theologian, Gerstner became "very influential" in the RPCNA, whose leadership viewed him as a "co-laborer."[59] Indeed, Gerstner subsequently went on to speak or teach on numerous occasions at RPCNA churches, at Geneva College and at the Reformed Presbyterian Theological Seminary in Pittsburgh. According to White, Gerstner had a "substantial influence on the RPCNA," which by the 1950s had a somewhat "undefined theology."[60] White claims that Gerstner helped many RPCNA pastors to clarify where they "should be at theologically," noting that he helped "the RPCNA become more explicitly and dynamically Reformed." His initial work among the Reformed Presbyterians in the 1950s was unique for a UPCNA professor; Gerstner's efforts with the RPCNA marked just the beginning of a career throughout which he sought to have substantive relationships with smaller and more sectarian Presbyterian denominations.

Gerstner also spoke at several UPCNA liberal arts colleges in the 1950s. In October of 1956 the Sterling College newspaper, *Ye Sterlng Stir,* reported on the lectures that Gerstner gave for the school's spiritual life week.[61] His lectures dealt with Christ's divinity and how doctrine affected the practical aspects of the Christian life. One Sterling student, Jay Grimstead, recalled that he was "impressed with Gerstner's fast-talking, heavy-duty theological teaching."[62] At Muskingkum College, R. Douglas Brackenridge, remembers that "Gerstner stirred up the chapel crowd and that discussion afterwards was packed."[63] Apparently, Gerstner took on an agnostic student who challenged him. "Gerstner influenced me to attend Pitt-Xenia," Brackenridge later noted. He enjoyed the "intensity in Gerstner's classroom." Nonetheless, Brackenridge also recounted that he "was impressed with Gerstner's caring

College Hill Reformed Presbyterian Church from 1962 to 1970. In 1970 he became a professor of biblical studies at Geneva and later an administrator at the college. From 1992 to 2004 he served as Geneva's president. From 1988 to 1990 he served as president of the National Association of Evangelicals.

58. Weir, "Reformed Presbyterian Church of North America, Covenanter Synod," 211–12.

59. Spear, Interview with the author, August 9, 2011, Spear served as a professor of theology at the Reformed Presbyterian Theological Seminary from 1970 to 2005.

60. White, Interview with the author, May 15, 2012.

61. "Gerstner Speaks For Spiritual Life Week," 1.

62. Grimstead, Interview with the author, January 20, 2014.

63. Brackenridge, Interview with the author.

attitude." When he began PhD studies in history at the University of Glasgow he was grateful that Gerstner sent him twenty-five dollars a month for a year to help with expenses.[64] Gerstner's contributions to UPCNA higher education were recognized in 1955 when he received his first honorary DD from the UPCNA's Tarkio College located in rural northwestern Missouri.[65]

Gerstner was making a name for himself as a popular lecturer and chapel speaker, but he also wanted to contribute to the study of American church history. On June 20 and 21, 1956, Gerstner attended the "Calvinistic Conference" held at Calvin College and Seminary in Grand Rapids, Michigan. Gerstner joined a variety of conservative Reformed scholars to discuss the history and "status" of Calvinism in America and its future "prospects."[66] Gerstner delivered a revealing lecture entitled "American Calvinism Until The Twentieth Century." This lecture is important because it represents his first major analysis of the colonial New England theologian Jonathan Edwards (1703–1758) and American Calvinist thought in the eighteenth and nineteenth centuries. In his lecture Gerstner noted that "we of the Scottish Secession traditions, Reformed, Associated, and United Presbyterians, must admit [that we] have not produced any thinkers known far beyond our walls."[67] In his lecture he argued that "until recently" the most important and influential theologians in the "cause of catholic Calvinism" came from the "Presbyterian Church, U.S.A." Gerstner noted especially its "Old School" wing, the Princeton theologians.[68] Provocatively he claimed that the Old School' scholars were the "spiritual allies" of the great colonial theologian "Jonathan Edwards and original New England theology." Contrary to some other historians, Gerstner maintained that the innovative nineteenth-century theologian Nathaniel Taylor (1786–1858) broke with Edwards's theological tradition. To support his historical argument, he highlighted the evaluation of Sidney Mead (1904–1999), the Taylor biographer and Yale historian, who observed that it is possible to say that "Edwardeanism [sic] or consistent Calvinism was never *the* New England theology."[69] For Gerstner this showed that Edwards legacy laid elsewhere.

---

64. Ibid.

65. Gerstner, Curriculum Vitae.

66. Some of the other speakers included: Eugene Oosterhaven of Western Seminary (MI), Paul Woolley of Westminster Seminary (PA), Donald Tweedie of Gordon College and Divinity School (MA), and Cornelis Jaarsma of Calvin College (MI).

67. Gerstner, "American Calvinism Until The Twentieth Century," 15–16.

68. Ibid., 16, 37.

69. Mead quoted by Gerstner, "American Calvinism until the Twentieth Century," 30. See Mead, *Nathaniel Taylor*, x.

If Edwards's theology was not in continuity with nineteenth-century New England theology and the theology of Nathaniel Taylor, then where did the stream of Edwards's powerful thought flow? Gerstner believed that he had the answer. According to Gerstner, "The mantle of Edwards fell not on the Taylors, Bushnells, Parks, Beechers, and Gladdens, but on the Alexanders, the Hodges, Pattons, and Warfields."[70] The thirty-nine-year-old Pitt-Xenia professor argued that "Edwards lived possibly most purely and certainly most influentially in Princeton Seminary and Old School Presbyterianism." He did note that in the nineteenth century there were some "able Reformed thinkers" at Union Seminary (New York) "such as H. B Smith and W. G. T. Shedd." Moreover, there were other "faithful" Reformed thinkers and traditions in different parts of the country, but these were "not conspicuous."[71] The most "robustly" visible form of Calvinism up until 1900 was centered at Princeton. While some historians would agree with Gerstner's interpretation about the decline of Edwards's theology in New England, many would disagree that Edwards could be so strongly linked to the scholars of Old Princeton.[72] Gerstner's lecture gave solid historical evidence to support his argument of Edwardsean "degeneration" in New England. Yet on the Princeton connection his argument offered far less detail. Gerstner apparently reasoned that if Edwards's powerful Calvinism slowly dried up in New England, it must have lived on at Princeton. Gerstner rejected the position of Winfield Burggraff, a Reformed Church in America scholar, who contended that Edwards's subjectivity and views on the internal testimony of the Holy Spirit were the source of American pelagianism. Gerstner argued on the contrary that Edwards "safeguarded objectivity as carefully, if not more so, than Calvin himself . . ."[73] In his mind Edwards's objectivity was a match with Old Princeton's use of reason. This lecture reveals Gerstner's early views on Edwards and how he viewed Edwards through the lens of Old Princeton; this approach to Edwards would continue to be a significant aspect of his scholarship and thought. For Gerstner, Edwards and the Old Princeton theological tradition represented the continuity of evangelical Calvinism in America and these figures reflected the type of Reformed evangelical minds Gerstner hoped to revive in his era. His position is reminiscent of Orr's suggestion of a bond between deism and modernism.

Three months after his lecture in September 1956, the *New England Quarterly* published a book review by Gerstner which examined a study

---

70. Gerstner, "American Calvinism Until The Twentieth Century," 37–38.

71. Ibid., 38.

72. See Noll, "Jonathan Edwards and Nineteenth-Century Theology," 260–87.

73. Gerstner, "American Calvinism Until The Twentieth Century," 25.

edited by Harvey G. Townsend, a University of Oregon professor, entitled *The Philosophy of Jonathan Edwards from His Private Notebooks* (1955). Gerstner, the budding historian, found the book to be a "careful study" of various texts written by Edwards. He labelled the work a "valuable" and a "philosophically significant" study of Edwards.[74] Even though the review appears straightforward, the final paragraph includes a significant revelation. In the last section of the review Gerstner wrote that the book makes a "useful and essential contribution to the work that, as Dr. Townsend himself observed, still needs to be written: an adequate statement of the philosophical system of the great New Englander."[75] It appears that perhaps Townsend first suggested to Gerstner's mind that a serious study of Edwards's philosophy needed to be written. Gerstner would spend the next several decades seeking to answer Townsend's call. It appears that he pursued writing a major study of Edwards's thought for years; his efforts culminated in a massive three-volume work that was published near the end of his life.[76]

From 1950 to 1959, Gerstner produced sixty-one book reviews and thirty-six articles of varying length. Nearly all of these reviews and articles appeared in three publications: *The United Presbyterian, Interpretation,* and *Christianity Today*. Gerstner served as a corresponding editor for both *The United Presbyterian* and *Christianity Today*. During this period, Gerstner wrote forty-seven book reviews and twenty-two articles for *The United Presbyterian*, the UCPNA's main denominational periodical. The bulk of the reviews were short, popular reviews, but some others offered more detailed analysis. These reviews are significant because they offer a window into the young scholar's mind and his attitude towards various theological perspectives and church movements. In a 1952 review, Gerstner criticized the "thoroughgoing Ecumenicalism" he found in *On This Rock* (1951), a book written by a Methodist bishop, G. Bromley Oxnam. Gerstner was troubled by Oxnam's glossing over of doctrinal distinctives; Gerstner noted "the impression is too commonly given here and elsewhere that the denominational differences are always merely diversities while often they are downright contradictions."[77] Gerstner, who was facing church union in his own denomination, revealed his own anti-unionist sympathies in the review of

74. Gerstner, Review of ed Townsend's *The Philosophy of Jonathan Edwards from His Private Notebooks*, 423.

75. Ibid.

76. In volume 1 of Gerstner's *Rational Biblical Theology of Jonathan Edwards* (1991) he claims that Edwards was his "main—on and off—academic preoccupation for the last forty years." See Gerstner, *Rational Biblical Theology of Jonathan Edwards* 1:3. For more on this, see chapter 7.

77. Gerstner, Review of Oxnam's *On This Rock*, *United Presbyterian*, 2–3.

Oxnam's book. While Gerstner did hold that ecumenical relationships were "possible" and "desirable," he insisted that Oxnam's "ultra" ecumenical spirit was "narrow" and "extremely sectarian."[78] In another 1952 review he praised G. C. Berkouwer, a Dutch Reformed theologian at the Free University of Amsterdam, for his two works *Faith and Sanctification* (1952) and *The Providence of God* (1952), which he found to be "profoundly theological," and averred that the works of Berkouwer and other Dutch theologians were "impressive." Yet like Cornelius Van Til, the American Dutch theologian, he also criticized the Amsterdam theologian for his "disparagement of reason" and "depreciation of traditional apologetic." He wrote, " [t]here is a clear tendency to make 'faith' work overtime."[79] Gerstner warned his readers against theologies which criticized rationality in an effort to defend the faith. The Pittsburgh church historian's academic training, his PhD study of James McCosh, had led him to believe that reason was crucial in overcoming challenges to the Christian faith.

The Pitt-Xenia scholar noted that Carl Henry's *The Drift of Western Thought* (1951) was a "solid book" which was effective in "analysis and exposing shibboleths." In Gerstner's words, Henry—like McCosh—was especially gifted in showing that "science is not opposed to Christianity" and in explaining that theological "liberalism" is actually "quite dogmatic in its assumptions about nature, revelation, etc."[80] Gerstner reviewed Neal J. Hughley's *Trends in Protestant Social Idealism* (1948), arguing that that the book was a "radical interpretation of the social gospel."[81] In his review of F. Maxwell Bradshaw's *Scottish Seceders in Victoria* (1947) he noted that the book "was well worth pondering" because it gave an "interesting projection" of the United Presbyterians and their principles in Australia.[82] In 1953, he wrote a review of Edward Carnell's *The Theology of Reinhold Niebuhr* (1951). In this review he asserts that the book offered an "admirable view of Neo-Orthodoxy."[83] He found Carnell's work to be "scholarly in character" and "adequately critical." Gerstner wrote, "Carnell's work is another proof of a deep conviction of the reviewer, that learned conservative writers know Liberalism and Neo-Orthodoxy better and expound it more fairly than learned

78. Ibid., 3.

79. Gerstner, Review of Berkouwer's *Faith and Sanctification* and *The Providence of God*, 3.

80. Gerstner, Review of Henry's *The Drift of Western Thought*, 21.

81. Gerstner, Review of Hughley's *Trends in Protestant Social Idealism*, 3.

82. Gerstner, Review of Bradshaw's *Scottish Seceders in Victoria*, 17.

83. Gerstner, Review of Carnell's *The Theology of Reinhold Niebuhr*, 20.

men of these schools know and expound conservative Christianity."[84] "The chief value of this book" the Pitt-Xenia professor wrote "is in bringing the wide literature of Niebuhr in the scope of one volume." In a review of Bela Vasady's *The Main Traits of Calvin's Theology* (1951), Gertsner found fault with the Hungarian Reformed theologian's "terms and their explanations," noting they were "ambiguous."[85] He argued that "Vasady sees Calvin generally, as the historic Reformed churchmen have seen him," but that Vassady, who was influenced by Karl Barth, was using "confusing nomenclature." Clearly, Gerstner was exposing himself to neo-orthodoxy, but in his review of Vassady's book he seemed to struggle to understand its finer points.

There were other theologians Gerstner found far easier to grasp. In 1954 he labeled Herman Bavinck's *The Doctrine of God* (1951 reprint) as a "masterpiece" written by a "great Dutchman" who was "not merely a master historian of theology but a master theologian."[86] He added the claim that no one would doubt this who read Bavinck's "profound, exhaustive analyses and syntheses." Apparently, Gerstner was enamored with Bavinck's "detailed knowledge of philosophy" and grasp of the "history of doctrine." Gerstner recommended to his readers that they should not just "read" the book, but that they should also "meditate on it and live with it and know the God whose wondrous majesty it so nobly exalts."[87] Clearly Gerstner was inspired by Bavinck's theological scholarship. He was less inspired by John T. McNeill's *The History and Character of Calvinism* (1954), which he thought gave numerous "evidences of an inadequate grasp of the Calvinistic doctrinal heritage."[88] He could not understand how the Union Seminary (NYC) scholar "could conceive of Calvin's view of scripture as resembling the accommodation theory of Lessing." The Pitt-Xenia historian was also annoyed that McNeill made "no reference to the United Presbyterian Church in North America" in his "discussion of American Presbyterian reunions."[89] Gerstner's reviews of various theological works appear to have been motivated by a desire to influence UPCNA clergy and laypeople in a conservative direction and to remind them of their UP heritage. Presumably this was done so that the UPCNA would avoid church union.

In the April 1955 edition of *Interpretation*, a review by Gerstner of John Dillenberger and Claude Welch's *Protestant Christianity* (1954) appeared.

84. Ibid.

85. Gerstner, Review of Vasady's *The Main Traits of Calvin's Theology*, 22.

86. Gerstner, Review of Bavinck's *The Doctrine of God*, 22.

87. Ibid.

88. Gerstner, Review of McNeill's *The History and Character of Calvinism*, 22.

89. Ibid., 23.

The book, according to Gerstner, sought "to set forth Protestant beliefs in the context of history."[90] He noticed, however, that there was "more theology than history in the book." He praised the historians for their "exposition of ideas" and for the "meatiness of this work." Their book was unlike many other historical studies of theology which downplayed theology while narrating "the events associated" with theology "in great detail." Gerstner was impressed with some aspects of their discussion of Luther and lauded their "survey of the nineteenth century—the mission century" as "admirably done." He also wrote that the book well explained the "development of liberalism, especially in Germany." Despite the "many merits" of the study, he faulted these "specialists in the history of theology" for "too many misinterpretations."[91] He included several criticisms of the portrayals of the Reformers and the author's overly "sharp distinction" between Calvin and the "later Calvinists." Nonetheless, his strongest criticism was leveled against what he regarded as the authors's prejudiced view of "orthodox" Christians. He noted that the two scholars "are in the best modern fashion of making the 'orthodox' of all time, the 'Scholastics' and The Westminster Confession of Faith of the seventeenth century (p. 114), and the American 'fundamentalists' of today, the scapegoat of academic criticism."[92] He abruptly and somewhat strangely ended his review on a note of pique. He blasted the authors for arguing that the "orthodox" care only for precise theoretical statements, for holding that the orthodox maintained an "idolatrous view" of the Bible and for "drawing no distinction between God's predestination of faith and man's having it."[93] Gerstner believed that the authors' criticisms of conservative theological positions were not well reasoned and misrepresented the actual beliefs and views of "orthodox" Christians. This polemical ending seems out of step with the rest of the review and reveals the scholar's sensitivity to the criticism of views with which he sympathized.

During the 1950s, Gerstner also worked on several book projects. In 1958 he published an eighty-four page commentary on Ephesians for Baker Book House's "Shield Bible Study Series."[94] This work was aimed at the "average, educated reader" and geared to pastors, students, and laypeople.[95] Gerstner also engaged himself in larger projects. John Orr suggested to Gerstner that he should write an apologetic work that defended the faith.

90. Gerstner, Review of Dillenberger and Welch's *Protestant Christianity*, 219.

91. Ibid., 219–20.

92. Ibid., 221.

93. Ibid., 221.

94. Gerstner, *The Epistle to the Ephesians*.

95. Ibid., 1.

It seems likely that Orr felt the book was necessary because of the decline of the Old Princeton theological tradition. Even though Gerstner's expertise was in the history of theology and philosophy, he decided, on the basis of Orr's encouragement, to study and write on apologetics. Throughout the 1950s, Gerstner worked on this venture and Orr "read and criticize[d] the manuscript."[96] The young protégé felt uneasy about this task and repeatedly told Orr that he "was far better qualified than I" to write the book. Gerstner later explained that he wrote the book because Orr told him that "there was need for such a work" and because Orr's "suggestions have always carried the force of commands with me."[97] In a letter to Carl Henry, Gerstner commented that his "interest in apologetics is general," covering the traditional areas of the discipline.[98] In August 1958, he shared his apologetic arguments and received feedback from college students at Inter-Varsity's "Campus-in-the-Woods" in Ontario.[99] His volume would not appear until the beginning of the new decade, but during the 1950s he continued to think seriously about apologetics. In the 1950s, Orr and Gerstner both seemed to believe that a book which offered an evidentialist apologetic of the Christian faith might bring some certainty to the theological uncertainty of the era.

Gerstner's more specialized interest was the study of Jonathan Edwards and his thought. He believed that Edwards could help bring theological and spiritual renewal to the American church. Throughout the 1950s, he worked on a "monograph" that dealt with the evangelistic message of Edwards's sermons.[100] He called it a "pioneer work in a largely unexplored region." Gerstner would drive from his home in Ligonier, Pennsylvania, to New Haven, Connecticut, to examine Edwards's sermons in the rare book room at Yale University's library. While there in the summer of 1957, he purchased an "air-conditioner" to relieve himself of the heat.[101] On May 15, 1957 he went to New York City to hear Billy Graham preach in the opening service of the evangelist's crusade at Madison Square Garden. In a letter he told his wife that the "service on the whole was good" and that Graham's sermon "exalted the Bible," discussed "sin and the need of salvation by Christ." Nonetheless, he found Graham's preaching "offensively Armininian in its need of man's ability" to come to faith. Gerstner, who had become ill with a cold, wrote that he was the "only one of 18,000" who appeared to

96. Gerstner, *Reasons for Faith*, ix.
97. Ibid.
98. Gerstner, Letter to Henry.
99. Gerstner, *Reasons For Faith*, ix–x.
100. Gerstner, *Steps to Salvation*, 12.
101. Gerstner to Gerstner.

be "weeping throughout the sermon."[102] At Yale he was pouring over and analyzing Edwards's sermons. The specific and somewhat narrow issue that Gerstner wanted to address was whether or not Edwards was a "covenant theologian" or if he did "compromise with Arminianism."[103] In the context of Billy Graham's popularity and the resurgence of evangelicalism in the 1950s, Gerstner wanted to show that Calvinism and its doctrine of election were not necessarily incompatible with evangelism. Indeed, Reformed evangelicalism extended far back into American history.

In *Steps to Salvation* (1959), Gerstner sought to explain Jonathan Edwards's "evangelistic message." Gerstner noted that Edwards "was neither merely a predestinarian, nor merely an evangelist." He demonstrated that Edwards "was a predestinarian evangelist." In the 1950s, it seemed obvious to many people to associate Billy Graham and evangelists in general with a decision-orientated, Arminian theological position. He noted that it was "surprising how many men, learned and unlearned, supposed that if a preacher believes in predestination, he is not an evangelist." Yet Gerstner showed in *Steps to Salvation* that the Calvinist Edwards "preached, with equal vigor and insistence, the decrees of God and the responsibility of men."[104] Evangelism and God's sovereignty were not mutually exclusive. "He [Edwards] pressed his hearers for decision," according to Gerstner, but "conceived of the steps to salvation within the framework of divine decrees and without any violation of the decrees."[105] Gerstner supported his view of Edwards with detailed analysis of the New Englander's sermons. Each chapter of the book dealt with a particular aspect of Edwards messages. Some of the chapters included were: "The Divine Initiative," "Justifying a Scare Theology," "The Sinner's First Step to Salvation," "A Fatal Backward Step," "Other Wrong Steps," "Seeking Salvation," "A Calvinistic Interpretation of Backsliding," "The Covenantal Frame of Reference." In a review, Alan Heimert (1928–1999), an English scholar then at the Institute for Advanced Study in Princeton, wrote, "we shall be grateful to Prof. Gerstner for the present information on a period of Edwards's career that has been given too little consideration."[106] In his study, Gerstner brought out information from many of Edwards's unpublished sermons which he had analyzed in his trips to the Sterling Library at Yale.[107] Already in 1953 Gerstner was

102. Ibid.

103. Gerstner, *Steps to Salvation*, 14.

104. Ibid., 13.

105. Ibid., 14.

106. Heimert, Review of *Steps to Salvation*, 473.

107. Gerstner, *Steps to Salvation*, 11.

working on the Edwards manuscripts with Thomas Schaeffer, another key Edwards scholar, and sometime prior to 1957 Gerstner was made editor of the Yale volume on Edwards's sermons.[108] Gerstner's book, his knowledge of the content of Edwards's numerous sermons, and his contacts with other Edwards scholars, like Perry Miller, had given Gerstner somewhat of a reputation in the growing field of Edwards studies. It remained to be seen, however, if this evangelical could rise to the top of Edwards's scholarship.

In 1957 he and Edna welcomed a son, Jonathan Neil, into their family. The couple now had three children in their loving home. Edna was supportive of her husband's work. John noted, "I am grateful to my wife, who played father and mother to our three children so that I could give my undivided attention" to research on Jonathan Edwards.[109] As a professor at the only UPCNA seminary in the country, Gerstner had more to worry about than family issues and academic interests. In the 1950s, discussion of a denominational merger loomed large in the UPCNA and at Pitt-Xenia. Indeed, church union proposals were a topic in the UPCNA and had extended far back into the first half of the nineteenth century. In 1958 Wallace N. Jamieson suggested in *The United Presbyterian Story* that the reason why the UPCNA engaged in so many union negotiations was because United Presbyterians wanted to "witness to the underlying unity of all Christian churches."[110] In 1907 the PCUSA began talks with the UPCNA, but three years later these merger discussions were dropped.[111] At this point the UPCNA was hesitant to amalgamate itself with a larger Presbyterian body. Plans for a merger with the Presbyterian Church US (PCUS)[southern church] also cooled in 1913 because of the race issue.[112] In 1926 the southern Presbyterians again invited the UPCNA to engage in merger discussions and the UPCNA agreed.

In 1929 the southern PCUS met first and approved the union and sent it to its presbyteries for a vote. At the 1929 UP General Assembly the small denomination voted to study the issue further.[113] The southern PCUS presbyteries did not like this move by the UPCNA and voted the merger down. For this reason the UPCNA formally disbanded its study committee in 1931. From 1931 to 1932, the Northern PCUSA and the UPCNA tried to merge again and created a "Basis of Union." In 1934, the merger vote passed in the PCUSA General Assembly, but failed in the UPCNA General

108. Crocco, "Edwards's Intellectual Legacy," 314; Minkema email to the author.

109. Gerstner, *Steps to Salvation*, 11.

110. Jamison, *The United Presbyterian Story*, 207.

111. Ibid., 214.

112. Ibid., 214–15.

113. Ibid., 215.

Assembly largely because a majority of UPs were troubled by modernism in the PCUSA.[114] For ten years there was little discussion of church union in the UPCNA. Yet the ecumenical spirit remained in the UPCNA and church leaders like John McNaugher kept pushing for church union.[115] In 1944, the UPCNA invited the PCUS, the Associate Reformed Presbyterian Church (ARP), and the Reformed Church in America (RCA) to discuss union. The PCUS and the ARP quickly turned down the invitation, but the RCA, a Dutch Reformed denomination, was interested. In 1949 the UP General Assembly approved this union and sent it to the presbyteries. The presbyteries voted 74.5 percent in favor of the merger; this was just shy of the 75 percent required for the merger. Even though they did not receive the required percentage needed, the 1950 UP General Assembly approved the union overture. Nonetheless, the merger failed because the RCA classes voted down the plan of union, with twenty-three against and nineteen in favor of the merger. Another development in the UPCNA was the 1948 defeat of a proposal to become a member of the upstart National Association of Evangelicals (NAE).[116] In the 1930s and 1940s the UPCNA had refused to join with anyone.

In 1950, the year Gerstner joined the Pitt-Xenia faculty, the UPCNA accepted invitations to join in merger discussions with the PCUSA and the PCUS. Church Union failed with the Dutch Reformed RCA, but perhaps it would succeed with other Presbyterians. This full three-way plan of union collapsed in 1954 when the PCUS removed itself from the negotiations; the denominations had decided beforehand that if one church pulled out, then the plan would fail.[117] Despite the demise of these negotiations and past failures, the desire for church union remained strong for many. In 1955, the UPCNA voted to continue discussions with the PCUSA. This merger proposal appeared to frustrate Gerstner, whose faith had been nurtured in the UP church. Gerstner's primary reason for opposing the merger of the two denominations was theological. During his college and seminary days in the 1930s, Gerstner had been a keen observer of the "Presbyterian Controversy" between modernists, moderates, and conservatives in the PCUSA and was aware of what he considered to be extremely liberal elements within the PCUSA. In an effort to stop the merger, he warned readers of *The United Presbyterian* of what he regarded as "deep heresy" and "serious doctrinal

---

114. Ibid., 216.

115. Coleman, "The Life and Works of John McNaugher."

116. Carpenter, *Revive Us Again*, 298.

117. Jamison, *The United Presbyterian Story*, 217.

defection" in the PCUSA.[118] The main evidence that the young church historian used to make this assertion was the Auburn Affirmation (1924): a modernist theological statement, adhered to by progressive PCUSA theologians, pastors, and laypeople. In a 1956 article titled "What Is Wrong With the Auburn Affirmation?" Gerstner argued that the Auburn Affirmationists rejected doctrines such as the verbal inspiration of the Bible, the virgin birth of Christ, the satisfaction of Christ, the resurrection of Christ and the miracles of Christ even though these doctrines are "explicitly taught in their own Creed," the Westminster Confession of Faith.[119] In contrast to the progressive wing of the PCUSA, he noted that "our [UP] ministers have never thought" of these doctrines as "optional theories." He added that this is "why we oppose union now while hoping for union one day."[120]

For conservative Presbyterians like Gerstner, the Auburn Affirmation and the toleration of its signatories' views remained the most important proof that the PCUSA was doctrinally unsound. Indeed, throughout the 1930s, 1940s, and 1950s various Presbyterian scholars, ministers, and laypeople continued to criticize the modernist theological statement. In 1931 the League of Faith was founded within the PCUSA by 1,082 ministers and one of the group's stated aims was "[t]o oppose the attack made by the document commonly called 'The Auburn Affirmation.'"[121] In 1935, Gordon Clark (1902–1985), then a University of Pennsylvania philosophy instructor, argued that "[t]he reason the Auburn Affirmation is so important is that it constitutes a major offensive against the Word of God." In sharp language Clark added, "[i]t or at least its theology, is the root of Presbyterian apostasy."[122] In 1942 Daniel S. Gage (1864–1951), longtime professor of philosophy and Bible at Westminster College in Missouri, wrote that the Auburn Affirmation was "one of the most important ecclesiastical papers ever issued." He held that the PCUSA "decided to preserve outward ecclesiastical unity by permitting any private interpretation to be put on all the facts of Christianity." As a member of the PCUS, Gage criticized the Auburn Affirmation in the pages of the *Southern Presbyterian Journal* and the *Christian Union Herald* in an effort to oppose a merger of the two churches. He

118. Gerstner, "What Is Wrong with the Auburn Affirmation?," 15.

119. Ibid., 21.

120. Ibid.

121. "The Presbyterian League of Faith," 19.

122. Clark, "The Auburn Heresy," 7. Clark's essay was originally published in *Christianity Today* in July 1935. Later in July 1946 conservatives in the southern PCUS utilized Clark's critique for the *Southern Presbyterian Journal*. By the 1950s Clark had become a minister in the UPCNA and served as philosophy professor at Butler University in Indianapolis, Indiana.

argued that his denomination had in the past tried to "preserve both inward and outward unity." By "inward" Gage meant personal theological beliefs. He added, " [w]e must pay the price if we give up our real inward unity."[123]

The best "proof," Gage wrote, that the PCUS, if it joined with the PCUSA, would be "removing almost all doctrinal standards . . .[is] that the Auburn Affirmation be studied." Apparently, Gage believed that the Auburn Affirmation was a hollow theological treatise, which created ambiguity on even the most basic of doctrines, thus injuring the church's theological integrity. Because the PCUSA took no action against the Auburn Affirmation and it signers, Gage held that the statement "committed the Church U.S.A., to the widest permission of holding any theory any minister may wish as to the doctrines of the Church."[124] Another key critic of the affirmation was William Childs Robinson (1897–1982), longtime professor of church history at Columbia Seminary in Georgia, who had asked bluntly "[s]hall we stand . . . for the faith or shall we surrender our corporate testimony by uniting with Auburn Affirmationists[?]"[125] In a 1959 essay which appeared in the *American Journal of Sociology*, two sociologists, Sanford M. Dornbusch and Roger D. Irle, concluded that "the most frequent theme" among 1950s anti-unionists in the PCUS "was an attack upon the Auburn Affirmation."[126] Conservative opposition to the Auburn Affirmation was the primary reason the PCUS avoided mergers with the northern church in the 1940s and 1950s. In 1934 the UP General Assembly defeated, by a vote of 123 to 113, a proposal to have UPCNA presbyteries vote on a merger with the PCUSA. In the internal UPCNA debate over the merger, the Auburn Affirmation and modernist theology played a central role in stopping the proposed merger.[127] In June 1953 the Presbytery of Boston (UP), led by an evangelical pastor, George Murray (1895–1956), instructed the UP church union committee to ask the PCUSA to "discipline those who have signified their departure from the Reformed faith by affixing their signatures to the Auburn Affirmation, and require definite assurance of repentance on their part as a prelude to further Church Union negotiations."[128] For many Presbyterians the Auburn Affirmation aroused strong feelings of hostility.

123. Gage, "The Auburn Affirmation," 19.

124. Gage, "Dr. Lingle and the Auburn Affirmation."

125. Robinson quoted by Ernest Trice Thompson, *Presbyterians In the South*, 3:570.

126. Dornbusch and Irle, "The Failure of Presbyterian Union," 352.

127. Jamison, *The United Presbyterian Story*, 216. See also Christy, "The United Presbyterian Church and Church Union."

128. Presbytery of Boston (UP) Minutes quoted by MacLeod, *George Murray of the U.P.*, 107.

Even though there was sizable opposition to church union in the UPC-NA, Gerstner and his fellow anti-unionists were fighting an uphill battle: the UPCNA seemed ready for union, as past union failures and a continued ecumenical spirit kept the merger alive. In a letter to his wife Gerstner wrote that "Dr. Long rather sheepishly said" to him that a "good many voted in favor" of the merger at the 1956 General Assembly, but some of these delegates are people "who say they will vote against the union in presbyteries." Gerstner knew, however, that it was unlikely that the UP presbyteries would disapprove the merger. He noted, "I think it almost impossible that presbyteries would defeat the overture, but some are not absolutely sure."[129] His efforts to stop the union, like his attack on the Auburn Affirmation, proved futile, and the UP approved the merger with the PCUSA in 1957. The two denominations formally joined together in Pittsburgh on May 28, 1958.[130] Yet the vote was close, with only 57 percent of UP presbyteries supporting church union. In retrospect Gerstner offered a theory for why the UPCNA and the PCUSA achieved union and it had to do with Pitt-Xenia itself. He speculated that Eugene Carson Blake, the PCUSA's Stated Clerk, pushed hard for the merger because of the strengthening of evangelical commitment at Pitt-Xenia. Gerstner reasoned that Blake wanted to have church union with the UPCNA because if Pitt-Xenia's evangelicalism kept intensifying it would make the UPCNA more conservative, thus halting any merger.[131] One sign that there might be a measure of truth in Gerstner's hypothesis is that during the late 1940s and into the 1950s Blake did indeed play a role in refusing to allow faculty and graduates of Fuller Seminary (CA) into the PCUSA's Los Angeles presbytery.[132] Blake's harsh comments towards Bill Bright (who later founded Campus Crusade for Christ), at a committee on preparation meeting, led Bright to withdraw from the PCUSA ordination process.[133] It is conceivable that Blake was concerned about affairs at the UPCNA's lone seminary, not wanting it to develop into another Fuller, and therefore he campaigned for church union. After the momentous merger there were now over 600,000 Presbyterians in a single denomination within a two-hundred mile radius of Pittsburgh.

---

129. Gerstner, Letter to Gerstner, n.d.

130. "Once in a Century," 9.

131. Gerstner, Interview with Coffin, PCA Historical Center, 19.

132. On Blake's early opposition to Fuller, see Marsden, *Reforming Fundamentalism*, 102–7. The one Fuller professor whom Blake said he would lobby for in the LA presbytery was Vassady, a Hungarian Reformed theologian, who had helped found the World Council of Churches.

133. Richardson, *Amazing Faith*, 57–58; Turner, *Bill Bright and Campus Crusade for Christ*, 36.

The denominational merger posed a particular complication in the city of Pittsburgh because the PCUSA already had a seminary there. The PCUSA institution, Western Seminary, which had been founded in 1825, had a rich tradition of scholarship and many progressive voices. An examination of the 1,274 signatories of the Auburn Affirmation reveals that three Western Seminary professors had signed the modernist theological document.[134] Moreover, James Snowden (1852–1936), Western's longtime professor of theology, while not a signer of the document, had defended the affirmation and scorned its critics in various articles.[135] John Orr in his *English Deism* (1934) took Snowden to task for his lack of understanding of the differences between the liberal and fundamentalist theological parties, claiming that Snowden did not grasp the language of the debate and therefore the doctrinal division.[136] Orr wrote "[i]nclusionists, like Mr. Snowden, are prone to define Fundamentalism and Modernism as 'principles and processes and not results and doctrine.'"[137] Snowden's theological pacificism tended to play down differences and because of this influence, Western had developed a doctrinally liberal orientation and ecumenical spirit during the twentieth century. From 1926 to 1958 Western's professor of ecclesiastical history and the history of doctrine was Gaius Jackson Slosser (1892–1967) who had penned *Christian Unity* (1929)—a sympathetic history of ecumenism[138] At Western, courses on liberal theology were prominent and key progressive Protestants spoke at the school. Eugene Carson Blake (1906–1985), a progressive Presbyterian church leader and PCUSA stated clerk, was a frequent visitor to the seminary, offering lectures in 1952, 1953, and in 1956. In 1957 the managing editor of the *Christian Century* magazine, Theodore Gill, gave an address at the school. Western had an ecumenical spirit and aligned itself with the moderate and liberal streams of American Protestantism and Presbyterianism.

Pitt-Xenia faculty member Bob Kelley remembers "denominational leaders saying you can't have two seminaries in one city."[139] Western's mixture of liberal and neo-orthodox approaches to theology, however, made it

134. Quirk, "The Auburn Affirmation," 439, 442, 444. The three Western professors to sign the Auburn Affirmation were: Cully, professor of Old Testament; Eakin, professor of ecclesiastical history; and Farmer, professor of sacred rhetoric.

135. Ibid., 362. On Snowden, see McKinney, ed., *The Incomparable Snowden*.

136. John Orr, *English Deism*, 253.

137. Ibid.

138. Eshbaugh and Walther, "Western Seminary," 150. Slosser received his BA from Ohio Wesleyan University, a BD and a STM from Boston University, and a PhD from King's College, University of London.

139. Kelley, Interview with the author, May 22, 2012.

a very different institution from Pitt-Xenia. Kelly recalled that in fact Leitch "feared two things—the liberalism of Western and the dilution of UPs" on a united seminary faculty.[140] Indeed, the majority of the Pitt-Xenia faculty and their president hoped they could remain independent and avoid consolidation with Western.[141] Intense debate ensued in Pitt-Xenia faculty meetings and numerous proposals were made in an effort to save the seminary from uniting. Gerstner proposed that the seminary "relocate in Omaha" or some other city.[142] He also suggested that if the seminary moved, the faculty should "work for a dollar a year until we can get on our feet." According to Gerstner, "most of the faculty was willing to go along with me on that type of thing; they felt that strongly."[143] Gerstner was clearly unhappy with the merger, which seemed to intensify his own UP identity and his loyalty to the Pitt-Xenia tradition.

Robert Lamont (1920–2012), pastor of the large and influential First Presbyterian Church in Pittsburgh, met with the Pitt-Xenia faculty to discuss the consolidation of the two seminaries. Lamont straightforwardly told the Pitt-Xenia faculty, "you don't have a chance" of remaining separate from Western.[144] He firmly told them "you're up against master craftsmen" who know how to effect this change. By the late 1950s the relative harmony that existed on the faculty had been shattered by differing views of how to handle the issue of seminary consolidation. According to Kelley, the faculty seemed to be somewhat annoyed by their dean, Gordon Jackson, who appeared "to be in cahoots with denominational leaders."[145] Gerstner later recalled that two members of the Pitt-Xenia faculty agreed with the merger and consolidation of the seminaries: Theophilus Mills Taylor and Gordon Jackson. Taylor served on the Plan of Union committee and was an "enthusiastic apostle of union."[146] Apparently these two faculty members "had gone on record that they were going to leave the seminary if it refused to unite."[147]

140. Kelley quoted by Stuart, "Diminishing Distinctives."

141. Several additions were made to the Pitt-Xenia faculty in the 1950s. Bessie Burrows taught at Pitt-Xenia from 1953 to 1971. Howard M. Jamieson Jr. taught from 1955 to 1970. John M. Bald taught from 1957 to 1977. Malcom S. Alexander taught from 1958 to 1966. Harold E. Scott taught from 1959 to 1978. Howard L. Ralston taught from 1960 to 1972.

142. Gerstner, Interview with Coffin, 20.

143. Ibid.

144. Kelley, Interview with the author, May 22, 2012. Lamont was also a contributing editor to *Christianity Today*.

145. Ibid.

146. McKinney, "Many Streams One River," 558.

147. Gerstner, Interview with Coffin, 20.

Tensions ran high at Pitt-Xenia, and in May 1959 the school's board was scheduled to vote on combining the two seminaries together. Prior to this meeting, Gerster wrote a "very carefully" worded resignation letter. Before the meeting he handed the letter to Leitch and told him that if his resignation "could save the seminary" from merger, "you just produce that letter." Gerstner reasoned that some of the board members would not allow Pitt-Xenia to remain separate with Gerstner on the faculty, but perhaps they would be willing to allow the seminary to remain independent if Gerstner were not on the faculty.

President Leitch entered the meeting carrying Gerstner's letter in his pocket, but he also carried a secret. As expected, the board voted to consolidate the two seminaries and decided that the seminary would be located on the site of Pitt-Xenia's new campus. It was simply impractical for one denomination to have two seminaries in the same city. After the board made its historic vote, however, there was a surprising development. Leitch offered the board a resignation letter, but it was not Gerstner's; it was his own. When Gerstner heard the news, he was incensed; he believed that if Leitch had threatened to resign before the vote, things might have gone differently. Gerstner later recalled telling Leitch that "it would have made a difference to them if you'd told them."[148] "Nevertheless, he didn't tell them, and as soon as they voted for the merger, he tells them," Gerstner recounted. One board member told Gerstner, "It might have been a very different story—I'm not sure—but it might have been very different" if Leitch had discussed his resignation prior to the consolidation vote.[149] Leitch was given a year's sabbatical and then returned to the seminary to teach theology at the consolidated seminary in the fall of 1960. Many Pitt-Xenia faculty and staff were troubled by these developments, and some staff protested publicly. In September of 1959, Agnes Ballantyne the Pitt-Xenia librarian resigned her post in protest against the consolidation.[150] In a letter to Carl Henry, Gerstner wrote that he and Pitt-Xenia were in a "desperately crucial situation."[151] Kelley remembers how difficult the process was; he compared it to "sailing on a ship you liked and then all of the sudden you get a new ship and a new crew." Even though the consolidation of the seminaries was painful for Gerstner and his colleagues, he later recalled, "we hung in there."[152] He remained at the

---

148. Ibid., 21

149. Ibid.

150. McKim, *Ever a Vision*, 40.

151. Gerstner, Letter to Henry.

152. Gerstner, Interview with Coffin, 21.

seminary seeking to be an evangelical voice and experienced the fusion of the two seminaries.

Gerstner began the decade of the 1950s as an unknown professor of church history in the third largest Presbyterian denomination in the U.S. In just a few short years, however, he became a well-respected scholar and churchman in the UPCNA and in the wider evangelical world. His powerful speaking abilities helped him win admirers in both the classroom and in the church. As a young evangelical with a PhD from Harvard, Gerstner's future looked bright as a national evangelical leader invited him to be a part of one of their key ventures—*Christianity Today*. By all accounts he had a happy family and a loving marriage. Yet not all was well. His efforts to stop the merger between the UPCNA and the PCUSA were a failure. Trying to prevent something which has been in the works for years is often difficult. Likewise, when Gerstner attempted to avert the consolidation of Pitt-Xenia and Western, he was unsuccessful. These struggles no doubt were traumatic for Gerstner, who had attended UPCNA churches since his teenage years and who had worked with Leitch to build up and strengthen Pitt-Xenia as a center of evangelical scholarship. The evidence clearly shows that Leitch, Gerstner, and their associates were making Pitt-Xenia a more robustly evangelical school. His opposition to church and seminary union reveals his anti-unionist sympathies and concern with the PCUSA's liberal party. For evangelical Presbyterians the Auburn Affirmation remained a controversial document that actually impeded the church union movement. The numerous book reviews and several articles he wrote demonstrate that Gerstner was a conservative Protestant scholar who took competing viewpoints seriously. Yet by the mid-1950s, he had not yet established himself as a *bona fide* church historian. This was partly due to the fact he was devoted to apologetics. During the late 1950s, he worked diligently on two books which he hoped would put him on the scholarly map. Most importantly, Gerstner was teaching on Edwards and developing his views of the great colonial theologian. His enthusiasm for Edwards would continue. Despite the UPCNA-PCUSA merger and the seminary consolidation, Gerstner carried on with his academic work. By 1959, Gerstner had achieved some minor accomplishments. Moreover, he was now a scholar in the largest Presbyterian denomination *and* in the burgeoning evangelical movement.

4

An Evangelical Defender of the Faith
(1960–1969)

GERSTNER'S LIFE IN THE 1960S WAS CHALLENGING. HE EXPERIENCED THE end of the old Pitt-Xenia and the birth of the new Pittsburgh Theological Seminary (PTS). This transition led to the desertion of one Gerstner's closest allies and friends. During the 1960s he also assumed new duties and positions of leadership. He navigated through tensions both at PTS and in his newly formed denomination, the UPCUSA. His public identity as a churchman and as a scholar became better known though his writings and active participation in American church life. The strict piety he administered in his family life created some unrest and this added to the pressures he faced. By the end of the 1960s, Gerstner had responded to these challenges in some unexpected ways, and had even found ways to thrive in the midst of great difficulty by re-orientating his own approaches to some of the most significant church debates of his time. Gerstner faced the intellectual, theological, and ecclesiastical issues of his day with great fearlessness and this can be observed by examining his willingness to criticize a new UPCUSA confession. He stood for a sharply defined theology in a decade of theological change. In the tumultuous 1960s, Gerstner successfully laid the groundwork for the renewal of Presbyterian and Reformed evangelicalism by defending the faith openly and by inspiring students to join him in the struggle against liberal theology and what he considered to be the irrationalism of the age.

The consolidation of Pitt-Xenia and Western seminaries was taxing for Gerstner. He felt overwhelmed, recalling that, "Western was more academically competent than we are."[1] Western did have an accomplished faculty, and Gerstner later admitted that he and his Pitt-Xenia colleagues "were no

---

1. Gerstner, Interview with Coffin, 21.

match for them."[2] During the consolidation process a stereotype emerged of the two seminaries.[3] Pitt-Xenia was said to have "all the piety and they [Western] had all the intelligence."[4] Bob Kelley, professor of biblical languages, believed that Western was viewed as "bookish" whereas Pitt-Xenia was seen as consisting of "lightweights."[5] Gerstner held that the stereotypes had a measure of truth and noted that Western's theological viewpoint "dominated very, very quickly" when the schools came together. He later recounted that the seminary's new faculty hires were more progressive and that this was an indication of the school's leftward theological direction.[6] Gerstner still had a close evangelical ally in Addison Leitch, but something needed to be done to prevent what they both believed was the rapid liberalization of the seminary. In the spring of 1961, as tensions were mounting, the former president and now professor Leitch decided he would take a stand.

On June 20, 1961, Pittsburghers awakened to read a front page story in the *Pittsburgh Post-Gazette* with the headline "Seminary Too Liberal, Professor Says, Quits."[7] The story was a report on Leitch's actions at a seminary board meeting the previous day. On June 19, the PTS board met and voted to "hold a private session" in which Leitch "addressed the board."[8] According to the *Post-Gazette*, the meeting lasted for three hours, and the board approved Leitch's resignation from his position as professor of theology.[9] Leitch pulled no punches, telling the directors that "I believe that, theologically speaking, the seminary is taking the road to liberalism."[10] PTS administrators and faculty were pursuing "a kind of neo-orthodox pattern to which I cannot subscribe," he argued. Apparently, Leitch's analysis of the situation incorporated observations by Gerstner about liberal inroads. Leitch faulted the seminary for "playing down the pastoral office and playing up the scholarly office." The theologian argued that there was an ethical looseness on the campus and that the seminary was divorcing itself from the

2. Ibid.

3. This stereotype was repeated in several oral interviews and discussed by McKim in *Ever a Vision*, 31–32.

4. Gerstner, Interview with Coffin, 21.

5. Kelley, Interview with the author, 2 December, 2010.

6. Gerstner, Interview with Coffin, 21.

7. Rimmel, "Seminary Too Liberal, Professor Says, Quits," 1, 6.

8. "Minutes of an Adjourned Meeting of the Board of Directors," 2.

9. There is no mention of this event or Leitch's concerns in the two main seminary histories *Ever a Frontier* and *Ever a Vision*.

10. Leitch quoted by Rimmel, "Seminary Too Liberal, Professor Says, Quits," 1.

common layperson in the pew. He lamented, "I'm convinced that the modern layman, in his desire for deep Christian information, would rather have the arithmetic before the calculus." Leitch, a seasoned administrator and theologian, held that the newly created seminary was being too intellectual and separating itself from the church. In a letter he wrote to the trustees on June 8, he noted, "the present structure and future plans of the Seminary are no longer such as can enlist from me the enthusiasm and loyalty which the Seminary has the right to expect from her professors."[11] Clifford E. Barbour, PTS's acting president, responded to Leitch in the *Post-Gazette* claiming, "It is not true that we are going down the road to liberalism. The seminary is more conservative than it was 25 or 50 years ago."[12] Soon after, on June 25, the *Post-Gazette* reported that Pittsburgh Presbytery would not conduct an investigation of the seminary based on Leitch's criticisms and concerns.[13]

One board member, Henry C. Herchenroether Jr., later wrote that the board meeting with Leitch was convened because Leitch threatened to go to the "public press" and "explain his version of [the] destruction of true Presbyterian beliefs and practices caused by the denomination and seminary consolidations."[14] Yet Leitch's own June 8, 1961 letter to the seminary's board seems to contradict this interpretation. Leitch wrote, "We could involve ourselves in many claims and counterclaims regarding this decision which would be neither informative [n]or edifying. Suppose we just call it quits and walk away." He straightforwardly told the trustees he wanted his resignation to receive "as little publicity as possible."[15] On June 19, the seminary's board accepted his resignation "with regret." Overall, the trustees and administrators did not appear responsive to the criticisms Leitch made during the board meeting. Also, it is unclear how the *Post-Gazette* would have been able to report on Leitch's comments to the board since the meeting was held in "private session." One puzzling aspect of this event is that Leitch appeared to act alone. Apparently, Gerstner thought "Leitch's move was a bad one and pushed him hard not to leave."[16]

11. Leitch's resignation letter is located within the "Minutes of an Adjourned Meeting of the Board of Directors," 2.

12. Barbour quoted by Rimmel, "Seminary Too Liberal, Professor Says, Quits," 6.

13. "Launching Seminary Probe Denied," 3.

14. Herchenroether Jr., "Pittsburgh Theological Seminary 1959–1999," 10. Herchenroether graduated from Westminster College in 1942 and earned a law degree from the University of Pittsburgh School of Law in 1949. He served on the seminary's board of directors and as general counsel for many years.

15. Leitch's resignation letter is located within the "Minutes of an Adjourned Meeting of the Board of Directors," 2.

16. Stark, Interview with the author.

Gerstner was away in Germany when Leitch resigned, and no known evidence exists that Gerstner was thinking of resigning along with his friend. On July 19, Carl Henry wrote to console Gerstner, saying, "[y]ou will have your own complex of problems at Pittsburgh Seminary this coming year but you will also have a strategic and responsible opportunity."[17] Leitch's departure from the seminary must have been a tremendous blow to Gerstner, who looked up to the more senior scholar. Leitch turned down a job offer from *Christianity Today* and quickly decamped from Pittsburgh to take a position as professor of philosophy of religion at Tarkio College in Tarkio, Missouri.[18] Later in 1969 he married Elizabeth Elliot (1926–), a well-known evangelical missionary, and became a professor of theology at Gordon-Conwell Theological Seminary, near Boston.[19]

The conservative leadership at the seminary now fell to Gerstner, but the loss of Leitch proved to be disastrous for the three remaining self-consciously evangelical faculty members at the school.[20] Leitch was replaced by a rapid succession of talented and scholarly progressive theologians. In 1962, George Kehm (1930–) arrived to teach theology.[21] A year later, in 1963, Dietrich Ritschl (1929–) and Edward Farley (1929–) were appointed to teach the history of doctrine and theology respectively.[22] The addition of these faculty members following Leitch's retreat from the seminary led to a monumental change in the seminary's theological position. Clifford Barbour, PTS's acting president, wanted everyone associated with PTS to "[t]hink Big . . . looking ahead with great dreams" for the new seminary. "This is the beginning," Barbour wrote, and then noted that "[w]e are in the process of

17. Henry, Letter to Gerstner, July 19, 1961.

18. Henry, Letter to Gerstner, July 19, 1961.

19. "About Elisabeth."

20. The evangelical faculty members included Gerstner, James Leon Kelso, and Robert Kelley. Kelso was primarily focused on his archaeological work, but he was involved in the Presbyterians United for Biblical Concerns (PUBC) evangelical renewal group. Sometime in the mid-1960s Kelso penned a booklet that criticised the liberal social gospel movement. See Kelso's *The Case Against the Counterfeit Gospel*. Kelley was moderately evangelical, but he spurned church and seminary politics.

21. Kehm earned his BS from Queens College, a BD, STM and ThD degrees from Harvard University.

22. Ritschl studied at the universities of Tubingen, Basel, and Bern and earned his PhD at the University of Edinburgh. Edward Farley earned his BA from Centre College (1950), BD from Louisville Presbyterian Theological Seminary (1953), and his PhD from Union Seminary (NYC)/Columbia University (1958). He taught at Tusculum College, DePauw College, Pittsburgh Theological Seminary, and Vanderbilt University.

developing here a great theological university."[23] Barbour and his associates would zealously pursue their vision of a progressive "theological university." In August 1960, Barbour invited Pearl S. Buck (1892–1973) to speak as part of a November program for the combined faculty installation service.[24] In 1933 Buck had resigned as a PCUSA missionary to China due to a controversy over her radical theological views which she openly espoused. In a lecture to Presbyterians in January of 1933 she had denied the doctrine of original sin, appeared to reject Christ's deity, and was noncommittal about whether Christ actually lived.[25] As it turned out, Buck, who had become a celebrated author, was unable to lecture to the new faculty because she was traveling in Japan. While Leitch probably did not know about Barbour's letter to Buck, he observed what was taking place at the new PTS and was indeed troubled. Perhaps his alarm and criticisms of the seminary were partially the result of the guest speakers the school actually did entertain in 1960 and 1961. In an effort to be a truly "great theological university," the school brought in numerous progressive scholars to speak, and their presence gives clear evidence that the school was moving in a leftward theological direction. In March 1960, Paul Tillich (1886–1965), a Harvard theologian, gave two days of lectures, and in the May of that year, Liston Pope (1909–1974), the Yale Divinity School dean, gave the commencement address. In October 1960, Krister Stendahl (1921–2008), lectured at the seminary, and in May 1961, Eugene Carson Blake, the stated clerk of the UPCUSA, gave the graduation address. Three of the guest speakers, Pope, Stendahl and Blake, spoke on various topics, but found time in their remarks to denigrate conservative Protestantism, thus highlighting the school's theological direction.

Liston Pope, the Yale divinity school dean and ethicist, stated bluntly in his graduation address that PTS "has the promise of being one of the foremost theological seminaries in the entire country." Yet he also noted that "a good seminary . . . is not a kind of theological kindergarten."[26] He warned against "[s]trict biblical literalism and theological fundamentalism," saying that these "tendencies in American Protestant life appear to be resurgent" but that they seek to "condemn an intelligent school because it refuses to play its simple games." To be sure, he added, "Let them condemn; these approaches to the Christian faith have never yet produced a first-class educational institution in America, and there is no evidence

23. Barbour, *Annual Catalog of the Pittsburgh Theological Seminary of the United Presbyterian Church in the United States of America 1961–1962*, 4.

24. Barbour, Letter to Buck.

25. Longfield, *The Presbyterian Controversy*, 201.

26. Pope, "The 1960 Commencement Address," 14.

that they will do so in the future."[27] Pope's message was clear: evangelical Christianity was intellectually irresponsible, and the seminary needed to abandon past "provincialisms."[28] On October 20, 1960, Krister Stendahl, the Harvard New Testament scholar, lectured at the seminary on the "Uses and Misuses of the Bible."[29] Stendahl like Pope took "fundamentalism" to task by arguing that conservative beliefs about Scripture had turned the Bible into an "idol."[30] He noted that "fundamentalism" was actually a "very rationalistic form of idolatry." Preachers, he argued, should not declare "The Word of God says" but rather "God says in his Word." Conservative views of the Bible were attacked as bibliolatry, and a traditional understanding of the Bible as God's word was declared to be untenable. Stendahl's remarks were not necessarily radical within a mainline UPCUSA seminary, but his comments surely would have been disconcerting for more than a few of the former Pitt-Xenia professors and students who were raised and trained in a denomination that was not nearly as exposed to liberal theology.

In May 1961, Eugene Carson Blake, delivered a commencement address titled "Anxiety, Frustration, and Subconscious Hatred."[31] Blake was known widely for his progressive theological views and ecumenical leadership. What is somewhat strange is that Blake had been the Western Seminary commencement speaker five years earlier in 1956. Perhaps his presence signaled to the evangelical faculty from Pitt-Xenia that the seminary's administration was molding the new PTS in the image of the old Western Seminary. In his speech, Blake argued that the church was a "sea of hostility" and that ministers needed to be prepared for "personal hostility" from their congregations.[32] He recounted critical letters he had received from his detractors and lamented the "typical rigid theology" which was the result of "the poisonous presence of anxiety." Blake spoke for the Presbyterian leadership, and his words seem to indicate his distrust of the evangelical populists who no doubt filled many pews in the UPCUSA. Compared to what Gerstner had experienced at Pitt-Xenia, the new PTS was becoming a very different place. While Gerstner did not make any public statement at the time, he later recounted how troubling were the loss of Leitch and the progressive shift at the seminary.[33]

27. Ibid., 14.
28. Pope, "The 1960 Commencement Address," 18.
29. Stendahl, "Uses and Misuses of the Bible," 22–32.
30. Ibid., 24.
31. Blake, "Anxiety, Frustration, and Subconscious Hatred," 11–16.
32. Ibid., 13.
33. Gerstner, Interview with Coffin, 21–22.

During the 1960s, Gerstner had a busy home life. For the duration of the school year he was fully engaged in school work, but virtually every summer the family would vacation in Ocean City, New Jersey. Summers also allowed Gerstner to take short research trips, most often to the Princeton or Yale libraries. Gerstner relished scholarship, but he also loved sports. He would often take his son to Pittsburgh Pirates baseball games. Jonathan remembers his father and him going to watch Roberto Clemente and Hank Aaron, who were arguably the two best outfielders of the era.[34] Gerstner was also fond of dogs. The family canine was an enormously large harlequin Great Dane, which had a loud bark. As an animal lover, Gerstner opposed killing animals for pleasure and did not participate in the hunting that was common in Western Pennsylvania. As a couple, John and Edna supported each other, but Edna had her own interests and priorities. She was active in Bible studies and in a local missionary society. In addition, she participated in the Ligonier township poetry society and served on the board of a Presbyterian hospital in Pittsburgh.[35] Both parents were concerned about the religious climate in their home and much time was spent discussing spiritual matters. John and Edna held family devotions every day with their three children Judy, Rachel, and Jonathan. Scripture would be read, followed by questions and discussion over the text. Jonathan remembers that "some of these devotions lasted a few minutes, and others lasted for hours." John and Edna were also strict sabbatarians. They were committed to keeping the Sabbath holy and refused to attend sporting events, watch television, or eat in a restaurant on this day of rest. After Sunday worship, the family would return home for a large meal, after which they would all participate in devotions. The focus for the day remained on God. Edna worked hard to provide her children with Christian board games, activities, and books. As a lively youngster, Jonathan loved his parents, but found their strict sabbatarianism "not always easy."[36] John and Edna provided a loving family environment, but there was some discontent over their strictness. The rigidity in the Gerstner home paralleled Gerstner's theological conservatism.

The year 1960 was an important one for Gerstner. During that year, two of Gerstner's books were published: *Reasons for Faith* and *The Theology of the Major Sects*.[37] *Reasons for Faith* was published with the mainstream firm of Harper Brothers and *The Theology of the Major Sects* was produced by Baker, an evangelical publisher. These books were the culmination of years

34. Gerstner, Interview with the author, September 10, 2012.

35. Ibid.

36. Ibid.

37. Gerstner, *Reasons for Faith*, *The Theology of the Major Sects*.

of study and cast Gerstner as an apologist. His profile was now raised within the academy and the church. In his book *The Theology of the Major Sects* Gerstner analyzed the development and intellectual history of nine major sects. One of the most interesting aspects of his study was that Gerstner ranked the different groups in a specific order, each receiving its own chapter. Gerstner wrote, "[w]e begin with the sect nearest in thought to catholic Christianity and move on to consider sects further and further from the thought of catholic Christianity."[38] He considered "Seventh-day Adventism" closest to Christian orthodoxy and "Faith Healing" the most distant. He believed that faith healing could occur, but that it was not a miracle. His position was based on Warfield's argument that miracles ceased in the apostolic period.[39] The church historian's view reflected the exaltation of reason. He was also troubled by the "failures in faith healing" which he found to be "conspicuous."[40] It appears that Gerstner's negative attitude towards faith healing occurred because of the controversial career of Kathryn Kuhlman, a prominent Pittsburgh faith healer. For progressive Presbyterians the most disturbing aspect of the book was the fifth chapter, titled "Liberalism." Gerstner held that Protestant liberalism was a sect and was far removed from "catholic Christianity" because it denied central tenets of the Christian faith, reducing them to mere theories. In fact, his chapter on liberalism followed chapters on Seventh Day Adventism, Jehovah's Witnesses, and Mormonism. In the book's introduction Gerstner stated,

> Although the Jehovah's Witnesses and Mormons are very objectionable to evangelical theology in many ways, we consider them after Seventh-Day Adventists because they have preserved more of essential Christianity in their theology than any of the groups, including Liberalism, or Modernism, which is considered fourth.[41]

Gerstner wrote that Liberalism "reinterprets all of the traditional doctrines of Christianity in such a way as to de-supernaturalize them."[42] He added that its "fundamental motif" was its "anti-supernaturalism." According to the PTS professor, "this motif" was then applied to the "various topics of theology." For liberals, "[s]upernatural revelation is denied; the fall of man is rejected; the deity of Christ is abandoned; the traditional views of the

---

38. Gerstner, *Theology of the Major Sects*, 12.

39. Ibid., 12.

40. Ibid., 108.

41. Ibid., 113–14.

42. Ibid., 53.

atonement disappear. Salvation becomes a natural process and resurrection is transformed into a continuance of spirit."[43] Gerstner wrote that he defined liberal theology in the same way that J. Gresham Machen had done in his "classic critique," *Christianity and Liberalism* (1923).[44]

Addison Leitch reviewed the book for the *Pittsburgh Perspective* in September 1960 and held that "[t]he shock to many will be the discovery that Liberalism is classified as a sect." He added, "I leave Dr. Gerstner to defend himself in this matter." Leitch believed that Gerstner had presented "Liberalism" in the most "extreme" way and that this could "lead only to misunderstanding." Overall, Leitch believed that the issue of theological liberalism was more complex and that Gerstner's approach offered the "constant danger of being led astray by over-simplification."[45] Perhaps Leitch was worried that Gerstner's polemical approach would inflame the former Western faculty members with whom he hoped he could get along on a united faculty. In less than a year, though, Leitch's own patience with liberal theology would run out, and he would resign. Despite their minor differences, the two evangelical scholars remained friends.[46] Yet it is apparent that Gerstner was more willing in print to draw sharp contrasts with theological Liberalism than was Leitch. The most plausible reason for this fact is that Gerstner had received a more aggressively conservative theological education than Leitch. In the late 1930s, when Gerstner studied at Westminster Seminary, the school was a hothouse of anti-modernist sentiment and strict allegiance to the *Westminster Confession of Faith*.[47]

In a review of *The Theology of the Major Sects*, Lewis Spitz (1895–1996), a Concordia Seminary (MO) historian, praised Gerstner for providing "a sufficient amount of doctrinal material to make his book useful for the reader who does not have access to other sources."[48] One of Gerstner's main reasons for writing the book was "to provide a more thorough theological examination of the sects."[49] Spitz noted that, compared to preceding studies, Gerstner's book sought to "focus more attention" on the doctrinal issues. "Unfortunately his book does not achieve this aim," wrote J. Stafford Wright (1905–1985), a theologian at Tyndale Hall, Bristol, England.[50] Wright ar-

---

43. Ibid., 61.

44. Ibid., 53.

45. Leitch, Review of *The Theology of the Major Sects*, 29.

46. Gerstner, Interview with the author.

47. On this point, see Murray's biography *The Life of John Murray*, 85–102.

48. Spitz, Review of *The Theology of the Major Sects*, 655.

49. Gerstner, *The Theology of the Major Sects*, 12.

50. Wright, Review of *The Theology of the Major Sects*, 119–20.

gued that Gerstner provided a "fair amount of information about personalities, but not much about theology, except for Mormonism and Theosophy." The English scholar homed in on various errors in the book, but noted that "the whole book is not as bad as the reviewer might suggest." In a review for the *Westminster Theological Journal*, George W. Marston (1905–1994), an Orthodox Presbyterian pastor, wrote that he "recommends this book as a ready source of reference material."[51] The book could be helpful for pastors seeking better knowledge of the sects. Walter Martin (1928–1989), a leading scholar of the cults, criticized Gerstner for misrepresenting Seventh Day Adventists by not examining their most up-to-date doctrinal positions and therefore being too harsh. Martin wrote that the book "will prove useful on an introductory level," but was "limited in its scope and understanding of a complex and growing field."[52] Gerstner's work on the sects raised his profile, and later, Carl Henry, editor at *Christianity Today*, sought to tap Gerstner's knowledge of this area for his readers.[53]

In *Reasons for Faith* Gerstner tried to provide cogent arguments in defense of the Christian faith. The two-hundred-and-thirty-three page book offered twenty-five chapters. He examined unbelief and theistic arguments and laid out the evidence for God from special revelation, miracles, prophecy, and archaeology. He explored biblical religion in comparison to other religions, and he also examined the influence of Christianity in the world. Moreover, he offered four chapters which dealt with objections from "Evolution and Anthropology," "Determinism," "Biblical Criticism," and the "Shortcomings of the Church." The book was written as a popular apologetic for the "general thinking public and not for the specialists." Gerstner's apologetic approach was something of a throwback position among the UPCUSA seminary professors, who had by the 1960s largely embraced modernist or neo-orthodox theologies.[54] The Old Princeton theology and its apologetic method, which were associated with Benjamin Warfield and his associates, had by the 1960s been almost completely rejected by mainline northern Presbyterian seminary scholars. Nonetheless, Warfield's ideas persisted among some UPCUSA clergy, in Gerstner's writings and in Floyd Hamilton's *Basis of the Christian Faith* (1927), which was reprinted several times well into the 1960s. In fact, in 1964 Hamilton had revised and expanded his book and had it published with the mainstream publisher

---

51. Marston, Review of *The Theology of The Major Sects*, 242.

52. Martin, Review of *The Theology of The Major Sects*, *Christianity Today*, 174–75.

53. Gerstner, "Christian Science," 5–7.

54. Moorhead, "Redefining Confessionalism: American Presbyterians in the Twentieth Century," 72–86.

Harper and Row.[55] A recommendation by Gerstner of Hamilton's work even appeared on the book's 1964 dust jacket. Gerstner wrote that Hamilton's book was a "vigorous reaffirmation of the traditional Christian apologetic so much needed in our time."[56] Both Hamilton's study and Gerstner's *Reasons for Faith* were an effort to carry on a rational apologetic tradition that had been severely weakened within northern mainline Presbyterianism. In *Reasons for Faith* Gerstner wrote that he favored the older approach to apologetics "not because I have not read and wrestled with the new, but simply because I am not persuaded by the less rational approaches of today."[57] The Pittsburgh church historian continued to endorse a rational apologetic because he believed that liberal and neo-orthodox theologies created an irrational perspective that downplayed or rejected doctrinal boundaries and/or formulations of Christian essentials, thus hurting the church's witness to the world and those who were seeking answers.[58]

R. K. Churchill, an Orthodox Presbyterian pastor, noted in the *Westminster Theological Journal* that Gerstner's book was the product of "considerable erudition and ripe scholarship." Yet he faulted Gerstner for not citing the "weaknesses" of his apologetic position. Churchill, who apparently held a presuppositional apologetic position, stated that Gerstner's "philosophical notion of hanging God in the balance between existence and no-existence has no warrant in scripture."[59] Many conservative Presbyterians who embraced Cornelius Van Til's presuppositional approach found Gerstner's approach too rationalistic and therefore problematic. There was indeed a division within conservative Presbyterian circles regarding apologetics. Nonetheless, Gerstner and Van Til still respected each other. On February 20, 1960, Gerstner wrote a letter to Van Til, saying, "I am quite ashamed of the apparent slighting of your significant work in the [*Reasons for Faith*] bibliography." He added, "somehow the printer omitted the entire last section." The younger scholar made clear to his former professor "that, in spite of any appearances to the contrary, I appreciate you, your work, and your impact on my life—though I am unable to share your apologetic views."[60] Van Til responded on February 26, saying, "I deeply appreciate your remarks" and "your explanation." He ended the letter, noting: "You may have heard that it is a great sin to differ with Van Til on his views of apologet-

55. Hamilton, *Basis of the Christian Faith*. On Floyd Hamilton, see chapter 2.

56. Gerstner quoted in Hamilton's *Basis of the Christian Faith*, dust jacket cover.

57. Gerstner, *Reasons for Faith*, x.

58. Ibid., 9.

59. Churchill, review of *Reasons for Faith*, 53.

60. Gerstner, Letter to Van Til, February 20, 1960.

ics. You may also have heard that anyone who does and comes in striking distance of Philadelphia would have his head cut off. So I would advise you not to come near my office!"[61] Van Til was being humorous, but it is clear that not all Westminster graduates shared Van Til's apologetic method.[62] Even though Westminster Seminary was founded to carry on the legacy of Old Princeton, the seminary, under the leadership of Cornelius Van Til, discontinued the Old Princeton apologetic in favor of the presuppositional approach.

In the pages of the *Pittsburgh Perspective* Leitch praised *Reasons for Faith* as an "exceptionally useful tool," noting that "[o]ne wonders in vain where he could better turn to find so cleanly and briefly stated the arguments for God's existence, the possibility of miracles . . . ."[63] Later, in Leitch's book *The Winds of Doctrine* (1966), the scholar wrote that "[w]e need not make our proofs for religion absolute, and yet they exist, as Gerstner has pointed out in the title and content of his fine apologetic, *Reasons for Faith.*"[64] In a more critical review, Donald G. Bloesch (1928–2010), a theologian at the University of Dubuque Theological Seminary (Iowa), wrote that "Gerstner is at his best when he attempts to unmask the fallacies of determinism and skepticism" but he criticized Gerstner for "adjudging the truth about God . . . on the basis of whether or not it is reasonable." He argued that "[i]t is a real question how much the cause of Christ is served by this kind of apologetics since a faith which is based on even the most cogent of reasons rests upon a very fallible foundation."[65] In his book, Gerstner argued that many "thinkers seem to feel . . . that reason is an obstacle to faith." To combat this view, Gerstner wrote that his aim was to "present a rational approach to our deepest and most irrepressible need—God." He labored to show that there were solid reasons for believing. Nonetheless, he finished the book by noting that reason in the end can only take an individual so far. A rational understanding of the Christian faith can make no person a Christian; something else was needed. Gerstner asserted,

> But the non-Christian can only understand it [*Reasons for Faith*] as a[n] argument and nothing more than that. On the other hand, the person who understands the arguments and submits himself to Christ's will shall gain a knowledge which can come no other way. Thus a highly intelligent unbeliever

61. Van Til, Letter to Gerstner, February 26, 1960.

62. See Muether, *Cornelius Van Til.*

63. Leitch, Review of *Reasons for Faith*, 24–27.

64. Leitch, *Winds of Doctrine*, 30.

65. Bloesch, Review of *Reasons for Faith*, 332.

could well master this book so as to state the argument better than many a less gifted believer. But the believer, however few his gifts, will have more of this experiential knowledge than the most gifted unbeliever. Indeed it is not a matter of more and less, but of some and none.[66]

Gerstner was not a bald rationalist. He believed that spiritual factors came into play in a person's commitment to Christ. Nonetheless, he was uneasy with the idea that "irrationalism [could provide] a basis for faith." After citing a statement from Henry Sloane Coffin (1877–1954), a liberal Presbyterian homiletics professor at Union Seminary (NYC), Gerstner went on to write that "although the traditional foundations of religious faith have been badly damaged in the minds of many, they have gone on believing."[67] He noted that many of these individuals have an "irrepressible desire to believe even when one thinks the intellectual obstacles are insurmountable."[68] *Reasons for Faith* was an effort to remove the "obstacles" and offer a reasoned defence of the faith. His book signaled a late echo of the Old Princeton apologetic.

In 1965 Gerstner produced a short theology book that was aimed at laypeople. In *Theology for Everyman,* published by Moody Press, Gerstner insisted that every Christian must be a theologian. "No, they do not need to be professional theologians," Gerstner argued, but they "must have sound knowledge about God."[69] Gerstner wanted to reach a popular Christian audience and strengthen the average believer's commitment and grasp of basic doctrines such as the sinfulness of humanity, the deity of Christ, the atonement, and justification by faith. Gerstner affirmed conservative positions on these doctrines and the idea that the true church was the invisible church. He explained to his readers that the visible church could not be the true church because it was impossible to "search the hearts of professing believers." The Pittsburgh professor argued "we must remember that the true church, the saved church, the church in vital communion with Christ, is the invisible church."[70] The book offered brief and accessible treatments of the theological topics discussed. By publishing with Moody, Gerstner was able to exert some influence within the wider conservative evangelical and fundamentalist circles. One of Gerstner's strengths was his ability to speak to laypeople, but also to write to them in ways that could be easily understood.

66. Gerstner, *Reasons for Faith,* 232–33.

67. Ibid., 4.

68. Ibid., 10.

69. Gerstner, *Theology for Everyman,* 16–17.

70. Ibid., 106.

In the 1960s Addison Leitch also produced three books which aimed at reaching a popular audience: *Interpreting Basic Theology* (1961), *Winds of Doctrine* (1966), and *A Layman's Guide to Presbyterian Beliefs* (1967).[71] *Interpreting Basic Theology* provided brief analysis of various Christian doctrines such as "The Cross of Christ," "The Nature of Sin," "The Work of the Holy Spirit," and the "The Bible: The Word of God." The book's aim was to "encourage the out-and-out newcomer to the field of theology" and Leitch maintained mainstream evangelical positions on the issues expressed. In *Winds of Doctrine* the Tarkio College professor offered a sixty-two page treatment of the theology of Barth, Brunner, Bonhoeffer, Niebuhr, Bultmann, and Tillich.[72] He also provided some discussion on the "counter-movement" he described as "old orthodoxy." Leitch praised Barth's "Bible-centered" viewpoint, emphasis on sin and Christ-centered theology. There were many fine aspects to Barth's theology, Leitch argued, and yet there were also "novelties." For Leitch, who had observed the Presbyterian Controversy and the liberalization of his former seminary, Barth posed a problem. Leitch argued "those who come from the orthodox tradition" of Hodge, Warfield, Machen, Van Til, Henry, Carnell, Murray, and Ramm "*know* that the *orthodoxy* of Barth is *neo*." Leitch added,

> We are not ready to accept his [Barth's] radical criticism of the Bible. When he will consider as allegory or legend that which we claim to be sober history, just so long as the "Word" comes through, we begin to see our differences. Also, followers of Barth are too ready to accept Biblical truth as paradox. Perhaps the easy acceptance of paradox is too quickly and too easily the evasion of truth instead of the way to truth.[73]

From his perspective, the theologian believed that neo-orthodoxy was too evasive and did not produce the "sharpest kind of definition" which was needed on core Christian doctrines. Leitch's analyses of Barth's contributions were relatively positive and yet he was unafraid to express his criticisms. Just as Cornelius Van Til's negative assessment of Barth can be linked to his experience in the Presbyterian Controversy, so too can Leitch's criticisms of Barth be traced to his traumatic experiences at Pittsburgh Seminary in the late 1950s and early 1960s.[74]

71. Leitch, *Interpreting Basic Theology*; *Winds of Doctrine*, and *A Layman's Guide to Presbyterian Beliefs*.

72. The five chapters in the book were originally five lectures given under the G. Campbell Morgan Lectureship at the Winona Lake School of Theology in Indiana.

73. Leitch, *Winds of Doctrine*, 29.

74. The Presbyterian theological battles of the 1920s and 1930s greatly shaped

In regard to Brunner, Bonhoeffer, and Reinhold Niebuhr the problem again was "[w]hat is done inside that canon of Scripture is where the difference between orthodoxy and neo-orthodoxy become[s] drastically plain."[75] Leitch was quite negative in his assessments of Bultmann and Tillich. In his final chapter, Leitch argued that there was countermovement that stood for the "old orthodoxy and a reasoned theology." The theologian cited "Henry, Carnell, Clark, Ramm, and Gerstner" as leading the way "in maintaining the orthodox tradition," noting that there was "nothing 'neo' about them."[76] As a sign of continued theological renewal within conservative Protestantism, Leitch noted the work of *Christianity Today*, Westminster and Fuller seminaries, Wheaton College, the Young Life para-church ministry, and Intervarsity Fellowship. The former Pittsburgh-Xenia president and theologian ended his book by taking direct aim at the progressive UPCUSA theologians and church leaders. He argued that their "refusal to draw lines [theologically] because they make divisions, is an offense to Truth, which is by its very nature divisive." Leitch maintained that the evangelical countermovement in theology "is committed to giving meticulous and sharp study to the words of Scripture, the definitions of theology, the absoluteness of ethics, and the differentia of the churches." Leitch, who was one of the most prominent UPCNA scholars prior to the 1958 merger, was clearly aligning himself with the evangelical movement which he described as "an ecumenical movement centered around an appreciation of the authority of Scripture . . . ."[77] An analysis of *Winds of Doctrine* reveals Leitch's theological position and his belief that Gerstner was playing an important role in reviving evangelical theology.

In *A Layman's Guide to Presbyterian Beliefs* Leitch sought to offer brief commentary on various doctrines and how they are related to the Westminster Confession. He noted that with the new UPCUSA Confession of 1967 (C-67) "there maybe some clear departures from the *system* of doctrine of the Westminster Confession." In the midst of competing theologies within the UPCUSA, Leitch sought to help Presbyterians grasp a traditional Reformed doctrinal perspective. The book addressed such topics as the "The Bible," "The Sovereignty of God," "Social Action," and "The Church and the Communion of Saints." An added feature of the book was a brief critique

Van Til's life and mind, which resulted in his severe hostility to Barth. Van Til's negative analysis of Barth needs to be understood through the lens of the intense American Presbyterian controversy. On this point see Hart, "Beyond the Battle for the Bible: What Evangelicals Missed in Van Til's Critique of Barth," 42–70.

75. Leitch, *Winds of Doctrine*, 39.

76. Ibid., 60.

77. Ibid., 61.

of C-67. It appears that Leitch's main concern was that the new confession would create theological ambiguity in the church. He was perplexed as to how C-67 would relate to the older Reformed confessions in the newly created *Book of Confessions* and which ones would be authoritative. Rather than being a strident critic, Leitch calmly raised concerns about C-67's position on salvific reconciliation and its lack of stress on Christ's divinity.[78] Leitch's book appears to have been an effort to promote traditional Presbyterian beliefs among the laity in an environment of momentous doctrinal change. As Leitch moved forward, Gerstner also sought to make sense of the theological climate of the 1960s.

From 1960 to 1969 Gerstner produced nineteen book reviews, a noticeable decline from the previous decade of sixty one.[79] In March 1962 he wrote a revealing review of an edited volume titled *The Incomparable James Henry Snowden* (1961).[80] Gerstner's review appeared in the *Western Pennsylvania Historical Magazine* and offers several key insights into James Snowden (1852–1936) and the persistence of Presbyterian theological battles. Snowden had taught theology at Western Seminary from 1911 to 1929, was a significant figure in the region, and had achieved some measure of fame after debating with Clarence Darrow (1857–1938), a leading atheist, in Pittsburgh in 1928. In his review, Gerstner noted that the book was "comprehensive in its sweep" and a "fitting memorial" to Snowden. He then wrote that Snowden's "greatest and lasting significance is the stance he took during the 'Modernist-Fundamentalist' debate" that raged in the PCUSA and in the wider church during the 1920s and 1930s. Gerstner charged Snowden with suppressing the doctrinal issues in the controversy by "ignoring" them. He noted that Snowden largely agreed with Machen doctrinally and was "against the 'Modernist' [position], but this did not appear clearly."[81] Gerstner then asked "[w]hy" Snowden failed to rally the troops to the conservative cause. The reason, according to Gerstner, was "because Snowden confused the word 'Modernist' with a methodology, disregarding its content." Snowden's mistake was that he viewed modernism as a method of open-minded inquiry, rather than a position that denied core Christian convictions. The debate, from Gerstner's perspective, "concerned content and not methodology as Machen's book, *Christianity versus Liberalism* [sic], written in 1923, showed." Gerstner added,

78. Leitch, *A Layman's Guide to Presbyterian Beliefs*, 157–58.

79. The vast majority of his reviews appeared in *Christianity Today*.

80. McKinney, ed., *The Incomparable James Henry Snowden*.

81. Gerstner's Review of *The Incomparable James Henry Snowden*, 70.

> Probably more than any other one individual he [Snowden] has
> influenced the Presbyterian Church of this Valley to ignore the
> issue from that day to this. The great question is whether this
> issue will permanently ignore the Presbyterian Church.[82]

Gerstner was seeking to make sense of the fact that in the mid-1930s, not a single congregation in Western Pennsylvania had departed from the PCUSA to join what became known as the Orthodox Presbyterian Church. The review reveals Gerstner's basic theological agreement with J. Gresham Machen and his belief that the earlier doctrinal dispute was still ongoing.

For some, the most obvious example that the prior theological controversy had not been resolved occurred when the PCUSA and the UPCNA merged in 1958. At the 1958 General Assembly of the new UPCUSA, a decision was made to organize a committee which could formulate a new confessional position for the denomination.[83] The committee set out to create a new theological statement and later sought to reduce the Westminster Confession to simply one creed among many in a newly constructed *Book of Confessions*. Leading the way in confessional reform for the committee was Edward Dowey (1918–2003), a Princeton Seminary theologian.[84] Dowey had done his doctoral work under Emil Brunner (1889–1966), a dialectical theologian at the University of Zurich, and Dowey was zealous in his pursuit of theological reform. When he joined the Princeton Seminary faculty in 1957, he refused to take the faculty oath, which required faithfulness to the Westminster standards.[85] Dowey later said that he was able to join the Princeton Seminary faculty because "Dr. Mackay and Eugene Blake initiated an action by which the General Assembly standardized the method of installing professors in all the seminaries. That meant simply by reaffirming one's ordination promises."[86] Dowey, who clearly had an aversion to the Westminster Confession of Faith, became the chair of the revision committee and approached the project from a "Brunnerian" theological perspective.

He traveled the country urging confessional change and visited Pittsburgh Theological Seminary in September 1960 to give a lecture on

82. Ibid., 71.

83. See *Report of the Special Committee on a Brief Contemporary Statement of Faith*, 7.

84. See Wilkinson, "Edward A. Dowey, Jr. and the Making of the Confession of 1967," 5–22. Dowey earned a BA from Lafayette College (1940), a BD from Princeton Seminary (1943), an MA from Columbia University (1947), and a ThD from the University of Zurich (1949). He taught at Lafayette, Columbia, McCormick Seminary, and at Princeton Seminary from 1957 to 1988.

85. See Miglorie, "A Conversation with Edward A. Dowey," 95.

86. Ibid.

Reformed Confessions.[87] In his speech to the seminary Dowey declared that the Westminster Confession "contains serious constricting archaisms."[88] He was critical of the first chapter of the confession which dealt with the Bible. The Princetonian argued that "it was formal authority, conceived as the detailed inerrancy of the biblical 'autographs,' that was the chief theological casualty of the nineteenth century."[89] From his perspective the Westminster standards were outmoded, and this led to "contemporary displeasure" and frustration for many Presbyterians. Dowey maintained that it was an "obvious fact" that the vast majority of Presbyterians "no longer study the 'orthodox' thinkers" of the "seventeenth century."[90] He and many others strongly believed that confessional change was needed. The new confession of which he was the chief architect of would ultimately be named the Confession of 1967. One PTS theology professor, George Kehm, remembers that "almost all the faculty members supported C-67."[91] Apparently there was little opposition. Despite this, Gerstner opposed it, saying that the newly proposed confession was "anything but sound."[92] From his perspective, the confessional revision committee offered a low view of Scripture which sought to change traditional notions of biblical authority. To be sure, the committee emphasized that Christ was the "Word of God" and that the Bible was "given under the guidance of the Holy Spirit." The members of the committee, nevertheless, stressed the humanity of Scripture and steered clear of saying that the Bible was the "Word of God." Instead, they affirmed the neo-orthodox perspective that the Bible was the "norm of all other witnesses" to God. To combat this assertion Gerstner wrote, "We are in danger of making what Christ calls the Word of God (the Bible) of no effect by teaching that He is the Word of God."[93]

During the winter before the June 1966 UPCUSA General Assembly, where commissioners would vote on C-67, Gerstner criticized the proposed new confession. In a December 1965 *Christianity Today* article entitled "A Church Historian Warns," Gerstner argued that the committee's goal "probably was not revision but rejection" of the Westminster standards.[94] He wrote that adherents of the Westminster Confession of Faith

87. Dowey, "Revelation and Faith in the Protestant Confessions," 9–26.
88. Ibid., 25.
89. Ibid.
90. Ibid.
91. Kehm, Interview with the author, August 14, 2012.
92. Gerstner quoted by Medsger, "Presbyterians Examine Confession of Faith."
93. Ibid.
94. Gerstner, "A Church Historian Warns: Presbyterians Are Demoting the Bible,"

will be offended by this absence of the very clarity for which the Westminster Confession of Faith has always been justly famous. But whatever heresies may lurk in the shadows of vague language, all of them have not yet dared to come to the light. Through the obfuscations of the new creed the light of truth of the old ones will continue to shine to the glory of God and the comfort of those who still believe what they vowed at their ordination.[95]

Gerstner was deeply concerned with what he believed to be the new confession's ambiguity. He also objected to the committee's stated belief that the "the doctrine of inerrancy . . . placed the older Reformed theology at odds with advances in historical and scientific studies."[96] The problem with this position, in Gerstner's mind, was that the committee seemed to be saying that an errant, non-scientific Bible is our normative witness to Jesus, who is the Word of God. He wrote, "[w]e are being told that the scientifically and historically errant word of God is nonetheless the norm of all witnesses to the Word of God.) The committee shows wisdom in not seeking to illustrate this."[97] Gerstner reasoned that a Christian's understanding of Christ would be harmed if the Bible, which tells us about Christ, was regarded as a solely human book filled with pre-scientific errors and historical inaccuracies. He found the committee's words to be an "inaccurate, pejorative, [and] disrespectful-to-the-fathers-statement."[98] Gerstner maintained that "[t]here is a vast difference between an infallible witness to an infallible Christ and a fallible witness to an infallible Christ." In a 1968 essay titled "The Message of the Word," Gerstner wrote: "The Bible in which God has clothed His revelation of Himself is like the seamless garment in which the Son of man was clothed. To tear apart the Bible is to rend the robe in which the deity is dressed."[99] He believed that those who rejected the Bible's historical trustworthiness would soon reject what the Bible says about Jesus *and* matters of "faith and practice."[100] For readers of the *Post-Gazette* Gerstner declared that C-67 was "the greatest doctrinal disaster in the history

11.

95. Ibid., 11.

96. Revision committee statement quoted by Ibid., 11.

97. Ibid., 13.

98. Ibid.

99. Gerstner, "The Message of the Word," 176.

100. Ibid.

of Presbyterianism."[101] (Accepting a lower view of the Bible would ultimately undermine belief in Christ and the obligations of the Christian life.)

Critics of the proposed confession in the Orthodox Presbyterian Church believed that the anticipated confessional changes made by the UP-CUSA were a vindication of their past protests against latitudinarian theology within the mainline northern Presbyterian church (PCUSA). Cornelius Van Til, the OPC apologetics professor, who taught at Westminster Seminary, argued that mainline Presbyterians would now view the Westminster standards just as modern highways would tolerate the horse-drawn buggies of the Amish.[102] Edmund Clowney (1917–2005), another OPC scholar, held that C-67 created a "creedal museum."[103] They believed a collection of different confessions created doctrinal chaos.[104] Van Til wrote *The Confession of 1967* (1967) to warn conservatives in the UPCUSA.[105] In addition, the OPC purchased large advertisements in *Christianity Today* objecting to C-67 and claiming that the "Confession of 1967 emerges not as a contemporary restatement but as a radical revision that expresses something other than Christian faith."[106] In the advertisement, the OPC also stated, "Presbyterians are being asked to choose between the fleeting fascination of the latest theological vogue and the timeless relevance of the truth of God's Word."[107] For many members of the OPC, the confessional change gave concrete evidence that their protests in the 1930s were well founded and proved once and for all that the PCUSA really was not committed to the Westminster Confession of Faith.

Within the UPCUSA Gerstner became the most visible Presbyterian seminary professor to oppose C-67. One minor exception to Gerstner's status as the primary scholarly opponent was Arthur Cochrane (1909–2002).[108] Cochrane was a theology professor, originally from Canada, who

101. Gerstner quoted by Gaitens in "The Presbyterian Dispute," 4.

102. Muether, *Cornelius Van Til*, 195. Van Til served as an instructor of apologetics at Princeton Seminary for the 1928–1929 school year. In his informative book *Princeton Seminary in American Religion and Culture* (2012), Moorehead incorrectly notes that Van Til was offered a position at Princeton Seminary, but turned it down to go to Westminster Seminary (368).

103. Clowney, *Another Foundation*, 4.

104. For a historical summary of how the Orthodox Presbyterian Church reacted to the newly proposed confession, see Hart, *Between The Times*, 89–98.

105. See Van Til, *The Confession of 1967*.

106. "The Presbyterian Predicament" [Advertisement], 27.

107. Ibid.

108. Cochrane received his BA from the University of Toronto, a BD from Knox College (Toronto) and a PhD from the University of Edinburgh.

taught at the University of Dubuque Theological Seminary in Iowa. The Dubuque theologian offered some criticisms of the proposed confession in a 1966 *McCormick Quarterly* article by comparing it to the *Barmen Declaration* (1934), a statement made by German Protestants in opposition to the Nazi-supported "German Christian" movement.[109] Cochrane, who was an international authority on Reformed confessions, expressed his concern that C-67 seemed to be more about updating language and adjusting the UPCUSA's theology to the culture than confronting doctrinal heterodoxy within the church. Besides this, however, few mainline northern Presbyterian seminary professors voiced any criticism. Nonetheless, substantial opposition did arise from a variety of other sources. In 1965 the Presbyterian Lay Committee (PLC) was founded by J. Howard Pew (1882–1971), owner of the Sun Oil Company, to oppose the confession.[110] The PLC board, which was composed of several influential business people, purchased full-page advertisements in thirty of the country's largest newspapers expressing their opposition to C-67. Their advertisement declared to readers across the nation, "[t]he Confession of 1967 does not ring true. It is so filled with ambiguities, undefined . . . and obscure language that it becomes possible to rationalize almost any point the reader seeks to establish."[111] They added,

> [t]he Westminster Confession of Faith, on the other hand, is so clearly and succinctly stated that anyone who can read can understand its meaning. It does not require a group of intellectuals to explain it.[112]

The UPCUSA magazine *Presbyterian Life* took umbrage at this advertisement and considered the PLC's publicity campaign to be an "attack on the [proposed] confession."[113] Theophilus Mills Taylor, the General Council Secretary of the UPCUSA, stated, "[t]he advertisement is deliberately calculated to undermine the faith of Presbyterians in their historic form of democratic government."[114]

109. Cochrane, "Barmen and the Confession of 1967," 135–48. See also Cochrane's *The Church's Confession under Hitler.*

110. Eskridge, "John Howard Pew," 522–23; Wilkinson, "Edward Dowey Jr. and the Making of the Confession of 1967," 16. Wilkinson notes that Dowey spoke at the PUBC event in Chicago for two hours, but mentions nothing about his debate with Gerstner.

111. "A Call To Every United Presbyterian . . . ," 12.

112. Ibid.

113. "Lay Committee Advertisements Assail Proposed Confession," 23.

114. Taylor quoted in "Lay Committee Advertisements Assail Proposed Confession," 23.

Gerstner later wrote only one article for the *Presbyterian Layman* magazine, but he did take a leadership role in Presbyterians United for Biblical Confession (PUBC) [later Concerns], which also emerged in 1965 to oppose the proposed confession. He served as the initial editor of PUBC publications and along with Addison Leitch served on the PUBC's executive committee.[115] Debate over C-67 was intense within the denomination during the 1960s, and several events were held to discuss the new confession. In November 1965, the PUBC organized a two-day forum in Chicago on C-67 in the hope of offering a "critique aimed at making it [the proposed confession] more biblical."[116] Advocates of C-67 were also invited to attend. The *Chicago Tribune* reported that the PUBC's goal was to revise the proposed confession to make it "truly biblical, evangelical, and consistent with our Reformed faith."[117] The event attracted five hundred and thirty eight registrants and was held in one of Chicago's premier hotels, the Palmer House. Gerstner's participation in this event would thrust him on to the national stage. Numerous Presbyterian leaders and dignitaries attended the event, including William Thompson (1918–2006), the moderator of the UPCUSA. *Christianity Today* reported that John Mackay (1889–1983), the retired president of Princeton Seminary, spoke and urged the drafters of the new confession to take a "stronger stand on the Bible." Mackay received applause when he stated in his Scottish accent that "the Bible has greater literary and theological dimensions than is attributed to it in the proposed Confession." The new confession affirmed that the Bible was the "normative witness," but Mackay argued "it is much more. It is the authoritative source from which we draw."[118] Conservatives in the UPCUSA were no doubt pleased to have support from someone of Mackay's stature, but overall there was little scholarly opposition to C-67.

At the meeting, the arduous task of debating against Dowey fell to Gerstner. Inside the hotel's gold and white grand ballroom, Gerstner sparred with Dowey over the proposed confession. The *Christianity Today* reporter found Dowey to be "engaging and persuasive," but held that Gerstner was more "articulate" and "argumentative."[119] Gerstner's asthmatic condition combined with his own forcefulness made him sound somewhat gruff when he spoke. After watching Gerstner's performance one observer

---

115. Heinze, "PUBC Meets in Chicago to Discuss Confession," 27.

116. "A Confession? In 1967?," 36–37.

117. Philbrick, "Presbyterian Doctrine Plan Is Criticized," B11.

118. "A Confession? In 1967?," 37.

119. Ibid.

later described him as a "tremendous debater."[120] Later in 1966, Gerstner served as a delegate to the UPCUSA General Assembly in Boston, which also debated the confession.[121] By this point, however, it was clear that the new confession would most likely pass. There was little Gerstner could do. In April 1967, shortly before the confession received its final presbytery approval, Gerstner wrote to one of his former students, "I seem to favor continuing with the church and yet at the same time, it is pulling the flesh from my bones to do so . . . ."[122] The conservatives were able to effect a few changes in the proposed confession; these changes according to Gerstner, gave the document "some unmistakably alien, orthodox elements super-imposed on its basic structure."[123] In the end, his efforts to stop the passage of C-67 proved futile. Dowey declared that the "bitterness of the 1920s is practically gone. Fundamentalism is as dead as the social gospel."[124] In June 1967, the UPCUSA General Assembly ratified the new confession. Only 18 out of 184 presbyteries rejected C-67 and so it was adopted.[125]

Gerstner's critique of C-67 and his more general criticisms of liberal theology put him at odds with the theological direction in which PTS was moving. Edward Farley, a PTS theologian, had helped facilitate the theological changes at school, and later noted that the seminary "grew in liberalism in the 1960s."[126] During the 1960s, Walter Wiest (1920–), who served as professor of the philosophy of religion, remembers that Gerstner was "pretty quiet at faculty meetings" and "kind of excluded himself" from fellow faculty members.[127] Another colleague, George Kehm, a PTS theologian, observed that Gerstner was a "strict adherent of the Westminster Confession of Faith" who was "quiet at faculty meetings."[128] Farley found that Gerstner was "always ready for conversation" and "friendly," but considered him to be a "marginal" faculty member.[129] Gerstner's conservative theological position—opposition to C-67, commitment to the Westminster standards, and involvement in the evangelical movement—did indeed lead to Gerstner's

120. Beatty, Interview with the author.

121. Gerstner, Interview with Coffin, 25.

122. Gerstner, Letter to Stark, April 20, 1967.

123. Gerstner, "New Light on the Confession of 1967," 4.

124. Dowey quoted by Rogers and McKim, The Authority and Interpretation of the Bible, 440.

125. Coalter, "Confession of 1967," 65.

126. Farley, Interview with the author.

127. Wiest, Interview with the author.

128. Kehm, Interview with the author.

129. Farley, Interview with the author.

isolation on the faculty. After listening to Gerstner preach in chapel, H. Eberhard Von Waldow (1923–2007), a PTS Old Testament professor, emerged and said to one student, "this man Gerstner is a fanatic."[130] Apparently, some people found Gerstner's theology and vigorous preaching style too severe. One former student remembers that Gerstner spoke with intensity and that he sounded like a "machine gun."[131] Gerstner later said that his experience on the PTS faculty in the 1960s "was not a pleasant situation as far as the faculty was concerned." Nevertheless, he remembered "always" going to the faculty meetings "because I felt it was my duty."[132] At the faculty meetings Gerstner later noted, "I stayed silent . . . there was no point to arguing." Gerster said, "[i]f I saw something which was negotiable, I would talk, or something where it was absolutely necessary to have a 'negative' recorded or something like that, I'd do it."[133] But, for the most part, Gerstner remained quiet. He bluntly stated that his colleagues "appreciated my not talking too much, because it was a waste of time. They weren't going to pay any attention to it." With the exception of Bob Kelley, who was a more moderate evangelical, nearly all of Gerstner's fellow faculty members at PTS disagreed with his doctrinal conservatism.

In hindsight Gerstner's isolation on the faculty may not have been as bleak as he assumed. Even though Gerstner was considered on the periphery of the faculty, his profile continued to rise within the seminary, the UPCUSA, and the wider American church. During the 1960s, two important developments occurred which changed the course of his career. The first development was the rise of some strong admirers and followers of Gerstner within the PTS student body. One student, David Williams, came to the seminary as a non-believer, but soon converted to Christ under Gerstner's teaching.[134] During the 1960s Williams and other students organized a campus group which looked to Gerstner for guidance and theological mentoring. Jim Dennison attended the meetings, which were usually held on Wednesday nights, and recalled that Gerstner "helped students with the arguments made by liberal scholars."[135] In April 1966, Gerstner wrote a letter to a former student, Carl Bogue, and recorded his observation of some

130. Dennison, Interview with the author.

131. Stark, Interview with the author.

132. Gerstner, Interview with Coffin, 23.

133. Ibid.

134. Williams received his BA from Milliken University (Illinois), did graduate study in Wales and at Oxford University and then received his BD degree from PTS in 1968.

135. Dennison, Interview with the author.

"encouraging developments . . . among the student body." He wrote that the strength of the evangelical student group was "precipitated by the Confession of 1967, the death of God movement, and similar phenomena."[136] This evangelical student group had a lasting vitality, and several of the evangelical students who participated would make their mark as outstanding pastors, scholars, and national church leaders. Bogue, who graduated from PTS in 1965, became a leading Presbyterian Church in America pastor in Akron, Ohio, in the 1970s. After finishing a doctorate on Jonathan Edwards and the covenant of grace from the Free University of Amsterdam, Bogue lectured widely in various conservative Reformed institutions.[137] Dennison, also a close disciple of Gerstner, went on to become Gerstner's pastor at Pioneer Presbyterian Church in Ligonier, Pennsylvania. Later he served as librarian and lecturer in church history at Westminster Seminary in Escondido, California, and as professor of church history and biblical theology at Northwest Theological Seminary in Lynnwood, Washington.[138] Dennison later established himself as a key scholar of the Reformed Confessions and of the Reformed theologian Francis Turretin (1623–1687).[139]

The most prominent scholar, however, to have studied under Gerstner in the 1960s was R.C. Sproul (1939–).[140] In 1961 Sproul arrived at PTS and became especially close to Gerstner. When Sproul began his studies at PTS, he held to Van Tilian apologetics, but after his coursework with Gerstner, he "became convinced of Gerstner's classical apologetics."[141] Sproul remembers that they would "often discuss theology over dinner" and have "endless conversation into the early morning." In the classroom Sproul found Gerstner to be challenging, but Sproul showed signs of promise. The seminary dean urged Sproul to pursue a PhD in the seminary's joint doctoral program with the University of Pittsburgh. Ultimately, however, Sproul would take his

136. Gerstner, Letter to Bogue.

137. "Dr. Carl W. Bogue Jr.," Reformation International Theological Seminary. Bogue earned his BA from Muskingum College (1961), an MDiv from PTS (1965), and earned a ThD from the Free University of Amsterdam in 1975.

138. "James T. Dennison Jr," Northwest Theologicalcal Seminary. Dennison received his BS from Geneva College (1961), an MDiv from PTS (1968), and a ThM from PTS in 1973.

139. Dennsion, ed., *Institutes of Elenctic Theology*, vols. 1–3; Dennison, ed., *Reformed Confessions of the 16th and 17th Centuries in English Translation*, 1523–1552, vols. 1–4.

140. Sproul earned his BA from Westminster College, his BD from PTS (1964), and doctorandus status from the Free University of Amsterdam. In Dutch higher education doctorandus refers to a candidate for a doctorate.

141. Sproul, Interview with the author.

mentor's advice and pursue graduate study at the Free University of Amsterdam. Gerstner's relationship with Sproul would in due course prove to be highly beneficial to the older scholar. In 1971, Sproul started a vibrant study center, Ligonier Valley Study Center, and later a successful para-church organization known as Ligonier Ministries. Gerstner became involved in both of these enterprises. Sproul also taught at Westminster College (Pennsylvania), Gordon College (Massachusetts), Gordon-Conwell School of Theology, Reformed Theological Seminary (Mississippi & Florida) and Knox Theological Seminary (Florida). Together the pair would play a key role in the resurgence of Presbyterian and Reformed evangelicalism and the battle over inerrancy in the 1970s and 1980s. Sproul became a zealous promoter of Gerstner's thought and the person most responsible for continuing his legacy.

Another development which changed Gerstner's career occurred in January 1966, when Kenneth Kantzer (1917–2002), dean of Trinity Evangelical Divinity School (TEDS) in Illinois, wrote to Gerstner inviting him to teach at TEDS. Kantzer commented that "I personally would be overjoyed at the thought that the Lord might, in certain circumstances, lead you to join our faculty."[142] The TEDS dean, who was an old friend from Gerstner's Harvard days, was concerned that Gerstner might not be able to carry out his "work effectively" at PTS because the "school [PTS] is not noted for its orthodoxy."[143] TEDS had been founded by the Swedish Evangelical Free Church in 1897 and had remained a small institution until the arrival of Kantzer, who helped the school grow rapidly in the 1960s.[144] Gerstner accepted a position there as adjunct professor of church history. TEDS gave Gerstner the opportunity to interact with scholars and students in a strictly evangelical environment. For the next few years, Gerstner would teach at PTS during the week and then drive eight hours from Pittsburgh to the TEDS campus located in the northern Chicago suburb of Deerfield. At TEDS Gerstner taught evangelical students who came from a wide variety of denominations. His study habits led him to create a small library in his Volkswagen van and he attached a device to his steering wheel which allowed him to read while making the long drive. One Trinity student from the late 1960s, Leroy Birney, recalled that Gerstner was "very knowledgeable about church history," but that most of the students disagreed with his

142. Kantzer, Letter to Gerstner.

143. Gerstner, Interview with the author, September 10, 2012.

144. Martin, ed., *Trinity International University, 1897–1997*; Woodbridge and McComiskey, eds., *Doing Theology in Today's World*.

views on predestination.[145] Another Trinity student, John Ault, did not like Gerstner's "way of testing" students for exams, but was "impressed by his presentations" which helped give him a "good grasp of the flow of church history."[146] Gerstner appeared to enjoy his time teaching at TEDS.

Even though Gerstner felt that his new colleagues at PTS, the former Western professors, were more scholarly, that did not mean he was afraid to engage them. During the 1960s, Gerstner formally debated with members of his own faculty and scholars from other institutions. He challenged George Kehm on the issue of infant baptism.[147] He also engaged in separate debates with Markus Barth and Edward Dowey on C-67.[148] In addition, he debated with individuals outside Presbyterian circles. In front of a crowd estimated at 700 to 800 people Gerstner sparred with Robert G. Olson, a Rutgers University philosophy professor, on the existence of God.[149] He also formally debated about the Vietnam War with Frederick Flott of the U.S. State Department and Joseph Zasloff of the University of Pittsburgh.[150] Moreover, during the 1960s Gerstner remained in constant demand as a guest speaker and preacher. He preached in various Presbyterian churches, but also preached at many Christian Missionary Alliance, Baptist, and other evangelical churches.[151]

At home, John and Edna faced the challenge of keeping a vibrant piety. The 1960s were a tumultuous period, and the Gerstners worried about how society was shaping their children. Tension grew within the family over clothing styles and the family's lifestyle. Apparently, Edna was upset that her daughter Rachel was reading books that embraced the values of the counterculture. Rachel particularly struggled with her parents' Christian child-rearing. Judy, however, was more compliant with her parents' spiritual influence. The family home was on an eight-acre tract of land in rural Westmoreland County, Pennsylvania, and ten miles from Ligonier.[152] Jonathan remembers that "the home's location made it feel like we grew up on an island." John and Edna loved their children, but their family life was not perfect. Gerstner's home in the country provided Gerstner the opportunity

145. Birney email correspondence with the author, September 14, 2011.

146. Ault email correspondence with the author, September 13, 2011.

147. Kehm, Interview with the author, August 14, 2012.

148. "A Confession? In 1967?," 37;

149. Gerstner, "Enlightenment," Handout Church History.

150. A picture of this debate is located in the *The Annual Catalogue of the Pittsburgh Theological Seminary 1967–1968*, 31.

151. Gerstner, Interview with the author.

152. Ibid.

to work in isolation, but it also serves as metaphor for Gestner's loneliness on the PTS faculty.

From 1960 to 1969 Gerstner accomplished many important goals. He produced several books which made him a notable figure within the UPCUSA and the wider evangelical movement. Like the Princetonians, whose apologetic he embraced, he defended the gospel inside the halls of PTS, in the wider academy, and in the church. His writing for *Christianity Today* gave him a voice within the large and expanding American evangelical movement. He was an engaged scholar who fought against the revision that led to the Confession of 1967. His leadership in the PUBC meant that evangelical layman in the UPCUSA had at least one professor who could speak to their concerns. As a defender of an older apologetic, he was viewed by many as out of step with the more modern theologies of his day. It is easy to view Gerstner as a professor simply beholden to retrograde beliefs and ideas, or a crank committed to a seventeenth century confession. As an example of his "marginal" status, many will no doubt point to the fact that he was indeed on the periphery of the PTS faculty and the UPCUSA, both of which continued to move further and further to the theological left. There is certainly some truth in this view of Gerstner. In the world of mainline Presbyterianism Gerstner was on the conservative edge, but as Gerstner maintained his views he simultaneously helped position himself near the center stage of Reformed evangelicalism. During the 1960s he produced several protégés at PTS who went on to become noteworthy scholars and church leaders within Presbyterian and Reformed evangelicalism. The battles Gerstner lost led to new opportunities. His teaching at TEDS proved to be fruitful and strengthened his ties to the wider non-denominational evangelical movement. The flowering of Gerstner's ideas and the movements with which he was associated were just beginning.

5

The Shaping of Modern Evangelicalism (1970–1979)

As Gerstner entered the 1970s he had a mature awareness of the powerful forces that opposed his evangelical beliefs. He had endured through the consolidation of Pitt-Xenia and Western, the loss of Leitch, and the adoption of a new confession—C-67, to which he was strongly opposed. The decade of the 1970s, however, offered its own particular challenges to a church historian who was uncomfortable with the social and religious changes that the 1960s had produced. During the new decade Gerstner continued his ministry of teaching. He remained a full-time professor at Pittsburgh Theological Seminary and a visiting professor at Trinity Evangelical Divinity School (TEDS). Moreover, he began lecturing at a new evangelical ministry which his protégé R. C. Sproul had founded. Gerstner was a driven person who sought to pass on his evangelical faith to his students, to the wider church, and to the world. His energy and tireless defense of evangelical convictions made him a force to be reckoned with in various ecclesiastical and academic environments. He was unafraid to engage other scholars and welcomed intellectual exchange. His strategy was to oppose theological liberalism, promote Reformed theology within evangelicalism and the UPCUSA, defend rational apologetics, and use Jonathan Edwards and the Old School Princetonians to achieve the first three objectives. Gerstner was, indeed, an evangelical dynamo in the 1970s. Yet there were also weaknesses in his scholarship that revealed the church historian's troubled career. Despite the flaws, Gerstner moved forward energetically and became a shaper of evangelical belief and practice. The issue to be explored in this chapter is the different ways in which Gerstner helped mold American evangelicalism.

The evangelical movement in the 1970s experienced growing strength and increasing diversity. Evangelicals did not control mainline Presbyterian seminaries and were not entrenched in the denominational leadership. Nonetheless, there were signs that evangelicalism was rising in the 1970s and even having an effect on mainline denominations. During this period, evangelical groups expanded their strength within the mainline churches.[1] Throughout the 1970s Billy Graham, the famed evangelist, continued his evangelistic activity and helped bring unity to the evangelical movement across the denominational spectrum. The evangelical orientated Jesus People movement harnessed the power of the pop culture world, spread the Christian message in a myriad of fresh ways, and created new denominations like Calvary Chapel and the Vineyard Church.[2] From 1969 to 1977 the evangelical sports ministry, Fellowship of Christian Athletes, expanded from 1,000 to 2,000 local chapters and by 1978 held more than thirty-two national athletic camps.[3] Other evangelical college groups such as Campus Crusade for Christ and InterVarsity Christian Fellowship also expanded in the 1970s.[4] Evangelical growth led the secular magazine *Newsweek* to declare that 1976 was the "Year of the Evangelical."[5] The movement's strength was tangible in the 1970s and yet its unity was somewhat illusory because of deep theological divisions within the broader movement and within one of its sub-groups, Presbyterian and Reformed evangelicalism.

During the 1970s Gerstner continued to participate in debates. In the early 1970s he debated with James Olthuis, a philosopher from the Institute for Christian Studies (Toronto), at Geneva College on the theology of Herman Dooyeweerd (1894–1977), a Dutch philosopher.[6] Peter Steen (1935–1984), a Geneva College professor who organized the debate, was a passionate advocate for Dooyeweerd's thought, but was dismissed from Geneva College in 1973 for his views.[7] Wayne Spear, a Reformed Presbyterian theologian, remembers that Dooyeweerd's philosophy had become somewhat of a controversial topic in Reformed Presbyterian circles and Gerstner sought to stand firmly against alleged Dooyeweerdian subjectivism and for what he considered to be a more traditional Reformed viewpoint.[8] Accord-

1. Flowers, *Religion in Strange Times*, 41; Eller, "Special Interest Groups and American Presbyterians," 254–78.

2. Eskridge, *God's Forever People*.

3. "History," Fellowship of Christian Athletes.

4. Turner, *Bill Bright and Campus Crusade for Christ*; MacLeod, *C. Stacey Woods and the Evangelical Rediscovery of the University*.

5. Marsden, *Understanding Fundamentalism and Evangelicalism*, 63.

6. Spear, Interview with the author; Borger, Interview with the author.

7. Borger, "Pete Steen—legend or legacy?."

8. Spear, Interview with the author, September 9, 2011.

ing to Spear, many Reformed Presbyterians were troubled by Dooyeweerd's overly subjective views on Scripture which focused on the "grip of scripture," but did not take the "meaning of biblical words seriously enough."[9] Presbyterian and Reformed evangelicals continued to experience doctrinal divisions of their own, but so did the wider evangelical movement.

Perhaps Gerstner's most impressive debate in the 1970s occurred in the spring of 1977 when he travelled to his *alma mater*, Harvard University. There he debated with Krister Stendahl, a liberal Lutheran Bible scholar and dean of the Harvard Divinity School. They engaged each other on the topic of the "Authority of the Bible." An estimated fifty people attended the debate, which began with the singing of Martin Luther's classic Reformation hymn "A Mighty Fortress."[10] William Long, a student at nearby Gordon-Conwell Theological Seminary, attended the debate and remembers Gerstner's gruff manner and forceful style.[11] According to Long, Gerstner's basic line of reasoning was that the concept of biblical authority did not mean very much if it was not linked to the doctrine of biblical inerrancy, which Gerstner defined as "what the Bible says God says."[12] Gerstner and many other evangelicals maintained that the Bible was completely true and accurately communicated God's word to humanity.[13] From Long's perspective Gerstner and Stendahl simply talked past each other. During the 1970s liberal and moderate Protestants rejected inerrancy, but increasingly evangelicals were also expressing doubts or jettisoning the doctrine as well.

In the 1970s the flagship evangelical periodical *Christianity Today* propounded conservative evangelical convictions, under the work of Harold Lindsell, its editor and a former Fuller church history professor.[14] In 1975 George Marsden, a historian at Calvin College, argued that evangelicals' "intellectual isolation seems to be past," but that their "isolation itself has had the effect of preserving the principle of biblical authority that is a chief

9. Spear, Interview with the author, May 23, 2014. On this general point, see Frame's chapter on Herman Dooyewerd in *Cornelius Van Til*, 371–400.

10. Long, Interview with the author, January 6, 2011.

11. Long received his BA from Brown University, a MDiv from Gordon-Conwell Theological Seminary, a PhD from Brown University and a JD from Willamette University (OR). He served as a professor of religion at Reed College (OR) (1982–1988) and professor of history at Sterling College in Kansas (1990–1996). Later he served as a lawyer, a visiting law professor, and a writer.

12. Gerstner, *A Biblical Inerrancy Primer*, 9.

13. On this traditional evangelical view of Scripture, see Mark Noll, *Between Faith and Criticism*, 150.

14. Stanley, *The Global Diffusion of Evangelicalism*, 38.

source of evangelical strength."[15] Despite evangelicalism's biblical conservatism, divisions were intensifying and evangelical disunity had become glaring at the movement's most prominent seminary, Fuller. In the 1970s the California institution became a theological warzone as it debated inerrancy, moved away from the doctrine, and pursued a more moderate evangelical orientation.[16] In 1976 Lindsell published the *Battle for the Bible*, which strongly criticised Fuller's drift away from inerrancy. Lindsell's book created a firestorm of controversy within evangelicalism and not all inerrantists agreed with the book's aggressiveness. Carl Henry, the dean of American evangelical theologians, noted that the book was "relying on theological atom bombing."[17] Lindsell's militancy aside, Fuller was indeed now more focused on conservative criticism than with combating theological liberalism and Gerstner's former student, Jack Rogers, helped Fuller facilitate this strategic move.[18] It seems clear that Gerstner's writing and organizational efforts in the 1970s to promote inerrancy were performed to halt what he considered to be a weakening of doctrinal conservatism within the evangelical movement. It is not surprising that a combative scholar like Gerstner, who was so familiar with liberalism, would seek to check the moves of evangelical moderates. Gerstner's experiences at PTS and his witnessing of its liberalization in the 1960s and 1970s served to reinforce in his mind the perils of the supposed evangelical accommodation.

One key ally Gerstner had in these controversies over scripture was his former student from the early 1960s, R. C. Sproul. The younger scholar's studies had been interrupted by teaching and he ceased his work at the Free University of Amsterdam in 1969. What was distinctive about Sproul's teaching is that he was a strong advocate for the evidentialist apologetic views he shared with his mentor. By 1970 Sproul was serving as an associate pastor at the prominent College Hill Presbyterian Church (UPCUSA) in Cincinnati, Ohio. In 1971 Sproul accepted a challenge to start a Christian study center an hour southeast of Pittsburgh in Stahlstown, Pennsylvania. The institution was named the Ligonier Valley Study Center (LVSC). The call for the new center came from Christian leaders in the Pittsburgh area including Dora Hillman, the widow of J. Hartwell Hillman, an industrial tycoon.[19] Along with her support, Mrs. Hillman gave fifty-two acres of land

15. Marsden, "From Fundamentalism to Evangelicalism: A Historical Analysis," 138.

16. Marsden, *Reforming Fundamentalism*, 277–98.

17. Ibid., 288.

18. Ibid., 277–92.

19. Rowley, "The Ligonier Valley Study Center Early Years."

to launch the project. The heiress had become enthusiastic about Sproul after hearing him teach. According to Jack Rowley, a LVSC staff member, the center maintained an informal atmosphere where lecturers did not wear ties, but rather dressed like college students.[20] While many of the lecturers probably wore casual clothes, it seems unlikely that Gerstner did not wear a suit and tie. Gerstner maintained a formal gentlemanly style of dress throughout his career. Sproul wrote that LVSC was "a facility developed to make the resources of Christian scholarship available to today's laymen and pastors."[21] LVSC provided courses on theology, apologetics, and the Bible. For Gerstner and Sproul the Christian faith required believers to defend the faith apologetically. Leaders at the LVSC hoped to strengthen Christianity in the Pittsburgh region. Soon however, their dream would expand far beyond Western Pennsylvania.

In 1972 Gerstner, because of his close relationship with Sproul, became a lecturer at the center and was given the title of professor-at-large.[22] Gerstner lectured at different times, but during the summers he taught every Monday night and offered instruction on "theology, philosophy, and apologetics."[23] Sproul and his wife, Vesta, began the study center with Jim Thompson, who had worked as an engineer with Proctor & Gamble. Thompson's involvement proved to be highly beneficial for LVSC because Thompson and later Jack Rowley helped to develop a strong audio and media ministry for the center and soon thousands of cassette tapes of Sproul's teaching were being sent around the country.[24] Rowley came to Ligonier in 1977 from his position as the head of the television production facility in General Electric's Aircraft Engine Training School. His work at the center ensured that Ligonier would have a technologically advanced audio visual ministry. Scores of Gerstner's lectures on apologetics, church history, and theology were preserved and distributed. The multi-media capabilities of LVSC were slowly helping Sproul and Gerstner reach audiences outside Stahlstown.[25] Indeed, the Ligonier ministry would became not merely a provincial or regional operation, but rather a nationally known transdenominational ministry that would uphold and promote a Reformed and evangelical theological position.

20. Rowley, Interview with the author, March 4, 2014.
21. Sproul, "Foreword," Montgomery ed in, *God's Inerrant Word* , 9.
22. Rowley, Interview with the author, March 4, 2014.
23. Rowley, "The Ligonier Valley Study Center Early Years."
24. Rowley, "The Ligonier Valley Study Center Early Years."
25. Ibid.

In the fall of 1973 the center hosted a "Conference on the Inspiration and Authority of Scripture."[26] The impetus for the event derived from what organizers felt was evangelical retreat from biblical inerrancy. Important scholars were brought in to speak at the event and "more than 100 registrants" attended.[27] The symposium resulted in the "Ligonier Statement" on biblical inerrancy and an edited book, *God's Inerrant Word* (1974), containing articles from conference presenters.[28] The "Ligonier Statement" asserted that the Bible was the "inspired and inerrant Word of God" as opposed to neo-orthodox or liberal Protestant views on scripture. Those who signed the "Ligonier Statement" and lectured at the event included Gerstner, Sproul, John Frame, Peter R. Jones, John W. Montgomery, J. I. Packer, and Clark Pinnock. Frame was a theology professor at Westminster Theological Seminary in Philadelphia. Jones was professor-elect at the Faculté Libre de Théologie Reformée in Aix-en-Provence, France. Montgomery was a newly elected professor of law and theology at the International School of Law in Washington, DC.[29] Packer, a Reformed Anglican theologian, served as associate principal of Trinity College, Bristol, England. Pinnock was professor-elect of systematic theology at Regent College, Vancouver, Canada. Gerstner and Packer were the most senior scholars among the group.[30] These conservative professors' main concern was with evangelicals who were moving away from the doctrine of inerrancy, thus placing evangelicalism in a situation "fraught with extreme peril."[31] From their perspective American Christianity had been injured by efforts to reject the doctrine of biblical inerrancy and something needed to be done to stop the bleeding.

In the editor's introduction to *God's Inerrant Word*, Montgomery cited defections from the inerrancy position at North Park Seminary in Chicago and at Concordia Seminary in St Louis.[32] He also added that the "United Presbyterian Confession of 1967 is the inevitable consequence of the deterioration of belief in biblical inerrancy in the Presbyterian Church U.S.A. in the 1920s."[33] Sproul, who convened the event, argued that liberal biblical

26. Sproul, "Foreword," 9.

27. *Perspectives*, 19. *Perspectives* was published by the Institute for Christian Studies in Toronto, Canada.

28. Montgomery, ed., *God's Inerrant Word*.

29. In 1979 the International School of Law became the George Mason University, School of Law.

30. "Contributors," *God's Inerrant Word*, 282.

31. Montgomery, "Editor's Introduction," *God's Inerrant Word*, 13.

32. Ibid.

33. Ibid., 14.

criticism had led to "confusion, skepticism, and despair" and that this encouraged churches to adopt "relativistic theology in order to accommodate the loss of authority."[34] In the midst of what they perceived was the theological chaos of the 1970s these evangelical inerrantists hoped to reassert the Bible's authority and truth by arguing in favor of biblical inerrancy. Specifically, they were worried about the "anti-inerrancy trend in evangelical Protestantism" because it would "corrupt evangelical witness here and abroad."[35] Significantly, Fuller Seminary had moved away—after much rancor—from more conservative forms of inerrancy in the 1960s.[36] The "Ligonier Statement" was also formulated against the backdrop of infighting over the doctrine within the Evangelical Theological Society (ETS), a scholarly organization founded by evangelical inerrantists in 1949.[37] Some ETS members were uncomfortable with the strict inerrancy that the society maintained and were expressing their concerns and even resigning over the issue. Another sign of the broadening of evangelical scholarship was the founding of the Institute of Biblical Research (IBR) in 1973.[38] E. Earle Ellis (1926–2010), then a professor of New Testament at Bethel Theological Seminary in St Paul, Minnesota, established IBR in an effort to orientate evangelical biblical scholarship more towards the arena of professional biblical scholarship. IBR had more doctrinal flexibility due to the fact that its focus was not on theological issues, but rather on biblical studies.[39] The efforts of Sproul, Gerstner, and the other scholars who gathered for the Ligonier event were an attempt to shape evangelical Protestants' views on the Bible's authority by insisting on the principle of inerrancy.

In the battle for inerrancy Gerstner hoped to alleviate evangelical anxiety over the issue by offering analysis of B. B. Warfield's position. At the meeting Gerstner spoke on the topic of "Warfield's Case for Biblical Inerrancy." Gerstner, who had studied directly under one of Warfield's students, John Orr, most probably wrote on Warfield because of his knowledge of the theological context in which Warfield operated. Gerstner surveyed the opinions that various scholars had towards Warfield in order to demonstrate that "Warfield is one of the greatest champions of biblical inspiration."

---

34. Sproul, "Foreword," 9.

35. Montgomery, "Editor's Introduction," 14.

36. Marsden, *Reforming Fundamentalism*, 197–230.

37. Worthen, *Apostles of Reason*, 52–53.

38. Stanley, *The Global Diffusion of Evangelicalism*, 93. IBR held its first meeting in 1970, but was not launched until 1973. On the founding of IBR, see "A Brief History of IBR."

39. Noll, *Between Faith and Criticism*, 158–59.

Yet he also noted that "many (if not most) modern scholars" had rejected Warfield's "method of proving" the Bible's inerrancy. These scholars rejected what they considered to be Warfield's "scholastic rationalism" and his alleged false association of inerrancy with the Westminster Confession of Faith.[40] He also contrasted Warfield's position with the Dutch Reformed presuppositonalism of Abraham Kuyper and Cornelius Van Til. Warfield, unlike his Dutch colleagues, held to "traditional arguments for God" rather than presupposing God as the starting point in apologetic method. From Warfield's perspective he was not an innovator, but rather a theologian who stood in continuity with Calvin and Christian apologists down through the centuries.

Gerstner also contrasted Warfield's views with the work of Karl Barth (1886–1968), the great Swiss Reformed theologian. Gerstner asserted that "[n]owhere was the antithesis between old and new orthodoxy sharper than in these two positions regarding proof and these two persons, B.B. Warfield and Karl Barth."[41] Warfield and Barth were both reacting against liberal theology and yet the two scholars took different paths. For Warfield God's self-revelation in nature (natural theology) was intimately connected to God's special revelation and the two forms of theology could not be separated, as they were in Barth's theology.[42] To make his point, Gerstner cited a quote from Warfield in which the Princetonian wrote:

> Without general revelation, special revelation would lack that basis in the fundamental knowledge of God as the mighty and the wise, righteous and good, maker and ruler, of all things, apart from which the further revelation of the great God's intervention in the world for the salvation of sinners could not be either intelligible, credible, or operative.[43]

Gerstner summarized Warfield's position, noting that "[m]an knowing his Creator to exist, could well understand God speaking to man the sinner in the role of Judge and Savior." For Warfield natural theology provided a very basic understanding of God that nevertheless helped a person know and understand Christ. Moreover, the supernatural miracles of the Bible were "the crux of Warfield's case for special, supernatural, divine revelation."[44]

40. Gerstner, "Warfield's Case for Biblical Authority," 116–17.

41. Ibid., 127.

42. Ibid., 127–28.

43. Gerstner, "Warfield's Case for Biblical Authority," 127. This quotation from Warfield was taken from Warfield's essay, "The Biblical Idea of Inspiration" in the collected posthumous volume of his essays *Inspiration and Authority of the Bible*, 75.

44. Ibid., 128.

The Bible was not merely a witness to Christ (Jack Rogers's position), but rather offered miraculous *"proofs of a person, the divine Christ"* (Warfield's position).[45] Gerstner noted that in Warfield's mind miracles corroborated God's special revelation in Christ.

The Pittsburgh church historian, perhaps anticipating his critics, also labored to show that Warfield was indeed a "theologian of the heart." Although he did not cite any names, Gerstner argued that Warfield was often characterized as "coldly scientific." For this reason Gerstner attempted to show that Warfield believed that personal religion was absolutely essential for true theological understanding. To prove his point, Gerstner cited a statement from Warfield in which the Princeton theologian claimed that "supernatural redemption itself would remain a mere name outside of us and beyond our reach, were it not realized in the subjective life by an equally supernatural application."[46] Gerstner argued that in Warfield's view there must be an "inseparability of the Word and the Spirit."[47] Warfield was truly following the path laid out by Calvin. As Gerstner moved forward, he and his fellow inerrantists sought to play a key role in the revival of Warfield's version of biblical inerrancy within American Christianity. Gerstner was working to ensure that the Old Princeton theology, one of America's longest lasting doctrinal systems, would persevere through the onslaught of post-World War II thought, which continued to challenge traditional Christian doctrine, moral norms, and social structures.

In the second half of the twentieth century Gerstner and conservative Protestant theology especially struggled with women in ministry. The Pittsburgh church historian formally debated on the topic of female pastors with David Scholer, a Fuller Theological Seminary New Testament scholar who was a proponent of women's ordination.[48] Gerstner stood against women's ordination and his views on this issue intensified in the 1970s. In the 1970s PTS had a growing number of female students on campus. In 1967 there had been twenty-one women enrolled, but by 1972 that number rose to thirty-seven.[49] In November of 1972 the seminary established a Task Force on Women which would "sensitize and educate the seminary community to the concerns of seminary women." As PTS moved forward, it purposely sought to recruit women students. These changes at PTS correspond to the

45. Ibid., 129.

46. Warfield quoted by Gerstner, "Warfield's Case for Biblical Inerrancy," 139.

47. Ibid.

48. Scholer, "My Fifty Journey with Women and Ministry in the New Testament and in the Church Today."

49. McKim, *Ever a Vision*, 88.

more general social shifts in gender that were taking place in the 1970s. In 1972 the United States Congress passed Title IX, an amendment to the Higher Education Act, which withheld vital federal funding from schools and colleges that discriminated on the basis of gender.[50] There was now a sweeping expansion of women's athletic programs in American schools. In the 1960s there were few women's studies programs on university campuses, but by 1975 the number had mushroomed to 150. In 1973 abortion in the first six months of pregnancy became legal as a result of *Roe v. Wade*, the landmark U.S. Supreme Court case. Also, in 1973 the Supreme Court ruled that employment advertisements were no longer allowed to indicate gender, which meant that jobs were for people and not gender specific.[51] Women's rights advocacy was growing within the culture and inside the mainline UPCUSA. In 1971 the first woman, Lois Star, was elected moderator of the denomination. Yet in 1972 women enrolled in UPCUSA seminaries for the Master of Divinity degree were less than ten percent of candidates. Two years later the UPCUSA's Council on Women and the Church was founded to help women become ministers.[52] Throughout the decade the UPCUSA sought to assist women with the ordination process and to change negative attitudes to female clergy. In 1978 the UPCUSA spent a half a million dollars in its Women in Ministry program to support female pastors and to gain their acceptance by the churches.[53] In the 1970s the fight for gender equality in the broader culture led to strong women's advocacy within the denomination and its seminaries.

Gerstner's opposition to women's ordination was increasingly out of step with his seminary's stance on the issue. To be sure, one women student later noted, "there was a small group on campus, students surrounding one professor, who did not accept me as a woman preparing for ministry."[54] Presumably it was Gerstner and his disciples who were opposed to the female seminarians. Gerstner later recalled that "[w]omen . . . would studiously avoid my classes."[55] His views on women's ordination were clearly not shared by PTS or his denomination. One lay person who was an acquaintance of the Gerstners was Jean S. Showalter, a publicist and member of the Wallace Memorial Presbyterian Church in Baltimore, Maryland. On July 22, 1978 Showalter sent a long letter to Edna Gerstner explaining why her husband's

50. Borstelmann, *The 1970s*, 86.

51. Ibid., 80.

52. Boyd and Brackenridge, "Presbyterian Women Ministers," 294.

53. Ibid., 294–95.

54. Quoted by McKim, *Ever a Vision*, 148.

55. Gerstner, Interview with Coffin, 22.

views on women's ordination were misguided. She stated forcefully that an "[o]rdained qualified woman, serving in the work of the Church, does not upset [the] created order or Biblical authority." Paul's teaching on the issue, she added, was a "personal preference" and not a command of God.[56] Despite her efforts, and despite seminary and denominational pressure to accept women as ministers, Gerstner exhibited little flexibility on the issue. He was willing to defend his position on this issue no matter how unpopular.

It appears that Gerstner's rigidity on the women's ordination issue stemmed from a well-known controversy in which he was involved. This dealt with one of his closest students: Walter "Wynn" Kenyon (1948–2012). Kenyon was the son and grandson of conservative UPCNA pastors. His father, Walter R. Kenyon, was a good friend of Gerstner. In 1970 Wynn graduated from Marietta College (Ohio), where he was known as an outstanding football player and wrestler.[57] He then entered PTS, where he became a disciple of Gerstner. At PTS Kenyon excelled academically and in 1973 graduated with honors.[58] Nonetheless, Wynn's entrance into the ministry of the UPCUSA became highly controversial because he did not believe in women's ordination. The northern mainline Presbyterian church had first ordained female elders in 1930 and female ministers in 1956.[59] Kenyon's opposition to female ordination aroused suspicions in Pittsburgh Presbytery and in its Committee on Candidates and Credentials (COCC). After Kenyon appeared before the COCC on February 14, 1974 the committee recommended to the presbytery that Kenyon should not be ordained.[60] Gerstner later noted, "[t]he committee felt that anyone who cannot ordain women has denied a principle so fundamental to our present Presbyterian system that he has rejected our Presbyterian system."[61] Advocates for women's ordination pushed for open mindedness towards women ministers, but would that tolerance extend to a conservative candidate like Kenyon?

Despite the COCC recommendation, the Pittsburgh Presbytery approved Kenyon's ordination by a vote of 147 to 137.[62] While listening to Kenyon express his thoughts on theology and women's ordination on the

---

56. Showalter, Letter to Gerstner.

57. Marietta College Athletic Department Obituary for Wynn Kenyon.

58. Rodgers, "Obituary: Wynn Kenyon / Became Beloved Philosophy Professor After Ordination Ordeal."

59. Zikmund, "Ministry of Word and Sacrament," 134–58.

60 *Maxwell v. Presbytery of Pittsburgh*, Remedial Case.

61. Gerstner, "Candidate Denied Ordination," 2.

62. *Maxwell v. Presbytery of Pittsburgh*, Remedial Case.

floor of presbytery, Jack Maxwell became "astonished at Kenyon's views."[63] He could not believe what he was hearing. Maxwell, who pastored the Presbyterian Church in Sewickley, Pennsylvania, and held a ThD in homiletics from Princeton Seminary, decided to take action against the presbytery's decision.[64] On February 25, 1974 he filed a complaint with his Synod's Permanent Judicial Commission (PJC) in an effort to reverse the presbytery's vote. George Kehm, a PTS professor, also disagreed with the presbytery's decision and helped Maxwell formulate arguments against the ordination of Kenyon. Maxwell remembers that "Kehm was in his corner and served as a consultant" for his appeal. On April 19, 1974 arguments were heard before the Synod PJC in Camp Hill, Pennsylvania. Gerstner defended the presbytery's action at the hearing, and Maxwell argued against the presbytery's decision. Maxwell's arguments proved persuasive, and the Synod PJC upheld the complaint. Yet Pittsburgh Presbytery and Gerstner would not back down. The presbytery appealed its case to the General Assembly PJC meeting in St Louis, Missouri. The GAPJC, the highest court in the denomination, ruled against Kenyon; it stated that Pittsburgh "[p]resbytery does not have the power to permit the ordination of Mr. Kenyon."[65] The GAPJC wrote unequivocally that "it is the responsibility of our church to deny ordination to one who has refused to ordain women." To be sure, Kenyon did not argue that the UPCUSA should not ordain women. The GAPJC admitted that he did "not seek to bind the church by his interpretations of Scripture." Instead, Kenyon's position was that he could not himself ordain a woman. Despite this caveat in his position, the GAPJC held that Kenyon could not be ordained. The opinion for the majority of the GAPJC stated, "[n]either a synod nor the General Assembly has any power to allow a presbytery to grant an exception to an explicit constitutional provision."[66] The presbytery's actions were "not in conformity with the requirements of the Form of Government." At the 1975 Cincinnati UPCUSA General Assembly the *Cincinnati Post* claimed that the Kenyon case was "THE MOST talked-about issue."[67]

---

63. Maxwell, Interview with the author.

64. Maxwell received his BA from the University of Texas at Austin and an MDiv and ThD from Princeton Theological Seminary. In 1976, shortly after his involvement in the Kenyon case Maxwell became the president of Austin Presbyterian Theological Seminary (Texas). He left the seminary in 1984 to become the pastor of Newton Square Presbyterian Church in Philadelphia. He retired from Newton Square in 2004.

65. *Maxwell v. Presbytery of Pittsburgh*, Remedial Case 1.

66. Ibid.

67. Adams, "Its Debate and Decision Day for Presbyterians," 28.

From Gerstner's perspective the denomination's refusal to ordain Kenyon seemed to be selective. In the February 1975 edition of the *Presbyterian Layman* Gerstner noted, "[o]ur denomination authorized the ordination of women to the eldership in the 1930s and to the ministry in the 1950s but until November 1974 the minority who disagreed with this decision was in no way debarred from her ministry."[68] Gerstner wrote that, before 1974, Presbyterians who were opposed to women's ordination "were thought, of course, to be in error but not so dreadfully in error that they could no longer function as officers." In a twelve-page pamphlet entitled *Ordination and Subordination*, Gerstner, Kenyon and three other Presbyterians explicitly tried to deny the charge of "male chauvinism," affirming that the "Bible teaches the equality of all humans."[69] Nonetheless, they also argued that "Scripture does not permit a woman to be ordained." Gerstner and his associates identified more with the complementarian position which asserted that "in the church and in the home women are placed in a subordinate position."[70] Their stated goal was not to try to "impose our beliefs upon others," but merely to "demonstrate" what they felt was the "real issue: Biblical authority." The denomination's rejection of Kenyon for ordained service only seemed to intensify Gerstner's opposition to women in ministry. From his viewpoint Kenyon was respecting the right of women to be ordained in the UPCUSA. Why then did they have to deny him his right to his view of scripture? Gerstner was troubled by a form of diversity he felt was not truly open-minded and excluded of one of his most prized students. Significantly, their openness to women ministers in the denomination serves as evidence that Kenyon and Gerstner were not as conservative as scholars in other denominations who argued for the total exclusion of women clergy. In the Kenyon case the UPCUSA appears to have been suppressing even moderately conservative forms of dissent.

Gerstner and Kenyon believed that women's ordination was not an essential aspect of Presbyterian polity. Gerstner argued that "Mr. Kenyon thinks that, important as is the ordination of women, it is not essential to our presbyterian system of government, (after all, presbyterianism existed centuries before the first woman was ordained)."[71] The ruling of the GAPJC in the Kenyon case was a watershed moment in the history of the UPCUSA: for the first time a candidate was denied ordination simply because he would not participate in the ordination of women. Even though his denomination

68. Gerstner, "Candidate Denied Ordination," 1.

69. Coho et al., *Ordination and Subordination*, 1.

70. Ibid.

71. Gerstner, "Candidate Denied Ordination," 2

would not allow his ordination, Kenyon remained in the denomination for many years. After earning his PhD in philosophy from the University of Miami (Florida), he taught theology, philosophy, and apologetics for over thirty years at Belhaven College [later University], an evangelical PCUSA liberal arts institution in Jackson, Mississippi, that had been strongly influenced by many PCA faculty members. Ironically Kenyon, who was denied ordination in the PCUSA, thrived as a theology professor in one of the denomination's colleges.[72] Kenyon became a professor at Belhaven and was named the school's teacher of the year several times. In 2003 Kenyon was made the "Humanities Teacher of the Year" by the Mississippi Humanities Council.[73] Kenyon, like Sproul, remained a strong advocate of Gerstner's theological views and continued the Gerstner legacy in the deep American south. Prior to his death in 2012, Kenyon listed on his faculty webpage that one of his areas of academic research was "John Gerstner."[74]

While Kenyon was denied ordination another one of Gerstner's protégés was on the verge of giving up his UPCUSA ordination. During the 1970s Sproul and Gerstner remained close through their work at Ligonier Valley Study Center and were excited about their new evangelical ministry. Gerstner, nevertheless, remained distraught over the theological direction of Pittsburgh Theological Seminary. LVSC provided, however small, an evangelical center of study, and Gerstner was by all accounts happy to be a part of the ministry, but not all was well. Both Gerstner and Sproul were deeply disappointed in the UPCUSA's treatment of Wynn Kenyon.[75] In 1975 when Sproul received a letter from the UPCUSA's stated clerk indicating that his objections in the Kenyon case were improper, he made the decision to leave the UPCUSA and join the newly founded Presbyterian Church in America (PCA).[76] In 1973 the PCA was established as a conservative offshoot from the southern Presbyterian Church US.[77] The southern Presbyterians who led the conservative revolt were troubled by liberal and neo-orthodox theologies in their church and by a possible merger with the

72. Rodgers, "Obituary: Wynn Kenyon / Became Beloved Philosophy Professor After Ordination Ordeal." Later, in the late 1970s Wynn Kenyon's brother, David, attended PTS, but ultimately decided it would be best if he studied elsewhere and transferred to Reformed Theological Seminary in Jackson, Mississippi.

73. "Belhaven College Professor Presents Humanities Council Lecture."

74. Kenyon, faculty page.

75. McKim, *Ever a Vision*, 147.

76. Sproul, Interview with the author.

77. Freundt, "Presbyterian Church in America," 198–99.

northern UPCUSA.[78] Gerstner believed Sproul was wrong to abandon the UPCUSA, and it became clear that the two did not agree about when it was appropriate to withdraw from a denomination.[79] In the mid-1970s Gerstner was firmly committed to the UPCUSA, but the Kenyon case was a great disappointment. Gerstner's reason for staying in the mainline church appears to have been connected to his longtime relationship to John Orr.

When Gerstner needed to consult someone about a weighty issue Gerstner would drive to New Wilmington, Pennsylvania and visit Orr. Orr, who was Gerstner's spiritual father and academic mentor, always encouraged Gerstner to stay in the UPCUSA and this advice apparently was influential in Gerstner's mind.[80] Even though Sproul and Gerstner did not agree about criteria for separation from the UPCUSA, they still worked together at LVSC, in the fight for inerrancy and in a college ministry. They were involved in an evangelical undergraduate student ministry, the Coalition for Christian Outreach (CCO), which began in Pittsburgh in 1971 and quickly became prominent in western Pennsylvania and Ohio.[81] CCO had a strong Reformed presence due to the large Presbyterian constituency in the region. Both men were trying to shape the evangelical movement by promoting a conservative brand of Presbyterian and Reformed evangelicalism in various arenas.

In February 1977 the International Council on Biblical Inerrancy (ICBI) was launched by Jay Grimstead (1936–), an energetic leader with organizational talents. Grimstead had grown up in the old United Presbyterian Church of North America and had graduated from the UPCNA-affiliated Sterling College (Kansas) in 1957.[82] In the mid-1950s Grimstead had met Gerstner and listened to him preach and lecture during a Sterling spiritual emphasis week. He was greatly "impressed by Gerstner" and the church historian's speaking abilities.[83] In 1961 Grimstead graduated from Fuller Seminary and then began a twenty-year career with Young Life, a large para-church youth ministry. He conducted outreach to students at Stanford University. By 1968 Grimstead came to believe that evangelicalism

---

78. See Nutt, "The Tie That No Longer Binds," 236–58; Smith, *How Is the Gold Become Dim.*

79. Sproul, Interview with the author.

80. Beal, Interview with the author. Beal is John Orr's daughter.

81. On the history of the Coalition for Chrstian Outreach, see *Celebrating the CCO.*

82. Grimstead, Interview with the author. On the history of Sterling College, see Tom and Christine Buchanan, *Sterling College.*

83. Ibid.

was becoming "soft theologically."[84] He was specifically concerned about Fuller Seminary's drift away from the inerrancy position.[85] His doctrinal conservatism intensified as he studied at the LVSC in 1973. When he began his doctor of ministry degree at Fuller in 1975, he was alarmed at his *alma mater's* opposition to a conservative understanding of biblical inerrancy. In order to combat what he felt was Fuller's drift to the left, he started the Reformation Study Center in 1976. In September 1976, he wrote to Harold Lindsell (1913–1998), editor of *Christianity Today* and R. C. Sproul suggesting that someone should organize a national conference that would defend inerrancy and address alleged evangelical accommodation on the inerrancy issue. Sproul responded positively.[86]

Grimstead decided to push forward and was able to gather a stable of evangelical scholars and church leaders for the fledgling organization's first meeting in Mt Hermon, California. The initial group who gathered included Gerstner, Greg Bahnsen, Norman Geisler, Karen Hoyt, A. Wetherell Johnson, J. I. Packer and R. C. Sproul.[87] Bahnsen (1948–1995) served as professor of apologetics and ethics at Reformed Theological Seminary in Jackson, Mississippi. Geisler (1932–) served as professor of philosophy of religion at Trinity Evangelical Divinity School. Hoyt served as Grimstead's assistant and was later given the title of executive secretary of the ICBI. Johnson (1907–1984), the founder of Bible Study Fellowship and the other woman present at the first meeting, later stated that she joined the ICBI because "[f]or some time I had been vaguely concerned about the growing lack of confidence even among professing evangelical pastors of the final authority of the Bible, and the fact (accepted in past generations) that it was entirely without error."[88] The first meeting was held the day before the first conference began in February 1977. The meeting included prayer and a call by Grimstead "to form an army of scholars to oppose the liberal drift among evangelicals."[89] By the end of the conference, which had three hundred attendees, the International Council of Biblical Inerrancy was formed. A lengthy list of biblical scholars, theologians, and church historians who affirmed inerrancy was assembled. Grimstead then approached the various

---

84. Ibid.

85. On Fuller's decision to distance itself from the inerrancy position, see Marsden, *Reforming Fundamentalism*, 188–92, 208–19.

86. Grimstead, "How the International Council on Biblical Inerrancy Began."

87. Geisler and Roach, *Defending Inerrancy*, 22.

88. Johnson, *Created for Commitment*, 307.

89. Grimstead, Interview with the author, November 6, 2012.

scholars to see if they were interested in participating and joining their group.[90] A coalition was emerging.

In March 1977, the executive committee held its second meeting at the Pittsburgh airport. Gerstner was a founding member of the ICBI and stayed with the group serving on the executive committee. According to Grimstead, Gerstner was not the most vocal member, but he was one of the three most militant. Apparently, Gerstner wanted to strengthen the inerrancy position within evangelicalism, but he also wanted the ICBI to do battle with theological liberals. Gerstner told members that the best way to make inroads among liberals was to stage honest debates that would involve serious discussions of the issues.[91] As the ICBI moved forward, Gerstner took up his pen and fought with ink. The organization's first scholarly work was an edited volume titled *The Foundation of Biblical Authority* (1978).[92] James Montgomery Boice (1938–2000), pastor of the Tenth Presbyterian Church in Philadelphia, wrote a brief preface for the volume, and Francis Schaeffer (1912–1984), the influential evangelical thinker, provided a foreword.[93] The first chapter was written by Gerstner and entitled the "The Church's Doctrine of Biblical Inspiration." His stated goal for this important essay was "to show that the main historic path [of the Christian Church] has been total biblical authority." He argued that since the Bible is the "Word of God," it "is the *only* foundation for full *biblical authority*." The Pittsburgh Seminary professor noted, "[w]e realize that some who disagree with inerrancy are claiming inspiration for parts of the Bible, the so-called salvation parts."[94] He then labeled this view as the "partial biblical authority" position. Lamenting that some supported this position, he noted that they "add insult to injury to God's Word, they cannot tell precisely what parts of the Bible are inspired." He held that "some evangelical scholars not only favor partial biblical authority today but believe that the historic Christian church believed

90. Ibid.

91. Ibid.

92. Boice, ed., *The Foundation of Biblical Authority*.

93. Boice received his BA from Harvard University (1960), a BD from Princeton Seminary (1963) and a DTheol degree from the University of Basel in Switzerland (1966). He was the senior pastor of Tenth Presbyterian Church in Philadelphia from 1968 to 2000. Schaeffer received his BA from Hampden-Sydney College (Virginia), studied at Westminster Seminary in Philadelphia, but transferred to Faith Seminary in Philadelphia, where he received his BD. He served for many years as the leader of the L'Abri Christian study center in Switzerland. On the importance of Francis Schaeffer to the American evangelical movement, see Hankins, *Francis Schaeffer and the Shaping of Evangelical America*; Duriez, *Francis Schaeffer*; Little ed, *Francis Schaeffer*.

94. Gerstner, "The Church's Doctrine of Biblical Inspiration," 23.

it."[95] The primary purpose of his essay was to show, as best as he could, that the church down through the ages affirmed inerrancy.

Gerstner argued that inerrancy was the position of the early church fathers and highlighted Augustine's maintenance of the belief. He rejected the analysis of Jack Rogers, a UPCUSA theologian, who held that the early church fathers did not believe in inerrancy because they affirmed God's accommodation of language. In order to make his case, Gerstner used quotations from early church fathers and from Augustine. He noted "divine accommodation is misunderstood by Rogers." The historian argued "[l]anguage is so important that God condescends to 'baby talk' in order to be understood verbally."[96] Gerstner also used the written views of other contemporary church historians. Next he briefly noted that the theologians of the middle ages "held firmly to the church's inerrancy doctrine."[97] He used the words of a few theologians of the middle ages, but his analysis of the period was thin—filling only a few short paragraphs. Gerstner gave somewhat more attention to the Reformation and especially Luther. He wrote "that Luther and the Reformation were launched with a nonrational, fideistic push," but that "they soon sailed under [followed] the traditional reason/faith synthesis."[98] Despite "Luther's 1517 denunciation of Aristotle" and other comments made "in the same vein," Gerstner held that Luther's "basic position clearly came to be a harmonization of faith and reason." He noted that the disagreements about Luther's approach to the Bible in no way "change his view about the inerrancy of the Bible." Gerstner noted that W. Bodamer had revealed "hundreds of indubitable utterances of Luther" which showed his allegiance to inerrancy.[99] "W. Bodamer" was a reference to Walter K. Bodamer (1897–1968), a Wisconsin Evangelical Lutheran Synod scholar, who in 1936 had published an exhaustive study of Luther's views on verbal inspiration in the WELS journal *Theologische Quartalschrift*.[100] Gerstner believed that Bodamer's work was authoritative and could not be easily refuted.

As for Calvin, Gerstner produced some detail in describing his views and ultimately came to the conclusion that Calvin was an inerrantist. He argued, "nothing that modern opponents of inerrancy have presented, cited, deduced, or inferred in any way whatsoever shows that Calvin held

95. Ibid.

96. Ibid., 28.

97. Ibid., 32.

98. Ibid., 34.

99. Ibid., 35.

100. Gerstner cited Bodamer, "Luther Stellung zur Lehre von der Verbalinspiration."

any other view than the absolute inerrancy of Holy Scripture."[101] In order to strengthen his case, he wrote that Emil Brunner and Edward Dowey both "find verbal inspiration in Calvin."[102] Moreover, he added that Kenneth Kantzer's Harvard dissertation "may be the most thorough demonstration of Calvin's teaching on inerrancy."[103] He noted that John Murray and J. I. Packer, two Calvinist theologians, also agreed with this view. For Gerstner, inerrancy was not an outmoded doctrine that lacked continuity with the Reformation. Gerstner briefly mentioned two post-Reformation scholastic theologians, John Gerhard and Francis Turretin, and found that they too held to inerrancy and were the "natural development and fruition of the Reformation." Reflecting on the Westminster Confession of Faith, he added that "inerrancy is its indubitable teaching, although the word itself is not used but only equivalents."[104]

He also argued that Jonathan Edwards affirmed inerrancy along with the Old Princeton theologians. His view of Edwards's position was based on his study of Edwards' sermons. He wrote "[t]hat Scripture was inerrant for Jonathan Edwards no one who has ever read his works, especially his sermons, can doubt."[105] The church historian highlighted Edwards's words "All Scripture says to us is certainly true," and in the Bible "you hear Christ speaking." Gerstner's position was not solely based on his examination of Edwards's writings. He also noted that other historians such as George Gordon and John E. Smith had come to similar conclusions about Edwards's view of Scripture. The Old School Princeton theologians were also discussed. Gerstner argued against Rogers's contention that Warfield created an "unassailable apologetic stance" by holding that it was only the unavailable original biblical texts that were inerrant.[106] Gerstner responded with the following argument:

> First of all, since no evangelical scholar ever defended an infallible translation, where can the written Word of God be located but in the original texts or autographs? This was always assumed. Warfield was no innovator. It is true that some believed the text was transmitted "pure," but in that case we would have

101. Gerstner, "The Church's Doctrine of Biblical Inspiration," 40.

102. Ibid.

103. Ibid. See Kantzer, "John Calvin's Theory of the Knowledge of God and the Word of God."

104. Gerstner, "The Church's Doctrine of Biblical Inspiration," 42.

105. Ibid., 47.

106. Rogers quoted by Gerstner, "The Church's Doctrine of Biblical Inspiration," 48.

the autographa. There is no question in any case but that the autographs alone were the written Word of God. Warfield would be amused to be given credit for discovering the obvious.[107]

In addition, Warfield, according to Gerstner, "believed that we virtually did have the autographa in the form of a highly reliable text." This being the case, Warfield "did not consider himself, therefore, 'unassailable.'" The point was that the biblical text could be studied and Warfield was not hiding behind the autogrpaha to shield the Bible from criticism. Gerstner believed that critics of the "autographa" argument were misguided because Warfield, J. Gresham Machen, the great Presbyterian scholar and A. T. Robertson, the famed Southern Baptist scholar, were all New Testament critics. Conservative scholars did not automatically assume that the methodologies of biblical criticism undermined belief in the Bible's inerrancy. In fact Gerstner notes that " [i]nerrancy has almost always been maintained along with biblical criticism."[108] Just as Warfield and Machen adhered to non-naturalistic forms of evolution so too had they sought to practise non-naturalistic forms of biblical criticism.[109]

Throughout the chapter Gerstner repeatedly argued against the view of Jack Rogers, a former student of his and since 1971 a professor of philosophical theology at Fuller Theological Seminary. In Gerstner's mind, part of Fuller's continuing drift away from inerrancy had been caused by his former pupil. He mentioned Rogers's name forty-three times in his twenty-nine page essay. Gerstner seemed to believe that Rogers was the scholar most responsible for pushing evangelicals to the left on the issue of inerrancy.[110] Rogers called those who affirmed inerrancy "historically irresponsible."[111] Perplexed by such a statement, Gerstner challenged his former student noting, "for Rogers to say that the statement that for two thousand years Christians have believed in the inerrancy of all scripture is 'irresponsible' is irresponsible."[112] Gerstner was venting his frustration with Rogers, who claimed that inerrancy was a "modern" invention. As a historian, Gerstner held firmly to the view that inerrancy was the classical view of the church.

107. Gerstner, "The Church's Doctrine of Biblical Inspiration," 48.

108. Ibid., 49.

109. On this point, see Gundlach's excellent and illuminating study of the Old School Princeton scholars, *Process and Providence*.

110. On Rogers's involvement in the inerrancy battle see Marsden, *Reforming Fundamentalism*, 285–86.

111. Rogers quoted by Gerstner, "The Church's Doctrine of Biblical Inspiration," 51.

112. Gerstner, "The Church's Doctrine of Biblical Inspiration," 51.

In the end, it appears that Gerstner's efforts to demonstrate that inerrancy was the traditional view of the church were hampered by the pique he exhibited towards Rogers. He accused Rogers of reducing the inerrancy issue to a "caricature." It seems clear that Gerstner viewed Rogers as theological traitor whose views increasingly bore a resemblance to those of the liberal faculty members at Pittsburgh Seminary. Rogers, a Pitt-Xenia graduate, had succumbed to the views of the old Western Seminary. Perhaps Gerstner even saw echoes of the Auburn Affirmation (1924) in Rogers' work. His final paragraph was direct and to the point:

> If Rogers and many with him do not believe the Bible is without error, let them continue plainly to say so and argue their case. But may God deliver us from evangelicals who follow the liberal practice of "flying at a low level of visibility." Evangelicals are already beginning to speak of errant inerrancy. But let the position not be confused with the historic consensus of inerrancy meaning "without error," PERIOD.[113]

Gerstner was an active disputant in the "Battle for the Bible" that raged within American Protestantism in the 1970s. His efforts led to the influential ICBI 1978 "Chicago Statement on Biblical Inerrancy."[114] This quarrel over the Bible reveals that the "Presbyterian Controversy" of the 1920s and 1930s lived on.

Not only was he a key inerrancy warrior in the conflict, but he had also mentored and taught some of the key scholars on the opposite side of the issue—most notably Jack Rogers and Donald McKim. While Rogers and McKim were not close to Gerstner, they had significant contact with their former professor. Rogers had studied with Gerstner in the 1950s. McKim graduated from Westminster College (Pennsylvania) in 1971, from PTS in 1974 and later finished a PhD at the University of Pittsburgh. McKim remembers that Gestner was "very kind to me" and even recommended McKim to write articles for a revised version of the *International Standard Bible Encyclopedia* (ISBE). He appreciated Gerstner's help and later noted that he "liked Gerstner personally."[115] Nevertheless, McKim opposed Gerstner on the issue of inerrancy. In 1979 Rogers and McKim produced a significant book that sought to challenge the inerrancy position—*The Authority and Interpretation of the Bible*.[116] That this book flowed from the pens of two

---

113. Gerstner, "The Church's Doctrine of Biblical Inspiration," 52.

114. Stanley, *The Diffusion of Modern Evangelicalism*, 107.

115. McKim, Interview with the author, October 18, 2010.

116. Rogers and McKim, *The Authority and Interpretation of the Bible*.

of Gerstner's former students shows the centrality of Gerstner to the inerrancy debate. For Gerstner the inerrancy debate was not a detached contest, but rather it was personal because of Gerstner's struggles at Pittsburgh Seminary. In Gerstner's mind, denials of inerrancy led directly to the type of progressive theological environment that Pittsburgh Seminary had produced and which he worked in, but lamented. No other scholar in America could claim to have so many of their ex-pupils fighting on the front line of the "Battle for the Bible."

In order to combat the progressive doctrinal atmosphere at Pittsburgh Seminary and in the UPCUSA, Gerstner believed he needed to resurrect the theology of Jonathan Edwards, perhaps the greatest theological mind in American history. In a retrospective judgment Gerstner's son claims that his father believed that Edwards was the "key to the battle against theological liberalism."[117] Gerstner apparently believed that just as Edwards challenged the deists of his day, so too could Edwards be helpful in combating the deist offspring, doctrinal progressives. By connecting historical issues with perceived contemporary problems Gerstner was mirroring the work of his beloved mentor at Westminster College, John Orr. Orr in his book *English Deism: Its Roots and Fruits* (1934) had sought to show continuity between English deism and theological liberalism.[118] At a 1972 appreciation dinner for John Orr, Gerstner told an audience at Westminster College that "nobody owes as much to John Orr as I do." He added "the thing you should remember as you notice some of the very conspicuous blemishes in me, is that they would have been much more noticeable if it had not been for John Orr."[119] It is clear that Gerstner had deep admiration for Orr. The problem was that Orr's scholarly model of relating the past to present issues proved problematic in Gerstner's scholarship because it seemed to focus his scholarship more on the quest for theological orthodoxy than on historical context and dispassionate analysis.[120] Gerstner was about to face a serious setback.

As editor of the Yale volume on Edwards' sermons since 1953, Gerstner occupied an important position within the field of Edwards studies. Yet

117. Gerstner, Interview with the author, June 9, 2010.

118. Orr, *English Deism*, 221–67. For more on Orr, see chapter 2.

119. Gerstner, John Orr Appreciation Dinner. Inside the dinner program Gerstner is listed as being in charge of the gift presentation. In 1973 Gerstner was awarded a doctor of humane letters degree from Westminster College.

120. Marsden has noted that Gleason Archer, a professor of Old Testament at Fuller and TEDS, viewed his Old Testament scholarly work in an apologetic fashion. On this point see Marsden, *Reforming Fundamentalism*, 224. Gerstner appears to have largely followed this approach in his own teaching and writing as well.

not all was well. Gerstner worked diligently to produce his edited volume of Edwards's sermons, but repeatedly his introductions and proposals were rejected by the *Works of Jonathan Edwards* editorial committee.[121] The committee was composed of Sydney Ahlstrom, Lyman Butterfield, Wilson Kimnach, Edmund Morgan, Norman Holmes Pearson, Paul Ramsey, Thomas Schaefer, and John Smith (chair).[122] Kimnach, a literary scholar who assisted Gerstner for a few years, thought that the problem was that Gerstner was "too explicit about being on the same wavelength as Edwards." Gerstner's strong advocacy of Edwards was becoming too pronounced. "Gerstner was always the proponent of Edwards," Kimnach noted.[123] A more critical approach was required by the committee. Another issue that arose, according to Kimnach, was that Gerstner was having problems accurately transcribing Edwards's handwriting in order to produce quality texts of his sermons.[124] Ultimately, the committee terminated Gerstner from his position on April 8, 1977. The committee report states:

> After considerable discussion the Committee voted that whereas there had been unanimous judgment in the Committee over a long period that with regard to both editing of sermon texts and preparation of introductions Mr. Gerstner's MSS had been unacceptable, and . . . the arrangement made to try to salvage the situation was proving unsatisfactory.[125]

The committee then asked the chairman to "communicate these decisions to Mr. Gerstner, with any necessary explanations, and to express to him the Committee's regret that they had become necessary." The decision was a serious blow to Gerstner personally. Yet it also, no doubt, wounded his professional reputation as an Edwards scholar. Gerstner had to some degree been marginalized at Pittsburgh Seminary, in the UPCUSA, and now even among other Edwards specialists.

Gerstner's struggles can be compared to the academic rebuff that George Eldon Ladd, the formidable Fuller New Testament professor, faced when his *Jesus and the Kingdom* (1964) came in for heavy criticism in an *Interpretation* book review by Norman Perrin, a New Testament scholar at the University of Chicago.[126] The sting of mainstream scholarly rejection lin-

---

121. Kimnach, Interview with the author, December 10, 2010.

122. Minkema, email to the author.

123. Kimnach, Interview with the author, December 10, 2010.

124. Ibid.

125. "Draft of Part of the JE Editorial Committee Meeting,"

126. D'Elia, *A Place at the Table*, 121–48.

gered in Ladd and Gerstner for the rest of their lives. The *Works of Jonathan Edwards* editorial committee replaced Gerstner with Kimnach as editor of the volume on Edwards' sermons. Gerstner's son Jonathan remembers that this was an "extremely painful" experience for his father.[127] Despite the disappointment, Gerstner would continue to write and lecture on Edwards. Gerstner's embarrassment over losing his editorial position seems to have fueled his subsequent scholarship and inerrancy campaign. Kimnach later remarked there was "no one more passionate about Edwards than Gerstner." He declared that Gerstner was "an apostle of Jonathan Edwards."[128] Gerstner's passion helped him persist in promoting Edwards and the Pittsburgh church historian continued to play a key role in reviving interest in Edwards in post-World War II America.[129]

In November 1975 Gerstner delivered the W. H. Griffith Thomas Lectures at Dallas Theological Seminary (Texas), a school deeply committed to inerrancy, on the topic of Edwards's apologetics. He discussed "An Outline of the Apologetics of Jonathan Edwards" in four lectures: "The Argument from Being," "The Unity of God" and two lectures on "The Proof of God's Special Revelation, the Bible."[130] In 1976 these lectures were published in *Bibliotheca Sacra*, the journal of Dallas Theological Seminary. In the first lecture Gerstner tried to establish that Edwards "was an eighteenth-century apologist in that classical age of apologetics." He added that the "truth about Edwards is, as his son Jonathan boasted, that he was more rational than most of his fellow Calvinists."[131] Gerstner was seeking to show that Edwards was a rational orthodox Reformed theologian, noting that "he tended to explain rationally what most other Reformed theologians were inclined to leave in 'mystery.'" Gerstner claimed that Edwards was "[m]ore idealistic [mind centred], comprehensive, and demonstrative in his argumentation than the Westminster divines, Bishop Butler or William Paley." He added

127. Gerstner, Interview with the author, June 9, 2010.

128. Kimnach, Interview with the author, December 6, 2012.

129. Hart, "Before the Young, Restless, and Reformed: Edwards Appeal to Post-World War II Evangelicals," 237–53. Hart discusses Gerstner's career as a major player in the revival of Edwards within the American evangelical subculture.

130. Gerstner, "An Outline of the Apologetics of Jonathan Edwards, Part 1: The Argument of Being," 3–10; "An Outline of the Apologetics of Jonathan Edwards, Part II: The Unity of God," 99–107; "An Outline of the Apologetics of Jonathan Edwards, Part III: The Proof of God's Special Revelation, The Bible," 195–201; "An Outline of the Apologetics of Jonathan Edwards, Part IV: The Proof of God's Special Revelation, The Bible—Continued," 291–98.

131. Gerstner, "An Outline of the Apologetics of Jonathan Edwards, Part 1: The Argument from Being," 4.

"Edwards, there can be no doubt, belonged in that tradition which is the general tradition of the Bible and the church."[132] He then attempted to show from Edwards's writings that the colonial theologian was a rigorous reasoner who, early on, came to the conclusion that God's existence was far more rooted in his being than in his causality [marks left in the world that point to the ultimate cause—God]. Gerstner based his position on several of Edwards works including "Of Being" (1721), "The Mind" (1723) and the "Miscellanies" (1722). In these writings Edwards argues for "the existence and necessity of God in terms of Nothing."[133] Edwards's argument was that God had to exist because it was impossible to have knowledge of nothing, humans whether they admit it or not have knowledge of God. The "Eternal Being" is then "revealed to be the Cause." Gerstner believed that Edwards's reasoning on God's existence was a first sign that Edwards was a rational apologist.

Gerstner's second lecture, which must have seemed dry to the students listening, dealt with Edwards "view of natural revelation." Purportedly this was the second step in Edwards' apologetic method. Gerstner noted that Edwards "sees virtually every attribute of God shining brilliantly in the things He has made . . . ."[134] Next, Gerstner discussed Edwards's thinking on natural theology and then delved into debates about Edwards's alleged pantheism. For Gerstner, Edwards's thought had to be viewed through the lens of Old Princeton because he reasoned that Edwards's thought had continuity with Old Princeton's evangelical Calvinism. In the end, Gerstner noted that Edwards sometimes sounded like a pantheist, but his views did not correspond to the five traits of pantheism that Charles Hodge, the Old Princeton theologian, identified.[135] Gerstner's second lecture was more cryptic than his first, and focused more on the issue of alleged pantheism in Edwards's theology than his apologetic approach. Gerstner sought to argue that Edwards was not a pantheist.

In Gerstner's third and fourth lectures, he explored Edwards' view of special revelation: Holy Scripture. Gerstner discussed the deist context and the view of many that special revelation was unnecessary "for the rational voyage of life." He noted that Edwards did not refute the deists by "an appeal to faith but by rational analysis."[136] Gerstner repudiated fideism in

132. Ibid.

133. Ibid., 7.

134. Gerstner, "An Outline of the Apologetics of Jonathan Edwards, Part II: The Unity of God," 99.

135. Ibid., 107.

136. Gerstner, "An Outline of the Apologetics of Jonathan Edwards, Part III: The

Edwards because he thought it was clear from Edwards's writings that the colonial theologian did not distrust reason. As an example, Gerstner cited an essay in which Edwards sought to refute Matthew Tindal (1657–1733), a leading deist writer.[137] Gerstner wrote that Edwards wanted to show "the unreasonableness of Tindal's reasoning."[138] Tindall held that reason should analyze revelation and every doctrine and proposition. According to Gerstner, Edwards reasoned under the authority of the Bible because he believed that natural revelation is not sufficient and can lead to doctrinal confusion and a myriad of problems. Gerstner noted Edwards's belief that " [n]ature, apart from the Bible, leads to the 'grossest theological error.'"[139] According to Gerstner, Edwards made an "essentially twofold case for Christianity: its inherent rationality and its external confirmation [the Bible]." Edwards believed that "mystery is to be expected" in the Bible and that mystery might lead to some "apparent contradictions," but no "real contradictions."[140] In summary, Gerstner held that Edwards's apologetics started with God's being, then proceeded to his "general revelation" and after that to the "fully and miraculously accredited special revelation." For Gerstner Edwards was a rational theologian who could speak to the irrationalism of the late twentieth century. Gerstner used Edwards to influence evangelical thought, but he also sought to shape evangelicalism with his own perspective.

In 1975 David Wells and John Woodbridge, two evangelical professors, brought together a bevy of scholars for a volume that would explore evangelical identity, history, and beliefs. Prior to the appearance of this volume, evangelicalism had received only limited attention by scholars.[141] Wells and Woodbridge justified the relevance of their book *The Evangelicals* (1975) by pointing to a "current resurgence of evangelical Protestantism."[142] Scholars who wrote essays for the volume included Martin Marty, Robert Linder, Sydney Ahlstrom, and George Marsden, both evangelical and non-evangelical authors. The first essay was written by Gerstner and entitled

Proof of God's Special Revelation, The Bible," 196.

137. Gerstner incorrectly labeled this miscellany as "The Sufficiency of Reason as a Substitute for Revelation." The correction title is the "The Insufficiency of Reason as a Substitute for Revelation."

138. Gerstner, "An Outline of the Apologetics of Jonathan Edwards, Part III: The Proof of God's Special Revelation, The Bible," 196.

139. Ibid., 200.

140. Ibid., 201.

141. Some earlier books included Shelley, *Evangelicalism in America*; Bloesch, *The Evangelical Renaissance*.

142. Wells and Woodbridge, "Introduction," 9.

"The Theological Boundaries of Evangelical Faith."[143] Gerstner's foray into teaching at Trinity Evangelical Divinity School (TEDS) had provided him with an opportunity to interact personally with various evangelical scholars. In turn, Wells and Woodbridge, who both taught at TEDS, invited Gerstner to tackle the issue of evangelical theology. Gerstner argued in his essay that "[e]verything that American Protestants once considered essential in Christian faith was conveyed by the word *evangelical.*" He added that by the 1960s, however, things had changed in American Protestantism. Theologians no longer could decide on "the very essentials of Christianity." Moreover, he noted that "it is certain that during the 1960s the Christian faith was debated against the background of declining congregations, diminishing financial resources, collapsing seminaries, and widespread, unsightly capitulation of Christian faith to secular assumptions."[144] As a mainline evangelical scholar, Gerstner argued for a robustly doctrinal evangelicalism that provided sharp distinctions rather than theological ambiguity.

Gerstner claimed to have felt pessimistic about the prospects of evangelicalism in the 1960s, but by the 1970s he had become optimistic about its vitality. He observed that out of the 1960s "unexpectedly emerged a robust evangelicalism that so many prophets had announced could never survive a thoroughgoing secular age."[145] Next, Gerstner explored the origins of the word "evangelical." He noted that it "derives from the Greek *euangellismos,*" which means good news or gospel. During the Reformation the word "evangelical" became prominent because Martin Luther "reasserted Paul's teaching on the *euangellismos* as the indispensible message of salvation." Gerstner then explored the evangelical movement from the seventeenth to the twentieth centuries. He noted that up until the nineteenth century, there was more "tacit than expressed doctrinal content to evangelicalism;" often all Protestants were regarded as evangelicals. The doctrinal formulations of the "The Evangelical Alliance" meeting in London in 1846 revealed that "though the movement was single-minded, it was not simplistic."[146] He held that Charles Finney (1792–1875), the great revivalist, was an ominous force for evangelicalism because he spread Pelagianism, which "subverted the Reformation's understanding of grace precisely because it denied the Reformation's view of man." Finney was singled out for criticism because his career revealed, in Gerstner's estimation, how detrimental errant theology could be to evangelicalism. Even though Unitarianism and liberal Protestantism

143. Gerstner, "The Theological Boundaries of Evangelical Faith," 21–37.

144. Ibid., 21.

145. Ibid.

146. Ibid., 24–25.

provided challenges to evangelicalism, Gerstner argued that Finney became "the greatest of nineteenth-century foes of evangelicalism."[147] Clearly, Gerstner's Reformed theological perspective shaped his view of evangelical history and belief. For Gerstner non-Reformed sections of American evangelicalism threatened the movement's traditional doctrinal character.

He held that, after Finney, "evangelicalism underwent a major change in meaning."[148] Apparently, Gerstner believed that new definitions of evangelicalism became more descriptive and less theological, thus diluting what Gerstner believed was the true identity of evangelicalism. "With the appearance of Moody, Sunday, and Graham, however, evangelicalism recovered from the distortion of Finney, but it has never since returned to its original, pristine character," he wrote.[149] For Gerstner, evangelicalism had theological boundaries that, if crossed, hurt the movement. Gerstner formulated his views in the midst of his own struggle against liberalism at Pittsburgh Seminary and in the UPCUSA. In his judgment Karl Barth posed a problem for evangelicalism in the twentieth century. Gerstner maintained that "it is plain that Barthians are not evangelical in an historical sense."[150] The Pittsburgh church historian held, "[i]f the term evangelical can include Karl Barth as well as Carl Henry, Emil Brunner as well as Jonathan Edwards, Oscar Cullman as well as John Wesley, then we must give it a definition so broad as to be somewhat meaningless."[151] Gerstner's mention of Wesley indicates that he viewed Wesley as being within the mainstream of the movement. The Pittsburgh church historian was appreciative of Wesley, but not Finney. For Gerstner, evangelicalism was a diverse movement, and yet he viewed it also as a movement with doctrinal standards. To be sure, in 1975 he lectured at the Evangelical Theological Society annual meeting on the topic of "Evangelicalism: Pure and Mixed."[152] Gerstner was happy with the resurgence of evangelical faith he observed in the 1970s, but he hoped that the movement would not transform into something else by compromising its core theological convictions.

"The five points of fundamentalism," he noted, "remain central to evangelicalism, for all five relate to the person of Christ."[153] The five points

147. Ibid., 27.

148. Ibid.

149. Ibid.

150. Ibid., 35.

151. Ibid.

152. Evangelical Theological Society: 27th Annual Meeting Program, December 29–31, 1975.

153. Gerstner, "The Theological Boundaries of Evangelical Faith," 30.

he mentioned were the "five fundamentals" affirmed by the PCUSA in 1910 and included the miracles of Christ, the virgin birth of Christ, the satisfaction view of the atonement, verbal inspiration, and the bodily resurrection of Christ. In the conclusion of his essay he wrote:

> In an age that is characterized by a loss of meaning and an uncertainty about religious values, it is important for evangelicalism to offer a choice, not an echo. It is important for it to be clear where it has always been historically clear; it must become creative, able to stir the hearts of men again, powerful, and able to open to the limitless depths of God's own being.[154]

Gerstner then closed his essay with a quotation from the "greatest of all American evangelicals, Jonathan Edwards," who urged that Christians should not trust in themselves for their salvation, but rather in Christ.[155]

Some scholars believed that Gerstner's analysis was misguided. Donald Dayton (1942–), an evangelical Wesleyan theologian, bluntly criticized Gerstner's essay in his *Discovering An Evangelical Heritage* (1976).[156] Dayton argued that Gerstner's "perspective has not only contributed to the decline of Evangelical social witness . . . but has also tended to distort Evangelical historiography."[157] From Dayton's viewpoint, Gerstner was guilty of equating evangelicalism with the Old Princeton School. He argued that Gerstner's view was too simplistic and that evangelicalism was more strongly influenced by "Finney and Oberlin than Hodge and Warfield." Dayton observed that "when American church historians use the term 'Evangelical" they generally refer to the Arminian, pietistic revivalism that was epitomized in Finney and marked the end of the cultural dominance of the 'old Calvinism' preserved in the Princeton theology."[158] While there is much truth in Dayton's analysis, it is also clear that parts of Arminian Wesleyanism had drifted away from evangelicalism (Oberlin and liberal Methodists), and thus the reason for Gerstner's emphasis on doctrinal standards (a common conservative Reformed theme). For evangelicals like Gerstner, who were so acutely affected by the Fundamentalist-Modernist Conflict, evangelicalism

154. Ibid., 35.

155. Ibid., 35–36.

156. Dayton, *Discovering an Evangelical Heritage*. Dayton earned his BA from Houghton College (NY), a MDiv from Yale Divinity School, a MA from the University of Kentucky and a PhD from the University of Chicago. Dayton served as a theology professor at Asbury Seminary (1969–1972), North Park Theological Seminary (1972–1979), Northern Baptist Seminary (1979–1997) and Drew University (1997–2004).

157. Dayton, *Discovering an Evangelical Heritage*, 138.

158. Ibid.

had to be anchored in clear doctrinal foundations or else in their minds it would drift off into the type of liberal Protestantism he had come to know so well at PTS and in the UPCUSA.

In the *Christian Scholars Review*, Donald Bloesch offered a more charitable assessment of Gerstner's essay, arguing in a perceptive way that "[a]lthough he [Gerstner] sometimes appears too censorious in his judgments, he is certainly right in maintaining that evangelicalism must not lose its historical distinctives if it is to make an impact on the present theological scene."[159] Nevertheless, Bloesch thought Gerstner went too far in his criticisms of Finney, holding that "[i]t would be more proper to contend that there are nonevangelical elements in Finney's theology, but certainly in his zeal for the conversion of souls he shows an evangelical passion that should be emulated."[160] Bloesch's critique was perhaps the most prescient and seemed to offer a winsome reconciliation between the two evangelical parties. Reginald Bibby, a sociologist from the the University of Lethbridge (Alberta, Canada), was more critical of Gerstner's essay.[161] In a review for *Sociological Analysis* Bibby noted, "[t]o equate evangelical belief with such doctrines as the virgin birth and substitutionary atonement and to cross out the likes of Karl Barth is to invite arguments galore." He added, "[t]he reader is left with the distinct impression that 'this' is only what 'some' evangelicals believe."[162] To his credit, Gerstner did recognize there were many "different expressions" both within evangelicalism and its theology, but Gerstner failed to explore these varieties at length. His essay led to disputes over the doctrinal boundary lines of evangelical theology.

As the reviews flowed in, the book which included Gerstner's chapter essay faced criticism. Bibby accused the essays of offering "pro-evangelical tones" and "sermonizing." In a review essay, Mark Noll, a former student of Gerstner and now a history professor at Trinity College (Illinois), observed that "readers who lean to Arminianism may find" Gerstner's essay simply "contentious and wrongheaded." Opposition to Gerstner's article, according to Noll, "is proof enough that serious questions need to be asked about the

159. Bloesch, Review of *The Evangelicals*, 81. Bloesch received his BA from Elmhurst College, a BD from Chicago Theological Seminary and a PhD from the University of Chicago. He served as a professor of theology at the University of Dubuque Theological Seminary (1957–1993).

160. Bloesch, Review of *The Evangelicals*, 82.

161. Bibby received his BA from the University of Alberta, a BD from the Southern Baptist Theological Seminary, a MA from the University of Calgary and a PhD from Washington State University. He has served for many years as a professor of sociology at the University of Lethbridge.

162. Bibby, Review of *The Evangelicals*, 364.

depth of evangelical theological unity."[163] Noll judged that Gerstner's writing was not as good as that of the book's non-evangelical writers. He noted, "[o]f the evangelical authors, only Marsden writes as well as these non-evangelicals." While Noll made numerous criticisms of *The Evangelicals*, he was generally quite positive about the book. In a significant sentence, Noll held that "the book should take its place as the single most important resource for both evangelicals and non-evangelicals who want to come to grips with conservative Protestantism in twentieth-century America."[164] Noll's praise aside, the book had to be revised. The most conspicuous revision in the book was that the editors added a chapter written by Vinson Synam, a Pentecostal historian, entitled "Theological Boundaries: The Arminian Tradition."[165] This chapter was added specifically to counterbalance Gerstner's article, which was re-titled "Theological Boundaries: The Reformed Perspective." Later, Dayton claimed that Gerstner offered the most "egregious rejection" of Finney by historians operating within what he describes as the "Presbyterian paradigm" of evangelical history.[166] He argued that "the 'Reformed' theological rejection of Finney, is perhaps the Achilles heel of much Reformed 'historiography' of 'American Evangelicalism.'"[167] Whether one agrees or disagrees with Gerstner's perspective, it cannot be denied that Gerstner's article sparked conversation amongst evangelicals about their identity in the 1970s. Dayton, who was troubled by Gerstner's views, subsequently spent much of his career advocating a "pentecostal paradigm" for evangelical history.[168] It seems clear that in the 1970s Gerstner became an important player in debates about the doctrine and character of evangelicalism. One sign of his stature was that he was invited to serve as a response group leader for the "Consultation on Future Evangelical Con-

163. Noll, "Catching Up With the Evangelicals," 21.

164. Ibid.

165. Synam, "Theological Boundaries: The Arminian Tradition." Synam earned his BA from the University of Richmond and a MA and PhD from the University of Georgia. He taught history at Emmanuel College (Georgia), Oklahoma City Southwestern College, Oral Roberts University, and Regent University.

166. Dayton, "The Search for the Historical Evangelicalism," 16. For further information on this debate see Horton, "Is Evangelicalism Reformed or Wesleyan? Re-Opening the Marsden-Dayton Debate," 137–55; Olson, "The Reality of Evangelicalism: A Response to Michael S. Horton," 157–62; Horton, "Response to Roger E. Olson's Reply," 163–68.

167. Dayton, "The Search for the Historical Evangelicalism," 16–17.

168. Ibid., 12–33; Dayton, "Rejoinder to Historiography Discussion," 62–71; Dayton, *Theological Roots of Pentecostalism*; Winn, ed., *From the Margins*; Dayton and Strong, *(Re) Discovering an Evangelical Heritage*.

cerns" at the Colony Square Hotel in Atlanta in December 1977.[169] By the late 1970s Gerstner had established himself as a partisan leader and shaper of modern evangelicalism.

The church historian also continued to have a presence on a key evangelical campus. As visiting professor of church history at Trinity Evangelical Divinity School in the 1970s, Gerstner sought to influence a cadre of evangelical scholars. One TEDS seminarian, Dennis Okholm, noted that Gerstner lectured on Jonathan Edwards in dark suits. With Gerstner's formal demeanor and style, Okholm recalled Gerstner tried to "channel [communicate] Edwards to his students."[170] Ron Frost, another TEDS seminarian, noted that Gerstner's teaching methodology "was striking and a bit terrifying: he would move progressively through the book [*Freedom of the Will* (1754)] by walking down the rows while pressing a given student to explain and assess the content at hand when our 'turn' arrived." Frost added, "[d]espite the daunting methodology, with Gerstner's bulldog presence, it was a stimulating and very helpful course."[171] A further TEDS student from the 1970s, David Buschart, remembers Gerstner eating with students and explaining to them why he stayed within the mainline UPCUSA. Apparently, Gerstner told the students that as long as the official confession of the UPCUSA was orthodox he would remain a part of the denomination.[172] David Wells, a native of South Africa who studied and later taught at TEDS, recalled taking Gerstner's course on Edwards book *The Freedom of the Will* (1754). He noted that Gerstner "latched you on to Edwards." Overall, Wells said he "enjoyed the course" and found Gerstner to be a "very engaging teacher."[173]

In the academic year of 1973 and 1974 Wells served as a fellow at Yale Divinity School. During that time Wells visited with his professor, and they would sometimes eat lunch together. He remembers Gerstner telling him how difficult his circumstances were at Pittsburgh Theological Seminary.

---

169. Hoke, "Consultation on Future Evangelical Concerns," C-5.

170. Okholm, Interview with the author. Okholm received his BA from Wheaton College, a MDiv and a MA from Trinity Evangelical Divinity School and a ThM and PhD from Princeton Theological Seminary. Okholm has served as a theology professor at Jamestown College (ND, Wheaton College (IL), and Azusa Pacific University (CA).

171. Frost, email correspondence sent to the author.

172. Buschart email to the author. Buschart received his BA from Wheaton College, a MDiv and a MA from Trinity Evangelical Divinity School and a MPhil and a PhD from Drew University. Buschart has served as a theology professor at the Canadian Theological Seminary and at Denver Seminary.

173. Wells, Interview with the author.

Wells observed that Gerstner slept in his Volkswagen van while visiting Yale.[174] Moreover, Kimnach recalls Gerstner driving long distances to teach and do research. He also recounted Gerstner sleeping in his van and at rest stops, eating sandwiches from truck stations, and wearing nondescript clothing and a leather jacket. Gerstner spurned amenities, considered himself to be a rugged individual and sometimes joked with his Yale friends that he was a "barbarian."[175] Apparently, Gerstner's attire changed when he was away from PTS and TEDS.

Another TEDS student over whom Gerstner exercised some measure of influence was Mark Noll.[176] Noll in the early 1970s was a MA student in church history at the suburban Chicago seminary and took several classes from Gerstner. Noll found Gerstner to be "very energetic and engaging" and a bit "eccentric."[177] The budding historian was "impressed by how seriously Gerstner took Edwards." He appreciated Gerstner's Reformed perspective and depth of learning. Moreover, he was amazed by Gerstner's teaching method, recalling that there was "terrific dialogue in classes." Gerstner taught Noll in the classroom and served as the second reader for his master's thesis on Melchior Hoffman (1495–1544), a German Anabaptist. During his oral exam, Noll remembers that Gerstner challenged him on some of his interpretations of Luther's theology. Ultimately, Noll had to rewrite a few pages to satisfy Gerstner's demands. Noll, who later became a noted American historian, believes that Gerstner had some influence on his understanding of American church history and on his 2002 landmark volume *America's God*. In that work Noll wrote, "I am pleased to acknowledge the

174. Ibid. Wells earned his BD at the University of London, a MDiv from Trinity Evangelical Divinity School and a PhD from the University of Manchester. Wells has taught theology at TEDS and at Gordon-Conwell Theological Seminary (MA).

175. Kimnach, Interview with the author, 6 December 2012.

176. Noll received his BA from Wheaton College, a MA from the University of Iowa, a MA from TEDS, and a PhD from Vanderbilt University. He later taught history at Trinity College (IL), Wheaton College and the University of Notre Dame. Ravi Zacharias, a well known evangelical apologist, studied under Gerstner at TEDS in the mid-1970s. Zacharias, Interview with John Carter, "On Leadership and Calling." Zacharias received his BTh from Ontario Bible College and a MDiv from TEDS. After teaching at Nyack Seminary in New York, he began his apologetics ministry and later helped found the Oxford Centre for Christian Apologetics at Wycliffe Hall, Oxford. It is also likely, but I have been unable to confirm, that William Lane Craig, another well-known evangelical apologist, studied under Gerstner at TEDS in the 1970s. Craig earned his BA from Wheaton College, two MAs from TEDS, a PhD from the University of Birmingham and a DTheol from the University of Munich. He subsequently taught at TEDS, Westmont College (CA) and Talbot School of Theology.

177. Noll, Interview with the author.

assistance on topics treated in these pages that I received many years ago at Trinity Evangelical Divinity School from . . . the late John Gerstner."[178] In addition, George Marsden, another evangelical historian, had some contact with Gerstner when he was a visiting professor at TEDS during the 1976–1977 academic year. Marsden, who also shared an interest in Jonathan Edwards and who later wrote the definitive biography of Edwards, noted that "[m]y one impression was that I could see that he might be more persuasive in person than I found him to be in print."[179] Gerstner appears to have been a respected teacher at TEDS, but there he was one evangelical professor among many.

The contrast between TEDS and the environment at Pittsburgh Theological Seminary was profound. TEDS had partial continuity with the Old Princeton tradition, whereas PTS by the 1970s had gone down a more progressive theological path. At PTS, Gerstner stood out for his outspoken evangelical views. Many students reared in conservative Presbyterian churches and homes knew that Gerstner was special. For evangelical students at PTS he was their leader and guide through the perplexing world of liberal doctrine and process theology. Andy Gerhardt, who studied at PTS from 1972 to 1975, was a member of the evangelical student group that was led by Gerstner. Gerhardt found Gerstner to be "very strident" but a leader who "kept evangelical students solid."[180] Another evangelical student from the mid-1970s was Bruce Mawhinney who remembers Gerstner challenging the process theologians at the seminary to debate with him—they refused. Mawhinney also recalled Gerstner's view that "many young pastors were wimpy." He remembers John and Edna traveling to a church in the middle of an ice storm in order for Gerstner to preach. Gerstner made it clear to Mawhinney that "ministry was a great opportunity" that should not be wasted.[181]

Mark Ross, a conservative PTS student, noted that Gerstner lived an "intense life" of study and teaching.[182] Ross, however, thought it was somewhat strange that Gerstner would occasionally sleep overnight in a chair in his office. According to Gerstner's son Jonathan, however, his father

178. Mark Noll, *America's God*, vii.

179. Marsden, email to the author. Marsden, *Jonathan Edwards*.

180. Gerhardt, Interview with the author. Gerhardt received his BA from Franklin and Marshall College and his MDiv from PTS.

181. Mawhiney, Interview with the author.

182. Ross, Interview with the author. Ross received his BA from the University of Pittsburgh, a MDiv at PTS and a PhD from the University of Keele (England). He has served as an associate pastor at First Presbyterian Church in Columbia, South Carolina and as a theology professor at Erskine Theological Seminary (SC).

regularly "slept in a chair for much of the last half of his life due to extreme asthma."[183] Don McKim, another PTS student, observed that Gerstner was "wound tight psychologically" [he was an intense person], but "could be very polite." McKim came to believe that Gerstner "had a very acute Christian conscience."[184] In June 1970 James Davison, one former student, wrote to Gerstner from the Netherlands. Davison, who was a graduate student at the Free University of Amsterdam, wrote "[b]y the way, I'm curious as to your comments on Dr. Schaeffer's type of orthodoxy and apologetics too."[185] Gerstner was often a helpful guide for a student trying to make sense of a particular thinker or school of thought. He was also an encourager to many evangelical students at PTS who felt overwhelmed by the progressive theological and political atmosphere they perceived at the seminary. On June 26, 1976 a *Pittsburgh Post-Gazette* story highlighted some radical activity by students and faculty that led to an unwanted "hippie image."[186] Specific problems the article mentioned included a professor's liberal views on censorship, a group of "long-haired seminarians who picketed the Presbytery" and a progressive seminary curriculum which allowed a person to graduate without taking a single theology class. For many traditional evangelical students PTS was a difficult environment. Yet the seminary did take steps to combat its image problem, creating a task force to study how the school could improve itself comprehensively. Ultimately, PTS was able to deal with its community image, funding shortages, curriculum problems, statement of purpose and relationship with parish churches.[187] By 1978 some of the more radical features of PTS were smoothed out in order to calm constituent fears and improve the seminary.

As Gerstner entered the late 1970s he was running out of steam. Steve Crocco, an evangelical PTS student from the late 1970s, remembers that Gerstner was not very social and would leave immediately after class was over. Gerstner appeared to be deeply troubled by continued developments at PTS. One sign that PTS was moving to the theological left in the late 1970s can be detected in a key faculty appointment. In 1977 PTS brought in Majorie Suchocki (1933–), a United Methodist, to teach theology. Suchocki was a former evangelical who had jettisoned what she felt was outdated doctrine and embraced process theology under her mentor John Cobb at

183. Gerstner, email to the author, March 7, 2014.
184. McKim, Interview with the author, October 18, 2010.
185. Davison to Gerstner, June 14, 1970.
186. Hodiak, "Theological Seminary Seeks an Image," 16.
187. For more on these issues see McKim, *Ever a Vision*, 75–150.

the Claremont Graduate School.[188] PTS was seeking to establish itself firmly as a more ecumenical and theologically progressive institution. In the last couple of years before his retirement in 1980 Gerstner had lost virtually all patience with his fellow faculty members. When Charles Partee arrived on the PTS campus to teach church history in the fall of 1978, Gerstner barely talked to him. Partee later recalled "that he had no real opportunity to get to know Gerstner."[189] He remembered Gerstner sleeping in the parking lot and what he believed to be Gerstner's general unhappiness. Gerstner no doubt was discouraged about PTS's theological direction, but perhaps some of Gerstner's disagreement was because the seminary, according to Partee, "had refused to give Gerstner a raise in the last few years."[190] Gerstner remained committed to teaching at PTS and for many years bore witness to those who did not agree with his positions, but near the end of his career at PTS he appears to have given up on the seminary.

One sign that Gerstner's scholarly and ecclesiastical efforts had been appreciated occurred in 1976, when R.C. Sproul edited a festschrift for his mentor entitled *Soli Deo Gloria*. This volume included essays by Cornelius Van Til, J. I. Packer, John Murray and Roger Nicole to name a few.[191] It was indeed significant that Van Til, who had been Gerstner's apologetic nemesis, contributed to the volume. In the preface Sproul gushed with admiration for his former professor and noted that Gerstner provides a "vivid example of one who stands in the midst of confusion as a 'bright and burning light.'"[192] Van Til contributed the first essay entitled "Calvin the Controversialist." Van Til held that Calvin was a great defender of the faith, but that his "theological effort was to set the biblical view of man and God squarely over against every form of man-centered philosophy."[193] Van Til contrasted the different apologetic strategies of Thomas Aquinas and Calvin and argued that Calvin's was the better way because it did not allow humanity to be the "rightful judge" over the "claims of Christ." Van Til wasted no time disagreeing with his former student. J. I. Packer provided the second essay which upheld a traditional view of the Reformed doctrine of justification. In Reformed the-

188. Dorrien, *The Making of American Liberal Theology*, 255–56.

189. Partee, Interview with the author, October 13, 2010. Partee received his BA from Maryville College (Tennessee), a BD from Austin Presbyterian Theological Seminary, a MA from the University of Texas at Austin and a PhD from Princeton Theological Seminary. He taught theology and church history at Buena Vista College (IA) and at Pittsburgh Theological Seminary.

190. Partee, Interview with the author.

191. Sproul, ed., *Soli Deo Gloria*.   get?

192. Sproul, Preface to *Soli Deo Gloria*, ed. Sproul, xi.

193. Van Til, "Calvin the Controversialist," 6.

ology, justification was not merely a "theological speculation but a religious reality." Packer surveyed some of the attacks on justification and perhaps he wrote on the topic because of the justification controversy surrounding Norman Shepherd, a theology professor at Westminster Seminary.[194] Philip Hughes, an Anglican theologian, wrote an essay on the sovereignty of God, and Thomas Gregory, a Westminster College philosopher, penned a piece on depravity.[195] Roger Nicole, the Reformed Baptist theologian from Gordon-Conwell Theological Seminary, wrote on inductive and deductive reasoning in relation to the Bible's inspiration. The festschrift offered insights on key themes in Refomed theology, but it also contained analysis of the Old School Princeton theologians and Jonathan Edwards. Andrew Hoffecker, a Grove City College (Pennsylvania) philosopher, wrote on "Beauty and the Princeton Piety" and Carl Bogue, a PCA pastor, evaluated Edwards and the covenant of grace.[196] Hoffecker demonstrated the spiritual life of Charles Hodge and Bogue showed Edwards's twin commitments to divine sovereignty and human responsibility. Edwards was no harsh Calvinist. The book served as a fitting tribute to Gerstner and reveals that by the mid-1970s he had achieved a high place among the Reformed evangelical scholars of his era.[197]

In the 1970s Gerstner continued to participate in different ways in the life of the church and in the halls of academe. He debated with the Harvard divinity school dean, fought for renewal in the UPCUSA, tried to set theological boundary lines around evangelicalism and gave his support and time to Sproul's growing Ligonier ministry. His teaching at TEDS allowed him to exert some measure of influence at that distinctively evangelical school. At PTS he mentored evangelical students and provided an evangelical perspective at a seminary that lacked a theological identity. His lack of success in trying to make PTS more evangelical allowed him to direct his energies into work with the Ligonier Valley Study Center. This ministry would carry on his theological vision in a popular way that reached the masses. Ligonier's growing-audio visual ministry of cassette tapes, VHS recordings, and radio

---

194. Packer, "Sola Fide: The Reformed Doctrine of Justification," 11–25. For an illuminating discussion of the Shepherd controversy, see MacLeod's *W. Stanford Reid*, 257–79.

195. Hughes, "The Sovereignty of God—Has God Lost Control?," 26–35; Gregory, "The Presbyterian Doctrine of Total Depravity," 36–45.

196. Hoffecker, "Beauty and the Princeton Piety," 118–33; Bogue, "Jonathan Edwards on the Covenant of Grace," 134–45.

197. Other essay in the volume were written by John Murray, Sproul, John Warwick Montgomery, Robert Coughenour, James Dennison, Jack White, and Kenneth Zaretzke.

broadcasts provided Gerstner with a way to be heard. Gerstner's promotion of Edwards, including both writing and teaching, was met with a mixture of deep disappointment and continued passion. His removal from the editorship of the Yale volume on Edward's sermons was painful, but led him, like George Ladd, to reorientate his scholarship away from mainstream academia and towards the evangelical world. He argued forcefully for biblical inerrancy and helped launch an organization to defend the doctrine (ICBI). His appraisals of American evangelicalism could appear wooden and narrow. Yet from another perspective his views and boldness seemed to ensure that a conservative Reformed evangelical position would not be lost in a cacophony of competing voices. In the 1970s Gerstner became a shaper of evangelicalism and he helped strengthen the vitality of Presbyterian and Reformed evangelicalism. The success and failures of the 1970s took their toll on Gerstner, but the aging church historian still had work to do.

6

Church Politics and a Reasoned Apologetic (1980–1989)

IN THE 1980S GERSTNER CONTINUED TO DEFEND THE FAITH THROUGH HIS preaching, teaching, lecturing, and writing. As a recent retiree from Pittsburgh Theological Seminary (PTS), he had the opportunity to pursue several writing projects and teaching opportunities that previously would have been impossible. This chapter will analyze these facets of his life, but also his participation in a well-known church court case where the limits of theological tolerance would be tested. At issue in this dispute was the effect the controversy had on the evangelical wing of the UPCUSA. During the 1980s, Gerstner also served as a theologian-in-residence at a church and continued to teach at several strictly evangelical institutions. His role in these schools will be evaluated and an analysis will be given on his apologetic approach and the apparent lack of change in his thought. His retirement was active; in completing some important works he continued to write with vigor. Moreover, he sought to communicate Jonathan Edwards's theology to a popular audience, thus amplifying the voice of the colonial theologian. During the 1980s, Gerstner continued to be the scholarly advocate for an uncompromising evangelicalism and thus helped to shape the Presbyterian and Reformed evangelical movement.

In 1980 Gerstner was sixty-five years old and decided, based on his age, to retire from Pittsburgh Theological Seminary. A year after Gerstner left PTS, an event was held to celebrate his retirement. The special occasion occurred on May 2, 1981 at Pittsburgh's stately Mt Lebanon United Presbyterian Church. The event was held in conjunction with a conference on Reformed theology. One organizer of the Gerstner celebration reported that "it was a wonderful evening and people from all over the country who have appreciated Dr. Gerstner's ministry were able to express that appreciation in a sincere and winsome fashion."[1] In addition, thirty-three letters of gratitude were sent to help celebrate the occasion. Gerstner, who had felt marginalized by PTS, was at last being formally recognized for his achievements. Numerous former students and colleagues expressed their admiration for Gerstner. In a letter, Richard C. Halverson, pastor of the Fourth Presbyterian Church in Washington, D.C., recognized that "[a]s far back as I can remember in my Christian experience you [Gerstner] have been a kind of a hero to me."[2] In another letter Earle McCrea, an Iowa Presbyterian pastor, told Gerstner, "you will always be the human voice of the Holy Spirit calling me into the ministry."[3] David Brown, a Pennsylvania minister, told Gerstner, "[y]our personal inspiration really changed my life and my ministry."[4]

Walter Kaiser, academic dean at Trinity Evangelical Divinity School, also articulated his esteem by telling Gerstner that he had "always been an inspiration to the students here at Trinity . . . as you have taught with a vivaciousness and an enthusiasm which is at once a joy to behold and a pleasure to enter into."[5] W. Fred Graham, professor of religion at Michigan State University, recalled that it "was in my first class in Church History at Pgh-Xenia that I experienced for the first time in my life that a Christian could be lucid, insightful, intellectually first-rate, and exciting."[6]

Tom Gregory, a religion professor from Westminster College (Pennsylvania), also wrote to say, "[s]o much that is good in the United Presbyterian Church, humanly speaking, can be traced to your faithful reformed teachings."[7] David Dorst, pastor of Pittsburgh's Beverly Heights United Presbyterian Church, remarked that Gerstner "provided the kind of emotional and spiritual support [evangelical students] needed to survive in a hostile environment [PTS]."[8] Johannes S. Vos (1903–1983), who had served as a missionary in Manchuria and later as professor of Bible at Geneva College and who was the son of Geerhardus Vos (1862–1949), the famed Princeton biblical theologian, also wrote to express his appreciation:

1. Dorst, To the Session of Mt Lebanon U.P. Church and MacDonald, May 4, 1981, Gerstner Papers, Chandler, Arizona.

2. Halverson, Letter to Gerstner, April 7, 1981, Gerstner Papers, Chandler, Arizona.

3. McCrea, Letter to Gerstner, March 27, 1981, Gerstner Papers, Chandler, Arizona.

4. Brown, Letter to Gerstner, April 27, 1981, Gerstner Papers, Chandler, Arizona.

5. Kaiser, Letter to Gerstner, April 9, 1981, Gerstner Papers, Chandler, Arizona.

6. Graham, Letter to Gerstner, April 16, 1981, Gerstner Papers, Chandler, Arizona.

7. Gregory, Letter to Gerstner, April 1981, Gerstner Papers, Chandler, Arizona.

8. Dorst, Letter to Gerstner, March 30, 1981, Gerstner Papers, Chandler, Arizona.

> Nothing is more difficult, or requires more devotion and cour-
> age than to witness consistently and faithfully for Jesus Christ,
> the Scriptures and the Reformed faith in the face of opposition.
> You have done it through the years. I want to honor you for
> your life and witness, and especially for your help on occasion
> to Geneva College.[9]

Gerstner must have been overwhelmed with all the praise that was showered upon him. The affirmations must have brought a great sense of satisfaction to him for his years of tireless and sometimes painful work at PTS and in his denomination.

Unfortunately, the joys of his retirement party were soon overshadowed by complaints about the event itself. During the festivities Gerstner apparently spoke and offered some comments about the state of the UPCUSA. Thirteen days after the event, Gerstner received an envelope from Myles W. MacDonald, the pastor of Mt Lebanon United Presbyterian Church. MacDonald began his May 15 letter noting that he "would prefer" not "to have had to write this letter because of my high regard and deep respect for you."[10] Nonetheless, MacDonald was upset that Gerstner had criticized the UPCUSA and that Gerstner and the organizers of the event had allegedly violated an earlier agreement that such matters would not be discussed. MacDonald stated that the "Session had made it explicitly clear . . . that we did not want the occasion to be used as a forum to denounce the UPCUSA." The pastor added that he was "surprised, shocked, and disappointed when I heard what you said." He then told Gerstner, "[m]y appreciation for your teaching and for you as a fellow Christian have not diminished, but I am bothered by the turn of events which took place that evening." He closed the letter by saying, "I sincerely pray, as I know you do, that the General Assembly will speak clearly, explicitly, and forcefully to the issues surrounding the controversy in the Kaseman case."[11] Gerstner would not escape controversy, not even at his retirement party. MacDonald's last sentence indicates that Gerstner's supposed controversial comments had something to do with Mansfield Kaseman and his acceptance into the UPCUSA as an ordained minister.

Just as Gerstner played a leading role in the C-67 conflict and the Kenyon controversy, he would again become a key combatant in the widely publicized Kaseman dispute. In the early 1980s perhaps no issue alarmed

9. Vos, Letter to Gerstner, n.d. Gerstner Papers, Chandler, Arizona.

10. MacDonald, Letter to Gerstner, May 15, 1981, Gerstner Papers, Chandler, Arizona.

11. Ibid.

the evangelical wing of the UPCUSA more than the ordination of Mansfield Kaseman, a United Church of Christ (UCC) pastor.[12] The UCC was known for having a largely liberal theological orientation and Kaseman shared the UCC's doctrinal tone.[13] In 1979 Kaseman was called to be co-pastor of the Rockville United Church in Rockville Maryland, a union congregation of the UPCUSA and the UCC. On March 20, 1979 he appeared before the National Capital Union Presbytery in order to be examined. What ensued set off a firestorm within some sectors of the denomination. In response to the question "Do you believe Jesus is God?" Kaseman answered by saying "No, God is God."[14] Kaseman later argued that he was attempting to make the point that Jesus is united to God the Father. He tried to defend himself, telling the Associated Press that "Jesus is one with God."[15] As a result of his response, however, a dispute over the nature of Christ erupted within the UPCUSA. The case which was profiled in *Time* magazine and reported in the national press led to wrangling in church courts over Kaseman's theology and acceptance into the UPCUSA. Gerstner paid close attention to the case as charges were soon initiated against the National Capital Union Presbytery for approving the minister's reception into the UPCUSA. The complaint was filed by Stewart J. Rankin, a UPCUSA minister, who like Gerstner was a former UPCNA clergyman.[16]

From 1979 to 1981 Gerstner served as counsel for the complainants. Gerstner would attempt to prosecute Kaseman. Rankin, Gerstner, and six elder complainants specifically challenged the presbytery's right to ordain Kaseman because they believed his theology did not fall within the confessional standards of the UPCUSA.[17] Kaseman, who was "embarrassed by the controversy," believed that his theology was "middle of the road;" he was "surprised by the more conservative elements in the UPCUSA."[18] The case eventually made its way to the Permanent Judicial Commission (PJC) of the denomination. The PJC ordered that Kaseman should be re-examined by National Capital Union Presbytery. On March 18, 1980 Kase-

12. Kaseman, BA Westmar College (IA), BD Andover-Newton Theological School, STM Yale Divinity School.

13. Wilshire, "United Church of Christ," 1199–1201.

14. Cornell, "Presbyterian 'Court' Backs Minister in Christ Dispute," 10; "Dispute Over the Deity of Christ," 78.

15. "Presbyterian Debate Jesus' Divinity," 3.

16. Rankin was a graduate of Temple Teachers College (1940) and Temple School of Theology (1941). He was ordained into the UPCNA in 1941.

17. The other complainants included elders Raymond Langille, Lee Mace, Robert Stadelhoffer, Alcott J. Larsson, J. W. McNamara, and James Reid.

18. Kaseman, Interview with the author.

man underwent a new examination and was "confirmed as a continuing member of the Presbytery" by a vote of 165 to 58.[19] Again, the complainants appealed to the PJC to reverse the decision of the presbytery, and some conservatives expressed their dismay. Five days before the PJC's verdict was rendered, Douglas Klein, pastor of the First United Presbyterian Church of Turtle Creek, Pennsylvania, told the readers of the *Pittsburgh Press* that "the Kaseman dilemma symbolizes the acute internal cancer which seems to be destroying the credibility of the church."[20] Ultimately, on March 6, 1981, the presbytery's decision to allow Kaseman's ordination was upheld by the PJC.[21] Gerstner and many other evangelicals believed they had lost another watershed case.

The executive presbyter of the National Capital Union Presbytery, Ed White, viewed the Kaseman controversy differently from many Presbyterian evangelicals. White believed that "conservatives weren't really concerned about Kaseman, but about women's ordination."[22] From White's perspective, the Kaseman issue became a cause célèbre for conservatives so that they could "create a situation where they could leave" the UPCUSA, justifying their actions by pointing to the alleged heresy of Kaseman. Conservative outrage over his Christological views "provided cover" for what Kaseman believed were "churches who did not want to recognize women on session." While there may be a measure of truth in White and Kaseman's claims, evidence indicates that Kaseman's acceptance into the UPCUSA did trouble conservative Presbyterians such as Gerstner deeply. To be sure, in the same month that the PJC made its decision, Gerstner penned a twenty-seven-page booklet which analyzed the Kaseman episode in detail.[23] Discouraged by his inability to prosecute the National Capital Union Presbytery and Kaseman effectively, Gerstner decided to raise the level of rhetoric against the

19. G-6.0106b (1) UPC, 1081, p. 113, Rankin v. National Capital Union Presbytery, Remedial Case.

20. Klein, "Letter to the Editor," *Pittsburgh Press*, March 1, 1981, B-4. Klein received his BA from Westminster College and his MDiv from Gordon-Conwell Theological Seminary. He later went on to become pastor of Grace Chapel (Michigan) and Faith Presbyterian Church (Colorado). He was moderator of the EPC in 2011 and 2012.

21. "Judicial Commission Upholds Presbytery's Reception of Minister," 1.

22. White, Interview with the author. White served as executive presbyter of National Capital Union Presbytery from 1972 to 1989. He received his BA from Wesleyan University (CT), an MDiv at Union Seminary (NY), and a DMin at McCormick Seminary.

23. Gerstner, *The Apostasy of the United Presbyterian Church in the United States of America.*

UPCUSA. From Gerstner's perspective, "Kaseman had been shown to be guilty of denying or refusing to affirm at least four essentials of the Christian religion: the sinlessness, bodily resurrection, vicarious atonement, and deity of Jesus Christ." Gerstner held that that he had denied these doctrines "[a]t Presbytery, Synod, and General Assembly levels."[24]

Moreover, Kaseman also communicated some of his views to the media, admitting to the *Pittsburgh Post-Gazette*, "I believe in the Resurrection without necessarily believing in the bodily resurrection" and also noting, "I have problems with the idea that he [Jesus] was sinless."[25] Kaseman was openly espousing his radical theological positions and disturbing conservative Presbyterians. In March 1981, while still dealing with the taste of defeat at church courts, the recently retired UPCUSA church history professor sought to use highly charged language in his booklet to express his indignation and to continue the controversy over Kaseman's acceptance into the UPCUSA. Gerstner made the most extreme charge possible against the UPCUSA when he alleged that the church had now become "apostate, officially."[26] This was a severe accusation, which was not shared by even most UPCUSA evangelicals.[27] Nevertheless, the UPUCSA continued to face unrest over the Kaseman affair, and Gerstner was clearly stoking the fires of turmoil.

In the wake of these events, several churches began to leave the denomination. The June 1981 edition of *Christianity Today* reported that sixty-six UPCUSA congregations had left or were thinking of leaving the denomination.[28] Official UPCUSA statistics do not fully account for the reasons why certain churches departed the denomination from 1981 to 1984 because denominational figures separate only dismissed churches from dissolved congregations. Many of the dissolved churches simply joined other denominations and some others folded. Numerous departing churches in Western Pennsylvania had some connection to Gerstner. While no evidence indicates a large schism within the UPCUSA in the early 1980s, there are clear signs that a deeper dissatisfaction was emerging. During this period some churches joined the doctrinally conservative Presbyterian Church

24. Ibid., 1.

25. Kaseman quoted by Hodiak, "Ministry Presbyterians Cite Biblical Authority Loss," 16.

26. Gerstner, *The Apostasy of the United Presbyterian Church in the United States of America*, 1.

27. Clapp, "Pressures Mount, Fissures Multiply as Major Presbyterian Realignment Looms," 36–37.

28. Moore, "Presbyterians Affirm Deity of Christ, Vow to Be Led by Historic Confessions," 32.

in America (PCA), and some others joined a fresh denomination formed in the midst of the Kaseman conflict. In 1981 this new denomination, the Evangelical Presbyterian Church (EPC), was created partly out of unease over the Kaseman decision. Edward Davis, the founding stated clerk of the EPC, noted that the "Kaseman case was an influential factor in the formation of the EPC, but not the only one."[29] According to Davis, two other major issues led to the creation of the EPC: the issue of freedom of church property and the issue of individual congregations' freedom to elect elders. These evangelicals did not agree with the UPCUSA's position that all property is held in trust for the denomination.

Moreover, some churches rejected a 1980 UPCUSA rule that church boards had to include women. In a March 22, 1981 *Pittsburgh Press* article, Calvin Gray, who became the first moderator of the EPC, explained that it was being formed because of the Kaseman case, the church property issue, and resistance to required gender quotas for church boards.[30] Mark Jumper, the son of one of the founders of the EPC, Andrew Jumper (1927–1992), remembers that the Kaseman case served as the "rock in the avalanche" for many people who joined the new denomination.[31] Clearly, the controversy over Kaseman was a major factor in the founding of the EPC, which held its first General Assembly in St Louis, Missouri, in September 1981 with twelve churches.[32] Even though the EPC started small, the denomination grew steadily, and by 1993 had 175 member congregations representing 52,360 members.[33] By 2013 the EPC had mushroomed to 419 churches

29. Davis, Interview with author, February 11, 2013. Davis received his BA from Nyack College (NY), a MDiv from Westminster Theological Seminary, and a DMin from McCormick Seminary. He served as the stated clerk of the Evangelical Presbyterian Church (EPC) from 1981 to 2000. He served as an associate pastor at Ward Presbyterian Church in Detroit, Michigan, prior to becoming stated clerk of the EPC.

30. Gray's comments are cited Sharpe in "Presbytery Bids to Heal Rift," A-4.

31. Jumper, Interview with the author. Jumper received his BA from Oral Roberts University, a MDiv from Columbia Seminary, a MA from the Naval Postgraduate School, and a PhD from Salve Regina University (RI). Andrew Jumper received his B.A. from the University of Mississippi, a BD and ThM from Austin Presbyterian Theological Seminary. A large collection of Andrew Jumpers's sermons can be found at the Preserved Wisdom website, <www.preservedwisdom.com>.

32. Heidbrecht, "Evangelical Presbyterian Church," 94. Heidbrecht argues the Kaseman decision was "the precipitating issue that led to the formation of the EPC" (94). Heidbrecht became involved in the EPC in the 1990s and served as the moderator of the EPC in 2006–2007. He received his BA from the University of Winnipeg, a MA from Wheaton College, and his PhD from the University of Illinois at Chicago.

33. Heidbrecht, "Evangelical Presbyterian Church," 94.

and approximately 140,000 members.[34] In the 1980s and beyond, the EPC became a key alternative for many churches departing from the mainline Presbyterian Church.[35]

While UPCUSA leaders were concerned with the defections, they received some relief in the summer of 1981, when the UPCUSA General Assembly took an action which most likely halted the departure of numerous other conservative congregations. At the UPCUSA's June 1981 General Assembly meeting in Houston, Texas, the denomination by a vote of 700 to 2 reaffirmed its belief in the deity of Jesus Christ by stating "that Jesus is one person, truly God and truly human" and the "second person of the Holy Trinity."[36] This statement was made to address concerns over the UPCUSA's theology in light of the Kaseman uproar. Louis Moore, a *Christianity Today* reporter, phoned Kaseman for his response to the GA's statement. From his Rockville, Maryland, home Kaseman responded by expressing his theological flexibility: "[i]t sounds good to me."[37] The *Pittsburgh Post-Gazette* declared, "Assembly Soothes Presbyterian Rift."[38] The assembly's action, according to Gerstner, "was most encouraging"; he now intended "to persuade other Concerned United Presbyterian members to withdraw the charge of apostasy."[39] Presumably "Concerned United Presbyterian members" was a reference to a western Pennsylvania chapter of Presbyterians United for Biblical Concerns (PUBC), a renewal group founded in the midst of the C-67 debate.[40] Gerstner, who was scheduled to participate in the assembly, released his comments from a Houston hospital where he was confined for over a week because of a back injury. Despite Gerstner's change of mind and despite his efforts to calm fears, some conservative Presbyterians continued to believe that the "apostasy" charge was accurate. On the night of June 11, 1981 some eighty conservative Presbyterians in Western Pennsylvania gath-

34. This information was provided to me in an, Interview with Ed McCallum, the EPC assistant stated clerk.

35. Fortson, who serves as a professor of church history at Reformed Theological Seminary in Charlotte, has written a history of the EPC *Liberty in Non-Essentials.*

36. 1981 General Assembly Statement quoted by Bohdan Hodiak, "Assembly Soothes Presbyterian Rift," 5.

37. Kaseman quoted by Moore, "Presbyterians Affirm Deity of Christ, Vow to Be Led by Historic Confessions," 32.

38. Hodiak, "Assembly Soothes Presbyterian Rift," 5.

39. Gerstner quoted by Hodiak, "Assembly Soothes Presbyterian Rift," 5. See also "Clergyman Withdraws Charge that Church Betrayed Faith," 4.

40. For a brief critique of the PUBC and its eventual assimilation into Presbyterians for Renewal, see Eller, "Special Interest Groups and American Presbyterianism," 268–74.

ered in a Ramada Inn near the Pittsburgh airport to discuss the assembly's actions. In his remarks Gerstner encouraged his fellow evangelicals to stay with the UPCUSA. He asked the crowd, "Did the general assembly repudiate apostasy?" Gerstner then claimed that it did and added, "I can't tell you how incredibly happy I am" with the GA's statement.[41] Frank Kik, the evangelical pastor of Eastminster Presbyterian Church in Wichita, Kansas, also reassured the audience,

> I am very pleased with the [GA] statement on the deity of Christ. . . . Now once again we are a confessional church. . . . We asked . . . the church to take a different direction. It has. . . . [I]f we pull out at this point, liberals will have every right to say, "We tried to accommodate you, but still you are not satisfied. You seem to have lost all of your integrity!"[42]

Despite these comments, the conservatives present rejected Gerstner's and Kik's analysis and voted that the UPCUSA was apostate. Apparently, for many of those assembled the Kaseman case caused great discouragement and extinguished whatever patience they had with the UPCUSA.

Harold Scott, Pittsburgh Presbytery's executive, was in attendance but became agitated when members of the group announced their apostasy verdict.[43] Scott told the *Pittsburgh Post-Gazette* that he completely disagreed with the vote and was shocked that "despite the forceful arguments to the contrary" the assembled conservatives had the gall to level such a judgment.[44] Gerstner inspired and influenced scores of conservative Presbyterians, but he could not always soften their criticisms of the UPCUSA or reason with them to remain in the denomination. This controversy reveals Gerstner as somewhat of a vacillator on such issues as the criteria for declaring apostasy and criteria for leaving a denomination. To be sure, Edward Davis, the founding EPC stated clerk has noted that "Gerstner's ambivalence about leaving became very confusing for many evangelicals."[45] As various conservative pastors and churches fled the denomination, Gerstner remained. The 1981 General Assembly statement combined with Gerstner's impassioned revelations of his own change of mind helped suppress what might have a much larger schism in the UPCUSA in the first third of the 1980s. Gerstner is revealed in the Kaseman controversy as a strong oppo-

41. Hopkins, "'Concerned' Faction Spurns Presbyterian Accommodation," 96.

42. Kik quoted by ibid.

43. Hodiak, "U.P. Church Vote: Apostate," 9.

44. Scott quoted by ibid., 9.

45. Davis, Interview with the author.

nent of doctrinal laxity, an advocate of theological boundaries, but conflicted about exactly when to withdraw from the UPCUSA. He did not succeed in prosecuting Kaseman. However, his efforts do appear—to some extent—to have influenced the UPCUSA General Assembly to affirm a Christological statement that adhered to classical Christian orthodoxy.

By the fall of 1981 Gerstner decided that a change of scenery was in order. His forays into church politics were making him weary and he needed a new challenge. Gerstner left Pennsylvania to accept an appointment as theologian-in-residence at Eastminster Presbyterian Church in Wichita, Kansas. Eastminster was a large church led by Frank Kik, the son of J. Marcellus Kik, who was a well known evangelical leader in Canada and then in the United States. The church pursued Gerstner for the new position because they thought this would release Kik to do other ministry work.[46] Eastminster members became aware of Gerstner's reputation as an evangelical scholar because of R. C. Sproul's involvement at the church as an occasional speaker. Sproul had continued to lead Ligonier Ministries and in 1984 moved the para-church organization to Orlando, Florida.[47] Bob Howard recalled that "John Gerstner did a lot of teaching at Eastminster" and had a "lasting influence on the congregation."[48] Howard also noted that "lots of people came to hear Gerstner teach" and that his "heavy duty Reformed teaching motivated a lot of people." Sometimes over two hundred people attended Gerstner's Sunday school class.[49] Howard, a well-known attorney at Kansas' largest law firm, found Gerstner to be a "courtly gentleman" with a "commanding presence." At one dinner party Howard observed Gerstner's graciousness when some specially cooked mushrooms were served. Apparently, Gerstner put several mushrooms on his plate in order to be polite, but later quietly slipped them into his coat pocket.[50]

Dick Gorham, one of the associate pastors at Eastminister, found Gerstner to be "quirky, but delightful."[51] Gorham regarded Gerstner as a "phenomenally brilliant" person who thrived in question-and-answer sessions. He also noted that Gerstner developed a reputation for sometimes chiding

46. Howard, Interview with the author.

47. Ligonier Ministries, "Introducing Dr. R.C. Sproul."

48. Howard graduated with a BA from Emporia State College (Kansas), and a JD from the University of Kansas. He has served as an attorney with the Wichita law firm of Foulston-Siefkin since 1959. He served as a board member and later chair of the Presbyterian Lay Committee from 1990 to 2010.

49. Gensch, Interview with the author.

50. Howard, Interview with the author.

51. Ghorum, Interview with the author.

a church member in group discussion. According to Gorham, Gerstner was not the most sensitive person, yet he found him to be caring. The visiting theologian-in-residence was often referred to as "Black Jack Gerstner" while serving the thriving Kansas congregation. Perhaps this nickname was given to Gerstner because of his sometimes gruff demeanour. Gerstner could appear polished, but he often had a rather brusque style. Gorham recalled how on one occasion Gerstner was exceedingly curt with an attorney who asked a question in a Sunday School class. It appears that throughout his career Gerstner could be frank with those he considered unwise or misguided. Suzanne Moody, an Eastminster member, recalled "learning a lot about Reformed theology" from Gerstner.[52] Another member of the church, Richard Todd, who served as a professor of history at Wichita State University, observed that Gerstner was a "very astute scholar, amenable, but also very opinionated."[53] Todd and Gerstner became friends, and the historian appreciated Gerstner's "straightforward" lecturing style. In 1993 a small segment of the church left to form a Presbyterian Church in America congregation. The new church, Heartland Community Church, "was deeply influenced by Gerstner's Reformed teaching" and formed because of concerns over "liberal theology in the PCUSA."[54] "Gerstner and Sproul both had an impact on many of the original founders of Heartland," Gary Gensch remembers.[55] Gerstner's evidentialist apologetic approach was also implemented at a large nondenominational Wichita congregation, Central Christian Church.[56] Eastminister remained, partially under the influence of Howard, a strong evangelical PCUSA church until the summer of 2012 when it moved to join the EPC because of what it considered the PCUSA's lack of scriptural teaching in regard to human sexuality.[57] In retrospect, Gerstner appears to have exerted a lasting influence on the congregation he served intermittently until 1989. He did this through his teaching and the many friendships he formed. According to Howard, Gerstner "had a strong personal influence on his life."[58] Later, Howard served as a board member and chair of the Pres-

52. Moody, Interview with the author.

53. Todd, Interview with the author. Todd received his ThB from Biola College, a BA from Sacramento State College, a BD from Fuller Seminary, and a PhD from the University of California at Berkeley. Todd served as a history professor at Wichita State University from 1963 to 1996. His speciality was the study of ancient history.

54. Franks, Interview with the author.

55. Gensch, Interview with the author.

56. Ibid..

57. On Easterminster's concerns, see Calovich, "Eastminster Church Decides to Break From Denomination."

58. Howard, Interview with the author.

byterian Lay Committee, a key renewal organization within the UPCUSA (later PCUSA).

After his involvement in the Kaseman case, Gerstner's participation in UPCUSA politics waned. Nevertheless, he continued to analyze the UPCU-SA, which by 1983 had merged with the southern Presbyterian Church U.S. to form the Presbyterian Church U.S.A. (PCUSA). Following the Kaseman episode, Gerstner focused his energies on lecturing, part-time teaching, and writing. One way that Gerstner's ideas continued to reach a wide audience was his relationship with Sproul's Ligonier Ministries. Jack Rowley, who served on the Ligonier staff, remembers "producing lots of Gerstner audio tapes" which were then distributed.[59] Gerstner's work became widely known to many people involved with the Ligonier Valley Study Center, where he continued to serve as professor-at-large. Gerstner affectionately referred to this group of individuals as the "Friends of the Gerstner Project." He was receiving encouragement from these laypeople and colleagues. In a November 1982 letter to supporters, Gerstner noted that he had been writing primers on various theological topics, was co-writing a massive book on apologetics, and writing "A History and Theology of Dispensationalism which will run in the neighborhood of 400 pages."[60] Gerstner wanted to shape evangelical attitudes towards dispensationalism. He also mentioned in his letter that he had not totally neglected his work on "what should be my magnum opus, Jonathan Edwards's Theology." Gerstner praised his group of followers by saying that "your support, prayers, and encouragement have enabled me to do this [his writing] at least twice as fast and competently."[61] In a letter, his former student Jim Dennison responded, saying that he was "[h]appy to hear of your progress on the Jonathan Edwards [book]." "It will be a joy to have it in print when complete," Dennison enthused.[62] Throughout the 1980s Gerstner continued to write and lecture and hoped to produce several significant books which would expand his influence.

In the 1980s Gerstner continued the inerrancy battle that he had helped launch in the 1970s. The fight for scriptural inerrancy had been the impetus for the influential Chicago Statement on Inerrancy (1978), which had been signed by over two hundred evangelical leaders.[63] Many conservative Protestants were intensifying their hold on inerrancy and

59. Rowley, Interview with the author.

60. Gerstner to Friends of the Gerstner Project. This topic will be addressed later in chapter 7.

61. Ibid.

62. Dennsion, Letter to Gerstner.

63. Geisler and William C. Roach, *Defending Inerrancy*, 22–23.

even two large denominations, the Lutheran Church-Missouri Synod and the Southern Baptist Convention, adopted firm stances on the doctrine.[64] Indeed, Gerstner had helped create the push for inerrancy and he did not relent in arguing for it. In 1982 Gerstner contributed the essay "A Protestant View of Biblical Authority" to a volume that explored Jewish, Roman Catholic, and Protestant perspectives on Scripture.[65] This essay, which was originally presented as a lecture at the University of Denver, argued that the classical Protestant doctrine of the Bible is that "[t]he Bible is the Word of God." He added that "the precise character of the authority of the Bible in the classic Protestant tradition can be stated in one word—inerrant."[66] Gerstner pointed to the Lutheran Formula of Concord, the French Confession of Faith, and the Thirty-Nine Articles of the Church of England to make his case. He also addressed modern Protestant deviations from inerrancy and noted the admission of Kirsopp Lake (1872–1946), a liberal New Testament scholar, that "[t]he Bible and the *corpus theologicum* of the Church is on the Fundamentalist side."[67] Gerstner complained that Protestant non-inerrantists were trying to "bring history into line with themselves." He countered their historical arguments by noting that "[i]f one were not knowledgeable, one could well imagine that inerrancy was unheard of until it was bruited abroad in the backwoods of America a century or so ago."[68] He also sought to answer objections to his position. The historian attempted to counter the argument of circularity by explaining the proper steps necessary to believe in the Bible's inerrancy.[69] For him the Bible was the inerrant Word of God because of Jesus' testimony, the witness of Scripture, the proposition that the Bible cannot err, and because inerrancy was the position of the historic Christian church.

64. Bebbington, *Baptists Through the Centuries*, 261–64; Noll, *The Old Religion in the New World*, 244–55.

65. Greenspahn, ed., *Scripture in the Jewish and Christian Traditions*.

66. Gerstner, "A Protestant View of Biblical Authority," 44.

67. Lake quoted by ibid. 46.

68. Ibid.

69. Ibid., 57–58. Gerstner's five steps are as follows: "1. The Gospels, not assumed to be inspired, are generally recognized as highly reliable sources. 2. From these sources, even allowing for errors and discrepancies, the picture of a miracle-working Christ emerges. 3. Miracles can be performed only by God. As Nicodemus observes: 'Rabbi, we know that thou art a teacher come from God: for no man can do these miracles that thou doest, except God be with him' (John 3:2 KJV). 4. Thus to use John Locke's expression, Christ's 'credit as a proposer' of doctrine is established. 5. It is this Christ who teaches that he is the Son of God and that the Bible is the Word of God."

He also contributed a short six-page response paper in an edited volume titled *Hermeneutics, Inerrancy, and the Bible* (1984). In this essay Gerstner critiqued a paper given by Paul Helm, a Reformed philosopher who served as a senior lecturer at the University of Liverpool. Helm's essay dealt with the role of logic in biblical interpretation. Gerstner agreed with Helm on how to respond to several arguments against using logic in understanding the Bible. Gerstner disagreed, however, with Helm's position that scripture is not dogma. "Logical interpretation does not make the Scripture dogmatic, it only shows what the dogmas are," Gerstner maintained; the Bible "asserts facts, principles, tenets, [and] systems." Gerstner's firm position that scripture was dogmatic and authoritative in nature made him unwilling to yield to alternative viewpoints. He noted that he felt "certain" Helm would agree with his position, but that he does not show it "by his words here."[70] Helm's essay, according to Gerstner, was only "slightly short of absolute perfection."[71] Gerstner's doctrinal position appears to have been very similar to Helm's theology because they agreed on the place of reason in relation to revelation.

In the 1980s Gerstner also kept trying to advance his apologetic position. His essays and articles paled in comparison to his *Classical Apologetics*, which was published in 1984.[72] This 356-page work was co-written with two of Gerstner's former students, R.C. Sproul and Arthur Lindsley.[73] Lindsley was a graduate of PTS and held a PhD from the University of Pittsburgh. He served as director of educational ministries at LVSC and the book was a product of Ligonier. *Classical Apologetics* was written to counteract secular ideology together with liberal and neo-orthodox theologies in mainline Protestantism. It also reacted against the presuppositional apologetics of Cornelius Van Til, as we have seen, which were influential in many conservative Presbyterian circles.[74] The book was organized in three sections. The first section dealt with issues surrounding natural theology. In the sec-

70. Gerstner, "A Response to the Role of Logic in Biblical Interpretation," 874.

71. Ibid., 873.

72. Sproul et al., *Classical Apologetics*. Sociologist James Davidson Hunter noted in his *American Evangelicalism* that Reformed-Confessional tradition is the most rational of the evangelical traditions. See his *American Evangelicalism*, 8.

73. Lindsley received his BS from Seattle Pacific University, his MDiv from Pittsburgh Theological Seminary, and his PhD from the University of Pittsburgh. Lindsley has served as the Director of Educational Ministries at the Ligonier Valley Study Center, Staff Specialist with the Coalition for Christian Outreach, President and Senior Fellow of the C. S. Lewis Institute, and as Vice President of the Institute for Faith, Work, & Economics.

74. On this point, see chapter 4.

ond section the authors dealt with theistic proofs, the deity of Christ and the infallibility of Scripture. The final section of the book was devoted to analyzing and refuting Van Til's presuppositonal apologetics, which, its authors held, downplayed reason. They asserted that "Christianity is rational." Nonetheless, they argued that "because it [Christianity] provokes passion, devotion, prayer, worship, and aspirations to obedience, its purely rational element can easily be submerged or concealed from view."[75] *Classical Apologetics* emerged in an intellectual and ecclesiastical context that appeared to spurn rational apologetic systems.

One of the strengths of the book was its interaction with various thinkers and schools of thought. Even though the volume had some technical language, it aimed to help both Christian scholars and lay people. Throughout the book the authors criticized what they described as "no-defense Christianity" or a "no-reasoned defense for Christianity." Dismissing fideism, they argued that "[a]pologetics, the reasoned defense of the Christian religion, is the job of every Christian . . . ."[76] "Apologetics acts as a bulwark against unbridled antitheistic ideologies and their cultural impact," Gerstner and his co-authors maintained. In their view, "secularism has called the enterprise [of traditional apologetics] into question." But they insisted that "[t]raditional apologetics is far from dead." *Classical Apologetics* was written to "define positively what apologetics is and what role it should have in the church."[77] Their classical apologetic method began by attempting to demonstrate the truth of theism based upon assumptions unbelievers hold in common with believers. The next logical step was to establish the truth of Christian theism from the historical evidence. Reason was an integral aspect of the two apologetic steps. They described their apologetic as "classical traditionalism (evidentialism)," and they sought to analyze and compare their method with Cornelius Van Til's "presuppositionalism."[78]

Van Til, longtime professor of apologetics at Westminster Theological Seminary, had developed his apologetic system as an effort to reject both liberal theology and conservative evidentialist apologetics. Van Til believed that the only way to find truth was not through rational argument, but by presupposing God and the truthfulness of Christianity.[79] Van Til had been strongly influenced by Herman Bavinck, a Dutch Reformed theologian.[80]

75. Sproul et al., *Classical Apologetics*, ix.

76. Ibid., 16.

77. Ibid., 12.

78. Ibid., 183.

79. Frame, "Cornelius Van Til," 163.

80. Muether, *Cornelius Van Til*, 115. On Bavinck's life and thought, see Gleason,

Bavinck's contribution to Van Til's thinking led him to offer a different apologetic approach from the old Princeton apologetic, which he regarded as too rational and not adequately biblical or Reformed. Gerstner's work in *Classical Apologetics* was a sign that some evangelical Presbyterians, while they appreciated Van Til's orthodoxy, still had lingering concerns over his apologetic method. In *Classical Apologetics* the Ligonier apologists argued that presuppositionalism was too innovative and was "virtually unheard of for eighteen centuries."[81] In addition, Gerstner and his co-authors asked "[i]f we presuppose rather than prove, have we not abandoned apologetics rather than performed it?"[82] They added "[p]resuppositionalism tends to avoid all the problems by a simple arbitrary presupposition of God."[83] The Ligonier apologists believed that "presuppositionalism is not only a departure from classical Reformed Christianity," but that it also delivers a "fatal blow to apologetics."[84] Apologetic differences within the conservative Reformed community were made apparent in *Classical Apologetics* and Gerstner was seeking to draw sharp contrasts.

In *Classical Apologetics,* Gerstner and his fellow writers also highlighted their differences with other key evangelical theologians. They briefly analyzed Carl F. H. Henry's thought in light of Van Til's apologetic. By the 1980s Henry, an American Baptist theologian, had become one of evangelicalism's top theological voices.[85] A sign of Henry's stature is seen in a 1983 biography of Henry that was published by Bob Patterson, a Baylor University theologian, in the Word Books Makers of the Modern Theological Mind series.[86] Through his prodigious writings and six-volume systematic theology—*God, Revelation and Authority* (1976–1983)—Henry was a force to be reckoned with.[87] Henry, like the writers of *Classical Apologetics*, was not enamored with Van Til's approach. The Baptist theologian criticized presuppositionalism, arguing that it "exaggerates the noetic consequences of the fall of man."[88] Apparently this meant that Henry thought that Van Til was too negative towards the role of reason in terms of sin corrupting the human mind. The Ligonier apologists noted that "[Gordon] Clark [a Presbyte-

---

Herman Bavinck.

81. Sproul et al., *Classical Apologetics*, 188.

82. Ibid.

83. Ibid., 326.

84. Ibid., 188.

85. Purdy, "Carl F. H. Henry," 260–75.

86. Patterson, *Carl F. H. Henry.*

87. Henry, *God, Revelation and Authority.*

88. Henry quoted by Sproul et al., *Classical Apologetics*, 337.

rian philosopher] and Henry have always been much more appreciative of the role of reason in the unregenerate." Nevertheless, they maintained that Henry's and Clark's position "reduces to fideism."[89] The Western Pennsylvania apologists argued that in Henry's mind " [r]eason is the 'instrument' which recognizes, organizes, and elucidates" but "does not *verify* revelation; and revelation is the source of all truth and its own 'verifying principle.'"[90] In other words, Henry held a high view of reason, but believed it did not have a role in validating the trustworthiness of scripture. The Ligonier trio clearly saw Henry as a theologian who ultimately fell within the presuppositionalist camp.

In a review David K. Clark, a theology professor at Tocco Falls College (Georgia), observed that the apologetic method shown in *Classical Apologetics* "differs significantly from an evidentialist approach, which moves directly to the establishment of Christianity on the common ground of historical data."[91] Clark's evaluation was shrewd because he recognized the difference between an evidentialism that involved steps (Gerstner's position) and an evidentialism that sought a more immediate provability of the faith. The Toccoa Falls professor pointed out the "generally convincing" and extensive argument the authors made about the "common-ground question." Apparently, this discussion was the reason why Clark did not consider Gerstner and his fellow authors to be bald rationalists. He argued that they began their apologetic method with what "essentially" was an "transcendental argument" on shared assumptions and then moved to the evidence. George Zemek Jr., a Grace Theological Seminary (Indiana) theologian, noted that Sproul, Gerstner, and Lindsley "certainly cannot be charged with ambivalence, but they frequently may be perceived by the reader as being arrogantly dogmatic."[92] Zemek found the authors to be too critical of other theologians with whom they disagreed, especially Van Til. Despite the fact the authors dedicated the book to Van Til and wrote favorably about him at several points, they argued that "the implications of presuppositionalism, in our opinion, undermine the Christian religion implicitly."[93] A Reformed apologist, who was a disciple of Van Til, Greg Bahnsen, found this criticism to be "quite harsh." Overall, Bahnsen censured the book as an "uncharitable and false representation" that failed to "interact meaningfully with

89. Sproul et al., *Classical Apologetics*, 337.
90. Ibid., 338.
91. Clark, Review of *Classical Apologetics*, 326.
92. Zemek Jr., Review of *Classical Apologetics*, 111.
93. Sproul et al., *Classical Apologetics*, 184.

presuppositionalism."[94] According to Bahnsen, the authors "have simply not taken the time to understand correctly what they have chosen to criticize." *Classical Apologetics* was revealing the tensions and apologetic differences within the conservative Reformed community of its time. In another review, John Frame, Reformed theologian and Van Til proponent, argued that Gerstner's "intense interest" and "scholary care" could "not be matched . . . by other critics of Van Til."[95] He noted, "[t]his book [*Classcial Apologetics*] is one of the most extensive critiques of Van Til to date, and I think of all the critiques of Van Til this one shows the most thorough research and the most accurate interpretation." Frame labelled *Classical Apologetics* as the "Ligonier Apologetic." In his review he held that the book "is rationalistic with a vengeance" and that the authors make "Fideism . . . the great enemy." Frame, however, believed that starting apologetic arguments with reason was as problematic as beginning with one's own personhood. He noted, "[b]ut just as 'starting with the self' leaves open the question of what criterion of truth the person should acknowledge, so 'starting with reason' leaves open the question of what criterion of truth human reason ought to recognize."[96] The problem, as Frame saw it, was that reason can operate "according to a number of different principles: different systems of logic, different philosophical schemes, different religious commitments."[97] Frame maintained that the Ligonier apologists did not deal adequately enough with how reason relates to principles that differ from reason. Frame argued that it is here that Van Til's presuppositionalism enters into the discussion and "demands that God's voice be heard in the selection of rational principles." "Reason" Frame wrote "is always involved in the human search for knowledge; but reason must always choose its standards, and that choice is fundamentally a religious one."[98] Rather than denying the intellect or playing down reason, what Van Til was doing, according to Frame, was supporting "a reasoning process which recognizes God's standards as supreme."[99]

On the whole, Frame found various points of agreement between Van Til and the Ligonier Apologists, but some other areas of disagreement. Frame noted the "chief difference is in the evaluation of autonomy." Apparently this meant that the Ligonier apologists relied more on reason, whereas presuppositionalists were more interested in showing how certain *a priori*

---

94. Bahnsen, "A Critique of Classical Apologetics."
95. Frame, "Van Til and the Ligonier Apologetic," 279–80.
96. Ibid., 285–86.
97. Ibid., 286.
98. Ibid.
99. Ibid.

commitments shaped beliefs. Yet he also noted that there "is much similarity in regard to general revelation and the noetic effects of sin." Frame, who was a key advocate of Van Til's apologetics, wrote that "there is plenty of room for mutual support and encouragement" between the two parties. Gerstner's long time opposition to Van Til's apologetic reveals the lasting continuity between the thought of John Orr and his protégé. The lack of change in Gerstner's mind reveals how powerful an influence Orr still exerted over Gerstner. Neither Cornelius Van Til nor Markus Barth could dissuade him from his apologetic perspective. Throughout his career he was exposed to a diverse range of theological perspectives, but he never jettisoned his earlier beliefs. Perhaps the best explanation for this constancy in his apologetic position can be traced to the changing attitudes towards Scripture that he witnessed over a forty-five year period in the mainline Presbyterian church. From his perspective neo-orthodoxy and liberal theologies were guilty of loosening the church's confessional commitment and led to the type of doctrinal chaos exhibited in the Kaseman episode.

It is obvious that the theologians of Old Princeton had a persistent influence on Gerstner's thought. This can be clearly detected in a 1984 essay he wrote, entitled "The Contributions of Charles Hodge, B. B. Warfield, and J. Gresham Machen to the Doctrine of Inspiration."[100] This essay appeared in an edited volume entitled *Challenges to Inerrancy*. The series editor wrote "[t]his book is part of a series of scholarly works sponsored by the International Council on Biblical Inerrancy."[101] Far from being merely dead theologians of the past, the Old Princeton theologians, as Gerstner saw them, spoke to the present, especially on issues relating to the inspiration of Scripture. Together, Gerstner argued, this group of Presbyterian theologians gave an "exceptional defense of inspired Scripture." Interestingly, in the beginning of his essay, the recently retired Pittsburgh Seminary church historian took direct aim at what he labeled the "New Princeton" scholars. Gerstner noted how "the modern Princeton faculty seems to find nothing more entertaining than the claim of old Princeton that no new ideas originated there."[102] He held that "[t]he current mockers, who are usually waiting to hear something new in Jerusalem, seem not have noticed that the most

---

100. Gerstner, "The Contributions of Charles Hodge, B. B. Warfield, and J. Gresham Machen to the Doctrine of Inspiration." Gerstner had previously written on Warfield in an essay titled "Warfield's Case for Biblical Inerrancy," 115–42.

101. Geisler, *Challenges to Inerrancy*, vii.

102. Gerstner, "The Contributions of Charles Hodge, B. B. Warfield, and J. Gresham Machen to the Doctrine of Inspiration," 347–48.

original stance today is the Old Princeton effort not to be original at all." Gerstner argued "[f]idelity to tradition is the novelty of our times."[103]

Old Princeton, according to Gerstner, was "ridiculed for that in which it gloried—its absolute lack of novelty in bibliology."[104] For Gerstner, who believed that inerrancy was the historic position of the Christian Church down through the ages, Hodge, Warfield, Machen, and other inerrantists were in the mainstream of the Christian tradition for holding to their conservative understanding of the Bible. From his viewpoint they were simply seeking to maintain theological continuity with the past. Gerstner added,

> [m]y feeling is that the institutional successors of Hodge-Warfield-Machen are even more rigidly opposed to the entrance of new (old that is) ideas than the Old Princetonians ever were. They stand as inflexibly for new errors concerning the Bible as the Warfieldians did for old truth—especially for the old truth of the inerrancy of holy scripture.[105]

Perhaps Gerstner was thinking here of his earlier battles with Edward Dowey, the Princeton theologian, who clearly had an aversion to the Westminster Confession of Faith and the theology espoused by Old Princeton. Gerstner's comments indicate that he saw his battles as being tied to the controversies surrounding old Princeton. Gerstner argued,

> The enemy of inerrancy had leveled Princeton (where there is not now a sole inerrantist survivor) and many other saints. Now the great counterattack has begun in the "The Battle for the Battle." The International Council for Biblical Inerrancy is the spearhead of the drive in which the Evangelical Theological Society and other movements and individuals are actively engaged. Almost all of those sense the need to go back to Warfield if they would then advance forward to meet today's needs.[106]

This passage gives evidence that Gerstner saw the struggles he was involved in as an extension of the earlier conflicts. He encouraged others to go back and embrace Old Princeton. "Revisiting Old Princeton," he held, is "taking one step backward in order to move two steps forward."

In his essay Gerstner promoted Hodge, Warfield, and Machen, saying "together they have raised a magnificent monument to the Word of

103. Ibid., 348.
104. Ibid., 347.
105. Ibid., 348.
106. Ibid.

God," and "[t]heir achievement was essentially a herculean" task.[107] Hodge, in Gerstner's mind, offered an "impressive" "defense of the infallibility of Scripture."[108] He noted,

> Lacking the profundity of an earlier Edwards and the preci-
> sion of a later Warfield, Hodge may well have been the ablest
> proponent of the historic, orthodox doctrine between those
> two giants. He took the torch from Edwards and though it was
> burning less brightly when he handed it on to Warfield it was
> still shining.[109]

Conspicuously absent from his analysis was any discussion of the New England theologians. Gerstner was attempting, as he did throughout his career, to connect Edwards to the Old Princeton tradition. He still held, as he had in 1957, that the New England theologians's modification of Edwards's theology resulted in a "matured liberalism," which cut itself off from Edwards legacy.[110] While this argument has merit because of the leftward drift in New England theology, it did not necessarily follow that Old Princeton was the heir of Edwards's robust theology. Gerstner's historical analysis was strained. The implication of his position was that it seemed to be more based on theological similarities than on any direct or genetic intellectual connection.

In Gerstner's analysis of Warfield he concluded that "[t]hough somewhat garbled, his [Warfield's] evidentialism met and survived the onslaughts of Kantianism, Darwinism, and Romanticism." Gerstner believed that Warfield was even more talented than Hodge. He noted Warfield's emphasis on the "supernatural" and his position that "miracles serv[ed] as facts from which revelation was inferred" rather than vice versa. According to Gerstner, "Warfield (and he interpreted the Westminster divine as the same mind of himself) argued the Bible offered *proofs of a person*, the divine Christ."[111] Warfield's evidentialism was rooted in the belief that scriptural miracles and citations were "proof of the confessional witness to Christ as divine and actually true."[112] While the focus of Gerstner's study was on Warfield's defence

---

107. Ibid., 347.

108. Ibid., 358.

109. Ibid.

110. Gerstner, "American Calvinism Until the Twentieth Century—Especially in New England," 35.

111. Gerstner, "The Contributions of Charles Hodge, B. B. Warfield, and J. Gresham Machen to the Doctrine of Inspiration," 365.

112. Ibid.

of inerrancy, it is clear that Warfield offered an evidentialist approach which Gerstner claimed avoided strict rationalism and mysticism.

Gerstner also analyzed Machen's apologetic perspective and work on the inspiration of scripture. He agreed strongly with Machen's defence of the Bible and the four steps in Machen's apologetic that Gerstner outlined. He noted that many scholars admired the cogency of Machen's arguments including Henry J. Cadbury (1883–1974), one of his Harvard professors. His Harvard professor's esteem for Machen's scholarship buttressed Gerstner's position that the scholarly views of Machen and Old Princeton were still intellectually viable. It may seem strange, but the evidence is clear that Harvard has actually been at different times a minor conduit for Machen's ideas.[113] One of the most perceptive and revealing contentions made by Gerstner dealt with criticism Machen faced from Lefferts Loetscher (1984–1981), a Princeton Seminary church historian, and James Barr (1924–2006), a British Bible scholar. "Machen is guilty they charge" Gerstner notes, "not only of a lack of charity . . . but to a lack of logic." Specifically, they claimed, Machen had committed the syllogistic sin of the "undistributed middle." According to Loetscher, Machen was wrong because he defined liberalism "in terms of the most radical, naturalistic implications."[114] Gerstner argued that Loetscher's charge carried no weight because he had "not given one instance in which Machen applies the term to a person who is not essentially naturalistic." He added that in his own *Theology of the Major Sects* "I discuss liberalism as a sect only after carefully defining it, as Machen did."[115] For Gerstner, Machen was not a reckless critic, but rather a careful scholar, whose views were even found sensible at Harvard.

Gerstner appeared to have a relatively high view of Harvard. The church historian apparently reasoned that if Harvard treated Machen's work

113. George Eldon Ladd, another evangelical student at Harvard in the 1940s, noted that it was at Harvard that he read Machen and wanted to imitate Machen's scholarship. Specifically, Ladd wanted to produce evangelical scholarship like Machen's that would be read in non-evangelical institutions. On this point, see D'Elia, *A Place at the Table*, 133, 220. It is also significant that Darryl G. Hart, the leading biographer of Machen, came to admire the Presbyterian scholar after reading his work in an early 1980s Harvard Divinity School class taught by William G. McLoughlin (1922–1992), the Brown University religious historian. Even though Hart had earned a degree from Westminster Seminary, it was not until he studied at Harvard that he read Machen's *Christianity and Liberalism* (1923) and recognized his brilliance and importance. On this point see Hart, "Defending the Faith."

114. Loetscher quoted by Gerstner, "The Contributions of Charles Hodge, B. B. Warfield, and J. Gresham Machen to the Doctrine of Inspiration," 379.

115. Gerstner, "The Contributions of Charles Hodge, B. B. Warfield, and J. Gresham Machen to the Doctrine of Inspiration," 380.

with respect, then it must be worthy of it. There were obvious theological differences between Gerstner and his Harvard professors and yet he seems to have respected their intellectual authority and the fair-mindedness they showed toward him and Machen. It is not surprising that Harvard influenced Gerstner's mind and that he would sometimes refer to his Harvard professors in order to strengthen his own position. His identity as a scholar had been greatly helped by his association with the school and he would not hesitate to make his connection to the famous academic institution known.

From Gerstner's perspective, the rightness of Machen's criticism of modernist theology was still vindicated by his old mentor John Orr, who had painstakingly traced the history of English deism and its relation to twentieth-century Protestant modernism. In 1987 Gerstner argued that "[Jonathan] Edwards not only justified the enlightened character of the orthodox position, but proceeded to demonstrate the unreasonableness of the deistic stance."[116] Theological modernism was not entertained by Gerstner's mind because he viewed it as a direct fruit of eighteenth-century deism, which he rejected. Gerstner agreed wholeheartedly with John Orr's statement that "[t]here is certainly enough in common between eighteenth century deism and twentieth century Modernism to indicate that the latter is in a large measure a continuation of or fruit of the former."[117] Machen's scholarly protests were well grounded in Gerstner's mind because the Old School Princetonian seemed to be attacking the theological offspring of deism.

Gerstner continued to teach at a school which had great respect for Old Princeton, Trinity Evangelical Divinity School. He taught at this institution at various times past his retirement at PTS. John Armstrong, who studied with Gerstner at TEDS in the early 1980s, found him to be a "master teacher." Yet he also remembers that Gerstner "blew up in class" on one occasion, labeling one student a "stubborn Arminian."[118] Armstrong developed a friendship with Gerstner and came to view Gerstner "as the main influence on the renewal of Reformed Theology in modern evangelicalism." Another TEDS student from the early 1980s, John Hoop, on the other hand, found Gerstner to be a "scary" and "intimidating" teacher.[119] He claimed

116. Gerstner, *Jonathan Edwards*, 18.

117. Orr, *English Deism*, 258.

118. Armstrong, Interview with the author, December 29, 2010. Armstrong received his BA and MA degrees from Wheaton College and a DMin degree from Luther Rice Seminary. He served as a pastor and in the 1990s became an evangelical leader and president of ACT 3 Ministries.

119. Hoop, Interview with the author. Hoop earned his BA from Miami University and a MDiv and MA from TEDS.

"Students would want to be prepared for Gerstner's classes." Hoop had observed that Gerstner's "reasoning was very tight" and that he took clear positions. Yet he also noted that Gerstner "filled the chalk board" in order to analyze and understand theological differences. Gerstner spent considerable time researching, studying, and expounding theological positions he did not necessarily hold. Sometimes Gerstner would defend views he did not agree with in order to increase participation. He wanted his students to be able to articulate the differing viewpoints. Gerstner continued his part-time teaching at TEDS until the winter of 1986.[120] He also taught some modular courses at Geneva College in the fall of 1986 and 1987.[121] Gerstner was busy working well past retirement.

Throughout the 1980s Gerstner continued to lecture and speak. In 1980 he gave the Jubilee Lecture at Westminster Theological Seminary and spoke on the topic of biblical authority at the University of Denver (Colorado). In 1981 he gave the commencement address at the Reformed Presbyterian Theological Seminary in Pittsburgh. Throughout the decade he spoke several times at the Philadelphia Conference on Reformed Theology. Darryl G. Hart attended one of the conferences and remembers Gerstner's "precision of thought" and "capacity to argue clearly."[122] Later, in 1983, he gave the Spring Lectures at Western Baptist Seminary in Portland, Oregon, and in 1986 he delivered lectures on virtue at Covenant Seminary in St Louis.[123] Moreover, in October 1987 Gerstner helped Sterling College in Kansas celebrate its one-hundredth anniversary by preaching the sermon at the Sterling Founder's Day Celebration Service.[124] The following month he delivered the Thornwell lectures at First Presbyterian Church in Columbia, South Carolina, on the topic of "The Bible: The Word of Life."[125] He also spoke at the Johnstown Reformed Conference in 1989 on the topic of "The

120. McDonald, Interview with White—TEDS assistant registrar, January 20, 2013.

121. Geneva College Course Flier, "Dispensationalism," 1986; Geneva College Course Flier, "Jonathan Edwards: Model for Renewal and Reformation in Church and Nation," 1987, Gerstner Papers, Chandler, Arizona.

122. Hart, Interview with the author, November 15, 2011. Hart claims that Gerstner had an "indirect influence on me through the Philadelphia Conference on Reformed Thought." Hart later become known for his biography of Machen entitled *Defending the Faith*. Hart received his BA from Temple University, his MAR from WTS, an MTS from Harvard University, and a MA and PhD from Johns Hopkins University.

123. Gerstner lists these lectures in his *Jonathan Edwards*, 10.

124. Bulletin, Founder's Day Celebration Service.

125. Bulletin, First Presbyterian Church Thornwell Lectureship.

Bible As the Word of God." Gerstner's was spreading his views across the country and in a variety of denominational and institutional settings.

In 1989 Gerstner also gave some additional lectures on the topic of hell at Sterling College. These lectures sparked some controversy. Thomas G. Reid, a Reformed Presbyterian pastor who attended the lectures, recalled Gerstner "combating differing views on hell" in a "very forthright manner."[126] Apparently, Gerstner was troubled by the perspective that John R. W. Stott (1921–2011) offered in a 1988 book entitled *Evangelical Essentials* (1988).[127] Stott, a prominent English evangelical leader, argued that hell was not a place of eternal physical punishment, but rather an eternal non-existence.[128] A minor controversy developed within evangelicalism over Stott's views and Gerstner was not afraid to express his alarm over the Englishman's departure from the traditional position.[129] In April 1989 Gerstner lectured at a "Reasons for Faith Seminar" at Coral Ridge Presbyterian Church in Ft Lauderdale, Florida.[130] Coral Ridge, under the direction of pastor D. James Kennedy (1930–2007), became a renowned PCA mega church, with 7,801 members by 1989.[131] Significantly, Coral Ridge and Kennedy founded Knox Theological Seminary in 1989, adding to the ever increasing list of evangelical Reformed seminaries. Several months after Gerstner's visit to Coral Ridge, an advertisement for Knox appeared in *Christianity Today* featuring a

126. Reid, Interview with the author, February 20, 2013. Reid earned his BA from Westmont College (California), an MDiv from Westminster Theological Seminary, a MTh from La Faculte de Theologia Reformee (France), an M.S. University of Pittsburgh and a DipTh Reformed Presbyterian Theological Hall (Northern Ireland). He has served as a pastor at Creevagh Reformed Presbyterian Church in Ballybay, Ireland, Quinter Reformed Presbyterian Church in Quinter, Kansas and at Presbyterian Reformed Church in Edmonton, Canada. Since 1996 he has served as librarian at the Reformed Presbyterian Theological Seminary in Pittsburgh, Pennsylvania.

127. Edwards and Stott, *Evangelical Essentials*.

128. This view had a long history in England. See Rowell, *Hell and the Victorians*, chapter IX.

129. Chapman has highlighted the controversy surrounding Stott's views in his biography of the Anglican clergyman—*Godly Ambition*, 145. In 1990 Gerstner published his criticisms of Stott in *Repent and Perish*, 57–64.

130. "Reasons for Faith Seminar," Coral Ridge Presbyterian Church.

131. This membership information was provided to me in an email from Alan Wibbels, Knox Seminary librarian, and Mariana Caro, Coral Ridge Executive office assistant. On D. James Kennedy's career see Davis, *The Truth That Transformed Me*. Kennedy earned his BA from the University of Tampa, his BD from Columbia Seminary (Georgia), a ThM from the Chicago Graduate School of Theology and a PhD from New York University. He served as pastor of Coral Ridge Presbyterian Church from 1960 to 2007.

portrait of Gerstner who would serve briefly as an adjunct professor of theology, thus expanding his ties to another evangelical Reformed institution.

Gerstner also maintained a relationship with the seminary he had attended, Westminister Theological Seminary (WTS). Samuel Logan, who served as a WTS church historian during this period, held that "Westminster was rigorously Van Tilian, but Gerstner still supported the seminary."[132] Logan argues:

> I would compare Dr. Gerstner's influence on the evangelical and Reformed scholarly world much as I would describe Perry Miller's influence on the secular scholarly world—even though most scholars, both evangelical and secular, now reject many of the details of Miller's analysis of American Puritanism, no one can question that it was his work in this field that led to the explosion of interest in early American intellectual history.[133]

Gerstner, who had some connections to Miller, created enthusiasm for Edwards and Reformed theology in the world of evangelicalism through his wide lecturing and contacts with numerous scholars, churches and academic institutions. His involvement with Westminster shows that he was willing to cooperate with scholars and institutions that did not necessarily hold to his apologetic views. While Gerstner was highly critical of presuppositionalism in print he did try, at some level, to work with those whom he disagreed.

Gerstner also continued to promote Edwards. During the early 1980s, Don Kistler, a college football coach, became interested in Ligonier Ministries because of advertisements he had seen in *Moody Monthly* and *Christianity Today* about R. C. Sproul. The brawny defensive coordinator, who had a growing interest in theology, soon ordered tapes of Sproul lectures, listened to them and was impressed. He continued to purchase more and more tapes, exposing himself to a conservative brand of Reformed theology. Soon Kistler, who had coached at Azusa Pacific, Central Methodist, and Wheaton, decided he needed to leave coaching and pursue study at the Ligonier Valley Study Center.[134] Shorty after arriving at Ligonier, Kistler was encouraged by

---

132. Logan, Interview with the author. Logan received his BA from Princeton University, his MDiv from Westminster Seminary, and his PhD from Emory University. From 1970 to 1979 he served as professor of history at Barrington College (Rhode Island). Later, he served as professor of church history at Westminster from 1979 to 2007. He was president of WTS from 1991 to 2007. In 2007 he became special assistant to the president and professor of church history at Biblical Seminary (Pennsylvania).

133. Logan, email correspondence to the author.

134. Kistler, Interview with the author.

the center's staff to study privately under Gerstner. Gerstner accepted the student and immediately instructed him to read the two-volume set of *The Works of Jonathan Edwards*, which were edited by Edward Hickman in 1834 and republished in 1974 by the Banner of Truth Trust. Kistler informed Gerstner that he had already read the volumes. Gerstner fired back, saying "read them again." As a student Kistler was given large doses of Edwards and later commented that "he studied theology by studying Edwards." Kistler, who had originally been a dispensationalist in an American Baptist church, embraced the Reformed faith and recalled being "converted [to Reformed theology] by reading Edwards."[135] From 1984 to 1988 Kistler served as the pastor of Pioneer Presbyterian Church in Ligonier, Pennsylvania, where Gerstner and his wife were members. Pioneer thrived and Kistler excelled in his ministry. Nevertheless, Gerstner encouraged Kistler to become a publisher.[136] According to Kistler, Gerstner told him it would be "sinful for him to stay in the pulpit" and that he should lead the new publishing firm. In 1988 Soli Deo Gloria Publications(SDG) was formed with Kistler as its head. SDG was an imitation and American version of the British Calvinist book house, the Banner of Truth Trust. SDG, like the Banner, specialized in reprinting Puritan and Reformed literature. Gerstner lent his stature to the new venture and served on the advisory board of SDG along with J.I. Packer, Eric Alexander, Roger Nicole, and Jack White. The formation of SDG was another way in which Gerstner hoped to spark interest in Edwards and in the Puritans. SDG became a part of the cottage industry of publishers who were involved in producing books about Edwards or works by him.[137]

In 1987 Gerstner penned a 135-page book which sought to communicate Edwards's theology to laypeople and scholars alike. He stated that his *Jonathan Edwards: A Mini Theology* was "meant to be a harbinger of things to come" as he hinted at the larger and more exhaustive study of Edwards he hoped to finish in the future.[138] His goal was to present Edwards's theology "based on the total corpus of Edwards's writings" in order to "give insights" into the main themes in his theology. Gerstner's first chapter evaluated Edwards's place in the history of Christian thought. The following chapters explored Edwards's views on different theological topics: Reason and Revelation, The Trinity, Man and His Fall, Sin, Atonement, Regeneration, Justification, Sanctification, The Latter Day Glory and Second Coming, Hell,

135. Kistler, Interview with the author.

136. Kistler, Interview with the author.

137. On the growth of interest in Edwards, see Hart, "Before the Young, Restless and Reformed: Edwards's Appeal to Post-World War II Evangelicals."

138. Gerstner, *Jonathan Edwards*, 10.

and lastly Heaven. Throughout the book Gerstner interacts with Edwards's writings and the ways in which Edwards's theology had been interpreted by historians and theologians. Gerstner was particularly bothered by the insistence of Peter Gay, a Yale historian, that Edwards had no place in the Enlightenment because he was committed to biblical faith. Gerstner believed that this criticism was leveled because some "[c]ritics assume that orthodox Christianity is fideistic and nonrational."[139] Gerstner emphasized that Edwards was a "rational" theologian who "could gain insights from contemporary philosophy." Edwards was being misunderstood, according to Gerstner, because scholars had a "misconception of traditional Christian orthodoxy."[140] From his perspective, neither Edwards nor Christianity was the enemy of reason.

In his introductory book on Edwards's theology, Gerstner defended the rational faith of John Locke, insisting that the great English empiricist affirmed "theistic proofs, miracles, the historic Adam, the historic Fall, the divinity of Christ, justification by faith, and many others."[141] "Edwards 'taking orders' from Scripture, therefore," according to Gerstner, "does not prove him not to be Lockean and a child of the Enlightenment in some respects."[142] Gerstner wrote that Perry Miller was "correct in noting that Edwards . . . was not only somewhat Lockean in his approach but that he even extended Locke's ideas to homiletics . . . ."[143] Gerstner tied Edwards to Locke in a effort to show that Edwards was a rational thinker whose thought was not anti-Enlightenment.[144] Enlightenment reason and an affirmation of historic Christian orthodoxy were not mutually exclusive. The belief that Edwards was an Enlightenment figure was a progressive historiographical position in the 1980s. Gerstner also showed that Edwards saw limitations in the use of reason. Using Edwards's own words, he noted that always trying to make faith comprehensible would "tend at last, to make men esteem the science of religion as of no value, and so totally neglect it; and from step to step it will lead to skepticism, atheism, ignorance, and at length to barbarity."[145] Edwards, so Gerstner's argument goes, had a high view of reason, but was aware of its shortcomings. Gerstner notes that "[t]he Calvinistic Edwards finds fallen men quite capable of seeing truth they do not love and therefore

139. Ibid., 14.
140. Ibid.
141. Ibid., 16.
142. Ibid., 16–17.
143. Ibid., 14.
144. Ibid., 15–16.
145. Ibid., 28.

rejecting it even as they formulate it."[146] Edwards emerges from Gerstner's short study as an advocate of reason, but not wholly uncritical of reason and thus never seduced by mere rationalism. Reason was important to Christian faith, but Gerstner argued "it cannot make the knowledge of God 'real' to unregenerate men," or "yield a supernatural, salvific revelation," or necessarily "determine what that revelation may or may not contain" or "even 'apprehend' divine revelation, though it may recognize its presence."[147] Here again, we see Gerstner spurning the charges of his critics and seeking to establish that both he and Edwards could not be called "bald rationalists." Gerstner offered in summary: "[y]et reason is a useful tool for any serious Christian, though the believer recognizes that the human mind must be satisfied with its limitations."[148]

In their review for the *Journal of the Evangelical Theological Society,* John Turner and Jennifer Goetz complained that in "the area of [historical] context we find this book wanting."[149] These reviewers also argued that the "result of insisting that Edwards is a Lockean" leads to "a confused muddle of a chapter." Gerstner, Turner, and Goetz noted, "refreshingly enthusiastic about his subject, is perhaps at times too immersed in Edwards to present his ideas clearly." In another review, Oscar Arnal, a theologian at Waterloo Lutheran Seminary (Ontario), accused Gerstner of using Edwards to "buttress Gerstner's own [theological] agenda."[150] Nonetheless, James Patterson, a historian at Toccoa Falls College (Georgia), praised Gerstner for producing "a systematic assessment of Edwards's theology" which "recent scholarship has failed to produce."[151] Mark Sidwell, writing in *Biblical Viewpoint,* also appreciated a study of Edwards's theology that was accessible to pastor and laypeople. He noted that Gerstner "outlines Edwards's views" in a "brief and comprehensible fashion."[152] Gerstner's presentation of Edwards's theology in popular form helped fuel the continued interest in the colonial theologian.

In a 1983 edited volume, *The Princeton Theology,* Mark Noll, Gerstner's former student who was now a historian at Wheaton College, noted that John Gerstner had "carried on the Old Princeton traditions in one form or another to this very day."[153] From 1980 to 1989 Gerstner continued to

146. Ibid., 27.

147. Ibid.

148. Ibid., 28.

149. Turner and Goetz, Review of *Jonathan Edwards*, 410.

150. Arnal, Review of *Jonathan Edwards*, 94–95.

151. Patterson, Review of *Jonathan Edwards*, 36–37.

152. Sidwell, Review of *Jonathan Edwards*, 104.

153. Noll, ed., *The Princeton Theology, 1812–1921*, 18.

pursue his goal of seeking to bring theological renewal to the UPCUSA and the American church more widely. Even though Gerstner lost the Kaseman case, the controversy that it ignited led to a growing sense of theological concern, especially among evangelicals. The 1981 General Assembly tried to alleviate some of the fallout by affirming an orthodox statement on Christ's divinity and humanity. Yet the divisions that the Kaseman affair produced continued to linger. Never again would Gerstner take such a public role in denominational affairs. His wavering on when to leave, the charge of apostasy and then its retraction left some evangelicals frustrated. The formation of the Evangelical Presbyterian Church and its growth were signs that there were fractures in the UPCUSA that would deepen. Gerstner's experience as theologian-in-residence at Eastminster Presbyterian Church in Wichita, Kansas, was by all accounts enjoyable and his time there allowed him to extend his influence in that noteworthy church. Gerstner's writing continued to focus on the need for an evidentialist apologetic that was unafraid to argue for Christian truth. His zeal to win theological debates and apologetic arguments made him less of a historian and more of a historical theologian with an axe to grind. He stood for unpopular causes and theological systems. Yet he also created enthusiasm for Edwards through his speaking and writing. In the UPCUSA his apologetic position and evangelical stance were marginalized. This was a great loss to a denomination facing an increasingly secular culture. While many Presbyterians would not agree with Gerstner's theology or his apologetic method, he did have the ability to help his hearers grow in their understanding of the Christian faith and the Reformed tradition. In an age of uncertainty his certainty was often reassuring to laypeople and pastors who needed a dose of spiritual and theological confidence. The days of Gerstner's speaking at the New Wilmington Missionary Conferences, lecturing in the halls of Pittsburgh Seminary or debating Ed Dowey or Markus Barth were now over. Nevertheless, Gerstner was able to pursue his vision of Presbyterian and Reformed evangelicalism through his books and other writings. He lived out the reality of his mission through teaching and lecturing with Ligonier Ministries, TEDS, Geneva College, and various other churches and seminaries which invited him to come and share his always fervent messages. His passion, rigidity, opinionated nature, and serious learning were not always appreciated, but they were the marks of his deep Christian conviction. The work of rugged "Black Jack" Gerstner would carry on.

7

Reformed Resurgence
(1990–1996)

JOHN GERSTNER ENTERED THE 1990S IN HIS MID SEVENTIES AND WORN OUT from the ecclesiastical skirmishes he had waged in the previous decade. Even though he had exhibited great patience with the PCUSA and its predecessor for over thirty years, he would no longer wait for the denomination to reform. In the final phase of his life, Gerstner made a clean break from the PCUSA. He thrust all of his energies into supporting the burgeoning world of Presbyterian and Reformed evangelicalism. During the 1990s this movement was continuing to grow and expand. As a visible leader in this evangelical faction, Gerstner wrote and published books that sought to defend conservative Reformed convictions and draw sharp distinctions. His writings during the last six years of his life addressed some controversial topics within evangelicalism, including the doctrine of hell, dispensationalist theology, and understandings of Jonathan Edwards, the famed colonial theologian. He set theological boundary lines within evangelicalism so that it would avoid the doctrinal mistakes he had perceived were present within mainline Protestantism. As he moved forward, he also promoted Edwards' thought and inspired many pastors and lay-people to become interested in the eighteenth-century theologian. During the 1990s Gerstner continued to propel his vision of Presbyterian and Reformed evangelicalism into the future.

Sometime during the early months of 1990, Gerstner decided that he needed to withdraw from the Presbyterian Church USA and join the Presbyterian Church in America (PCA). The PCA had been formed in 1973 as a conservative split off from the southern Presbyterian Church US.[1] On May 5, 1990 the senior church historian appeared before the Presbyterian

1. Freundt Jr., "Presbyterian Church in America," 198–99. See also Lucas, *For a Continuing Church*.

Church in America's Presbytery of the Ascension in order to be examined as a minister. Ascension was a regional presbytery that encompassed Northeast Ohio and Western Pennsylvania and was the first PCA presbytery to be located north of the Mason-Dixon Line.[2] The lone Yankee presbytery in the southern denomination had been founded on July 25, 1975 by ministers who objected to the exclusion of Wynn Kenyon from the ordained ministry of the UPCUSA.[3] Gerstner's desire to affiliate with the Ascension presbytery was a natural fit ecclesiastically and theologically. The presbytery meeting that included Gerstner's ordination examination was held at the Gospel Fellowship Church (PCA) near Butler, Pennsylvania. On June 8, 1990 the *Christian Observer* reported that Gerstner "was enthusiastically received into its [the presbytery's] membership."[4] Gerstner's entrance into the PCA occurred after several years of intense reflection about the PCUSA and his earlier claims of its apostasy. Apparently by the late 1980s Gerstner had become frustrated with the PCUSA. In 1988, Gerstner had begun a study of the PCUSA: he delved into its history and examined connections between its theology and its *Book of Order*.[5] As a result, in 1989 he developed a paper entitled "The Marks of the Church Applied to the PCUSA." In the conclusion of this paper, Gerstner held that the PCUSA had strayed from the traditional marks of a church in terms of word, sacrament, and discipline. He concluded that "the PCUSA is not a true Church," a harsh judgment from someone who had been so fully engaged in the PCUSA since 1958 and before that in the UPCNA.[6]

Gerstner circulated his paper broadly and invited individuals to demonstrate any error they could find. He added the caveat, that if no one could show him by January 1990 where he was wrong, he would leave the PCUSA. According to Gerstner, the only person to offer any "substantive" criticism of his paper's position was ironically Wynn Kenyon, his former student, who had remained a lay member of the PCUSA, but by now was a theology professor at Belhaven College (Mississippi).[7] Kenyon who had been the conservative cause of division was now challenging his mentor to stay

2. Bogue, Interview with the author, April 5, 2014.

3. "Ascension Presbytery (PCA)." See chapter 5 for a discussion of the Wynn Kenyon controversy.

4. Bogue, "Dr. John Gerstner Withdraws from the Presbyterian Church (USA)," 20.

5. Gerstner, Interview with Coffin, 31.

6. Gerstner quoted by Bogue, "Dr. John Gerstner Withdraws from the Presbyterian Church (USA)," 20.

7. Gerstner, Interview with Coffin, 31.

in the denomination. In the end, no one could change his mind. Gerstner decided to leave the PCUSA and join the PCA because, he said, "they were striving for a vigorous, expansionistic, evangelistic, Reformed faith."[8] From 1973 to 1990 the PCA had grown from 61,470 to 224,821 members.[9] Gerstner felt comfortable enough with the PCA to believe that "I might be able to make some contribution to it."[10] Several of Gerstner's former students, including R.C. Sproul and Carl Bogue, had already joined the PCA, and so the new communion offered him familiar faces and likeminded friends. Two months after being ordained in the PCA, in writing to John Frame, a longtime acquaintance, he noted, "[i]t's always a great pleasure" to be in contact with you, "[h]ow much more so on our coming together in the same visible church [the PCA] after so much fellowship in the invisible church."[11] Gerstner's strenuous efforts to renew the PCUSA from within were now concluded. He withdrew, finding new life in the PCA, and would remain a member of that denomination until his death six years later.

In 1991 Bradley Longfield's landmark book *The Presbyterian Controversy* appeared.[12] Longfield's study analyzed the immense ecclesiastical conflict that had taken place in the PCUSA from 1922 to 1936; his purpose was to give some historical explanation for the PCUSA's contemporary "theological fragmentation."[13] He deftly explored the powerful controversy that had effects on American Presbyterianism, the wider Protestant movement, and Gerstner. The historic crisis within the PCUSA had caused antagonism that had persisted. The church in the 1930s adopted a policy of "doctrinal inclusiveness" in order to avoid unceasing conflict, but this policy continued to trouble evangelical Presbyterians. They insisted that the denomination ought to maintain a more exclusive theological identity. Gerstner was one person within mainline Presbyterianism who even into the 1990s was still engaged in the earlier conflict. His *alma mater* Westminster Theological Seminary (WTS) had been formed in 1929 as a direct result of this significant controversy. After abandoning Pitt-Xenia as a student for Westminster Seminary in 1937, Gerstner had personally observed the conclusion and aftermath of the well-known dispute. As a United Presbyterian student, he was not directly involved in the ecclesiastical clash, but his access to observing it offered him a different perspective from that of

8. Gerstner, Interview with Coffin, 31.

9. Presbyterian Church in America Historical Center, Statistical Tables.

10. Gerstner, Interview with Coffin, 31.

11. Gerstner, Letter to Frame.

12. Longfield, *The Presbyterian Controversy*.

13. Ibid., 3.

many other Presbyterians, especially UP pastors and laypeople. On May 27, 1992 Gerstner revisited the famous conflict when he led a commencement symposium on Longfield's book on the campus of Westminster in suburban Philadelphia.[14] Paul C. Kemeny, who at the time was a teaching fellow at Princeton Theological Seminary, was present at the forum as a panelist and remembers Gerstner "getting up and presenting things in black and white, indicating who were the good guys and bad guys" in the historic controversy.[15] Gerstner held firm views about the conflict and it greatly shaped his view of the PCUSA.

Gerstner's theological sympathies were clearly on the side of Machen and those who founded Westminster. Machen may have been ultimately expelled by the PCUSA in June 1936, but Machen's ideas and influence had persisted.[16] In a video lecture, three years prior to the Westminster event, Gerstner said, "Machen is quite right; he shows that what goes by the name of liberalism . . . denies the deity of Christ, denies the supernatural basically."[17] "That book [Machen's *Christianity and Liberalism*] remains a classic," Gerstner noted; "when I was at Harvard for example in the early forties which was an absolute bastion of liberalism they used it, approved it, that was a good solid statement." He added that his Harvard professors, who were largely Unitarian, "did not want to be confused with orthodoxy" and therefore appreciated Machen's sharp distinctions.[18] Progressive Presbyterians, however, were alarmed by Machen's analysis.[19] Gerstner's admiration for Machen and his long-term commitment to Westminster were both confirmed by Gerstner's decision in the 1990s to become a member of the seminary's Western Pennsylvania President's Council—an advisory body. Samuel Logan, the president of WTS, noted that he "met with Dr Gerstner frequently" and appreciated the senior scholar's experience and input.[20]

14. Gerstner and Kemeny, "The Presbyterian Controversy," Fundamentalists, Modernists and Moderates.

15. Kemeny, Interview with the author. Kemeny holds a BA from Wake Forest University, an MA and MDiv from Westminster Theological Seminary, a ThM from Duke University, and a PhD from Princeton Seminary. Kemeny has served as a professor of religion and humanities at Grove City College since 2000.

16. On this point see Hart, "Make War No More?," 37–55; Frame, "Machen's Warrior Children," 113–46; Marsden, *Reforming Fundamentalism*, 31–52; MacLeod, *W. Stanford Reid*.

17. Gerstner, "20th Century: Theological Liberalism," Handout Church History.

18. Ibid.

19. See Longfield's *The Presbyterian Controversy*.

20. Logan, email correspondence with the author.

By the 1990s Gerstner had abandoned any hope of seeing evangelical reform in PCUSA seminaries. His entrance into the PCA gave him a greater sense of freedom and thus he became more openly critical of the mainline Presbyterian seminaries. For instance, in a 1992 interview he argued that the PCUSA seminaries regard the denomination's *Book of Confessions* as "meaningless," and he noted that the confessional "language is just not taken seriously" by most professors and students. His preference for supporting and being involved with Westminster, Knox, and other conservative seminaries stemmed from his opinion that "most of our mainline seminaries are training our youth to go into all the world to undermine the gospel."[21] Despite having taught in mainline Presbyterian seminaries for thirty years, Gerstner was now expressing, in perhaps an exaggerated fashion, his deep dismay at their evolution. In his old age, Gerstner, the new PCA minister, was speaking with less restraint and more bravado. Whatever the case, his somewhat inflammatory language resonated with many evangelicals who were concerned with and opposed to the theology that was emerging from mainline Presbyterian seminaries.

During the 1990s Gerstner was not alone in his criticisms of the liberal theological drift in PCUSA seminaries. Donald Bloesch (1928–2010), an evangelical UCC theologian who taught at a PCUSA seminary (Dubuque), was a stalwart critic, for a number of decades, of the progressive theology that emanated from PCUSA and other mainline seminaries.[22] In 1992 Bloesch observed that "[a]s mainstream academic theology veers ever more towards the left, a reaction is ineluctably setting in." While Bloesch acknowledged theological problems in "conservative circles" he argued that "[a] protest against the leftist perversions of the faith is understandable and welcome."[23] Bloesch, who had taught at Dubuque since 1957, lamented "[w]e are confronted by the rise of theological schools that no longer share a common [doctrinal] parameter."[24] John Leith (1919–2002), a PCUSA minister and longtime professor of theology at Union Seminary (PCUSA) in Richmond, Virginia, lodged similar complaints in his book *Crisis in the Church* (1997).[25] Leith's book argued that PCUSA seminaries were mar-

21. Gerstner, "20th Century: Theological Liberalism."

22 Some of Bloesch's works that reveal his concerns about liberal theology include, *The Invaded Church*; *Essentials of Evangelical Theology*; *Faith and Its Counterfeits*; *Crumbling Foundations*; *The Battle for the Trinity*; and his seven-volume Christian Foundations series.

23. Bloesch, *Theology of Word and Spirit*, 31.

24. Ibid., 33.

25. Leith, *Crisis in the Church*. Leith received his BA from Erskine College (SC), a BD from Columbia Seminary (GA), an MA from Vanderbilt University, and a PhD

ginalizing their own theological and church traditions, adopting secular approaches to education and becoming less accountable to the churches.[26] Leith argued that "[t]he irony of Presbyterian [PCUSA] seminaries is that academic freedom permits professors to call into question basic Christian doctrines" but "allows no freedom to challenge" liberal dogmas.[27] In a key sentence that revealed the aging theologian's grief, Leith argued,

> [n]o fundamentalist group in the South was ever as relentless in denying freedom for theology and ministry as the left wing of the Presbyterian Church (USA) has been to those who challenge their special dogmas, not only in the seminary but in the church.[28]

Leith was criticizing what he regarded as the progressive orthodoxy that had become prominent in PCUSA seminaries. The Union Seminary theologian's lament was a direct challenge to these schools' response to the secularization that was taking place in American culture. Gerstner's, Bloesch's, and Leith's censures aside, perhaps the most striking example of discontent with PCUSA seminaries was the proliferation of non-mainline evangelical seminaries rooted in the Presbyterian tradition.

Serving as a guest speaker and professor, Gerstner had connections with several of these schools. These institutions include: Fuller Seminary (California, 1947), Covenant Theological Seminary (Missouri, 1956), Reformed Theological Seminary (Mississippi, 1963), Sangre de Cristo Seminary (Colorado, 1976), Westminster Seminary (California, 1979), Whitefield Theological Seminary (Florida, 1980), Western Reformed Seminary (Washington, 1983), Greenville Presbyterian Theological Seminary (South Carolina, 1987) and Knox Seminary (Florida, 1990).[29] While some of these schools were small, sectarian, and unaccredited, others such as Fuller and Reformed had developed to become some of the largest seminaries in the United States and, indeed, in the world. By 2013 Reformed Theological Seminary (RTS) had over 2,700 students enrolled on five campuses.[30] The

---

from Yale University. Leith served as a visiting professor of theology at Columbia Seminary from 1957 to 1959 and professor of theology at Union Seminary in Richmond from 1959 to 1990.

26. Leith, *Crisis in the Church*, 13–19.

27. Ibid., 20–21.

28. Ibid., 21.

29. More recent examples that highlight this trend include New Geneva Seminary (CO, 1998), Redeemer Seminary (TX, 1999), Northwest Theological Seminary (WA, 2000).

30. "Founding," Reformed Theological Seminary.

rise of more general evangelical schools such as Gordon-Conwell Theological Seminary (Massachusetts) and Trinity Evangelical Divinity School (Illinois) are also signs of this tendency. The inability of evangelicals to control PCUSA seminaries led evangelical church leaders to found new schools; this initiative has resulted in the surprising growth and expansion of Reformed evangelical seminaries in the post-World War II era. A further sign of Reformed evangelical growth in the 1990s was the rise of Reformed University Fellowship (RUF), a campus ministry organization affiliated with the PCA. RUF's income in 1995 was $200,000, but in 2012 RUF received revenue of over $24 million and had a presence on one hundred collegiate campuses.[31]

During the 1990s Ligonier Ministries also expanded and continued to flourish. In 1995 Ligonier began broadcasting the "Renewing Your Mind" (RYM) radio program. RYM quickly expanded from fourteen stations to over three hundred nationally.[32] In 1998 Ligonier established an internet website which ultimately offered seventy-four of Gerstner's audio and video lectures.[33] These lectures dealt with various topics including church history, theology, and apologetics. Previously Gerstner's video and audiocassette lectures were distributed and sold, but the internet led to new opportunities. Gerstner's books and other writings were also disseminated by Ligonier. Sproul continued in his role as president of Ligonier Ministries, but his promotion of Gerstner as a scholar was occasionally overstated. Product publicity pieces by Sproul included his statement that, "[i]f God gave me the opportunity to apply my mind to the fullest for the next 250 years, I wouldn't begin to know what John Gerstner knows today."[34] Clearly, Sproul had a deep admiration for Gerstner, and that esteem in turn ensured that Gerstner's thought and scholarship would reach popular audiences through the audio-visual ministries of Ligonier.

In the last third of the twentieth century Ligonier steadily became the organization that was most responsible for the popularization of Reformed theology.[35] R. C. Sproul's accessible writings on Reformed theology and on

---

31. Shackleford, Interview with the author. Shackleford serves as the business manager of Reformed University Fellowship. He noted that the financial statistics are located in the March 5, 2013 RUF Permanent Committee Reports. Colin Hansen points out that in 1998 RUF was on only thirty-five campuses: see Hansen's, *The Young, The Restless, and The Reformed*, 66. Hansen briefly explores the rise of RUF and its growth at Yale University.

32. "40+ Years of Ministry—A Testimony of Grace (Video)," Ligonier Ministries.

33. Ibid.

34. Sproul statement on the back of John Gerstner's "The Theology of Jonathan Edwards," audiotape series.

35. No other Reformed seminary, church, denomination or para-church

Calvin have eclipsed those of distinguished mainline Presbyterian Calvin scholars. For instance, in 2008 Sproul had over 200,000 Google hits compared to 3,800 for Jane Dempsey Douglass, the esteemed Calvin scholar at Princeton Seminary.[36] In 2013 Gerstner had 134,000 Google hits whereas B. A. Gerrish, a moderate Calvin scholar, had only 6,350 hits and Edward A. Dowey, the neo-Orthodox theologian, had 69,300 hits.[37] These statistics offer some evidence of the extent of Sproul's and Gerstner's popular appeal. In 1990 Charles Colson (1931–2012), former presidential attorney and a leader in prison ministries, expressed the effect that Sproul's teaching had exerted over him. Colson noted,

> One day I took a set of tapes out by R. C. Sproul on the holiness of God. I played them on my VCR. Before those tapes were over, I found myself down on my knees before the majesty of a holy God, in awe that he would call any one of us to be his own.[38]

In the 1980s Colson had brought his fellow staff and inmates to learn at the Ligonier Valley Study Center and Colson continued to be influenced by Sproul.[39] As chairman of Prison Fellowship, Colson became a key evangelical leader and Sproul had an enormous impact on Colson's life and thought. Colson, in a letter to Sproul, wrote, "no one has had a greater influence on my Christian growth than you." Colson added, "I have studied at your feet for over fifteen years, devoured everything you have written and appreciated your ministry beyond words."[40] Moreover, Gerstner and Colson were featured speakers at the June 1990 PCA General Assembly in Atlanta, Georgia.[41] An additional indication of the Ligonier influence on Colson was his founding in 2009 of the Chuck Colson Center for Christian Worldview in Lansdowne, Virginia.[42] Ligonier's Reformed teaching was inspiring some of America's most prominent evangelical leaders.

A further sign of Sproul's influence can be seen in a 1995 book by Lynne and Bill Hybels, *Rediscovering the Church*. Bill Hybels, senior pastor

---

organization could match the media outreach of Ligonier Ministries.

36. Crocco, "Whose Calvin, Which Calvinism? John Calvin and the Development of Twentieth Century American Theology," 170.

37. This Google search was conducted on April 30, 2013.

38. Colson, "Keynote Address," 63.

39. Rowley, email to the author.

40. Colson quoted by Aitken, *Charles W. Colson*, 384.

41. "Clergymen Attend Assembly," B–7.

42. "About Chuck Colson (1931–2012)," Chuck Colson Center for Christian Worldview.

of one of America's largest churches, Willow Creek in the Chicago suburbs, and his wife recounted their attending Ligonier Valley Study Center in the 1980s. The Hybels wrote "it is no overstatement to say that R. C.'s teaching on the holiness of God was pivotal in Bill's spiritual development, both theologically and experientially."[43] They also recounted Sproul's teaching at Willow Creek in the 1980s and that "it was first through the ministry of Dr. Sproul that worship came alive at Willow Creek."[44] Rather than supporting the view that Ligonier was a small conservative Reformed ministry on the margins, the evidence indicates that this evangelical Calvinist institution was influencing the mainstream evangelical movement in some important ways. Ligonier was expanding and connecting itself to the larger evangelical movement.

Further signs of Ligonier's influence are seen in the fact that Sproul's "Renewing Your Mind" radio program was broadcast nationally, the only Reformed program to do so in the 1990s. Moreover, Ligonier has not been content to operate merely as a para-church ministry organization. Like other Reformed evangelical efforts, Ligonier later created new educational institutions: Ligonier Academy and Reformation Bible College. These schools were built on a beautiful thirty-plus acre campus with stately buildings in Sanford, Florida. Ligonier Academy, founded in 2009, offered a Doctor of Ministry (D.Min.) degree, and Reformation Bible College, established in 2011, offered bachelor's (B.A.) degree programs. The rise of these schools further expanded the theological vision that Gerstner and Sproul inspired and demonstrates the Reformed evangelical impulse of creating new institutions to carry on a particular evangelical theological tradition.

During the 1990s Gerstner served Ligonier Ministries as a professor-at-large. Gerstner lectured for Ligonier and helped produce taped video resources. In one of the videos, "Silencing the Devil," Gerstner took on Sproul, who played the devil's advocate. Sproul's responsibility was to argue that "truth is impossible, God is unknowable, the Bible is fallible, and that God's will depends on man's."[45] Gerstner energetically combated Sproul's arguments with forcefulness. Gerstner also produced various lectures for Ligonier Ministries. But it seems that the workload was becoming too much. In a devotional note apparently written to himself, Gerstner lamented "I was almost praying that I would have a heart attack or die or that something would give me an honorable excuse not to do those jobs."[46] Yet he perse-

---

43. Lynne and Bill Hybels, *Rediscovering the Church*, 98.

44. Ibid., 99.

45. Sproul and Gerstner, "Silencing the Devil," video.

46. Gerstner note, April 21, n.d., Gerstner Papers, Chandler, Arizona.

vered. In the early 1990s Gerstner's active retirement also led to his teaching as an adjunct professor of theology at the newly founded Knox Seminary in Orlando, Florida. Knox was founded by D. James Kennedy and the large Coral Ridge Presbyterian Church (PCA) (Ft Lauderdale, Florida).[47]

Kennedy, Coral Ridge's legendary senior pastor, "loved Gerstner" and decided to bring him to teach at the new seminary.[48] Samuel Lamerson, who studied at Knox in the early 1990s, notes that Gerstner was hired because "Knox was trying to bring in some bigger name scholars." Lamerson took an introduction to Reformed theology class with Gerstner and recalls his "energetic and clear teaching style." He noted that, with Gerstner, there was "no sense of pretence"; he was "very willing to answer questions and spar with students."[49] Ron Kilpatrick, who lived directly behind Gerstner in his Florida neighborhood, observed Gerstner's love for technology, watches, and gadgets. Somewhat strangely, he remembers Gerstner working on calculus problems.[50] It seems that Gerstner still had work to do and was seeking to stay in top mental shape.

During the last six years of Gerstner's life, he continued to speak in various venues. *The Pittsburgh Press* reported on March 1, 1990 that Gerstner was preaching at the Sunday services of the Alliance Church (Christian Missionary Alliance, CMA) in Upper St Clair, Pennsylvania. The CMA was an evangelical denomination, but not necessarily Reformed. Gerstner was willing to work with non-Reformed evangelicals. In September 1990 Gerstner gave a series of lectures at Faith Presbyterian Church (PCA) in Akron, Ohio.[51] In late April 1992 Gerstner spoke at the Soli Deo Gloria conference held at First Reformed Presbyterian Church in Pittsburgh. The theme for the two-day event was "The Mercy of God."[52] Elizabeth Elliot, the second wife of Gerstner's old colleague from Pittsburgh Theological Seminary Addison Leitch, was also a speaker at this event along with Don Kistler—a former student of Gerstner and the head of Soli Deo Gloria Publications. In October 1993 Gerstner spoke at the Johnstown Reformed Conference in Johnstown, Pennsylvania. This conference focused on the nature of the Christian church and included two other lecturers, Michael Horton and J. I. Packer. Horton, a budding Reformed theologian, would five years

---

47. Davis, *The Truth That Transformed Me*, 213–16.

48. Samuel Lamerson, Interview with the author.

49. Ibid.

50. Kilpatrick, Interview with the author.

51. Gerstner Lectures Flier, First Presbyterian Church, Akron, Ohio.

52. "The Third Annual Soli Deo Gloria Conference on The Mercy of God," brochure.

later complete his doctoral work on Thomas Goodwin (1600–1680) under Alister McGrath, the eminent Anglican evangelical theologian.[53] By 1993 Packer had established himself as one of the world's leading evangelical theologians and served as a professor at Regent College, Vancouver.[54] The titles of Gerstner's two lectures were: "Is the Roman Catholic Church a True Church?" and "How is Presbyterianism Related to Other Churches?"[55] Gerstner's work with these two scholars reveals that he continued to play a role in the wider Reformed evangelical movement.

In 1989 *Christianity Today* reported that "strong disagreements" were emerging within evangelicalism over the doctrine of hell and more specifically over a theological position formulated by John Stott, the Anglican clergyman referred to as the "pope of evangelicals." Stott's view was known as annihilationism, the view which denies eternal punishment.[56] As the debate unfolded, John White, a longtime friend of Gerstner and the President of the National Association of Evangelicals, asked Gerstner to write a book addressing the doctrinal controversy. In 1990 Soli Deo Gloria Publications released Gerstner's *Repent or Perish* which defended the historic position on the issue and analyzed differing views of the topic within the world of evangelical Protestantism. White, who wrote the book's foreword, stated that the "Evangelical community needs the clarity, logic and forthrightness that have always been the style of John Gerstner." White noted that he "asked John Gerstner to respond, especially to John Stott and Philip Hughes in reference to the annihilation doctrine."[57] In his book Gerstner explored the biblical view of hell alongside different views through church history. Gerstner analyzed the positions of numerous Christian scholars who either accepted or denied the traditional view of hell. Specifically, he examined what he termed the "conservative revolt against hell."[58] In his study he was troubled with the changing views of Philip Hughes (1915–1990), a South African who served as a visiting professor at Westminster Theological Seminary, who, he claimed, was "denying God's eternal punishment."[59] He also accused John

53. Horton has become a prolific Reformed theologian and has served as a professor of theology and apologetics at Westminster Seminary in California since 1998.

54. See McGrath, *J. I. Packer*; George, ed., *J. I. Packer and the Evangelical Future.*

55. Johnston Reformed Conference Flier, "The Christian Church."

56. "What Does It Mean to Be Evangelical," 60. On Gerstner's earlier criticisms of John Stott, see chapter 6, pp. 32–33.

57. White quoted by Gerstner, *Repent or Perish*, ii.

58. Gerstner, *Repent or Perish*, 29.

59. Hughes received MA and DLitt degrees from the University of Cape Town (RSA), the BD from the University of London, and a ThD from the Australian College of Theology. He served several institutions including Trinity College, Bristol, the

Stott (1921–2011), of a "flat rejection" of Jesus' teaching on hell.[60] Gerstner noted that he was "glad" that Stott did not want to dogmatise his views on hell. Nevertheless, Gerstner disagreed sharply with Stott's statement that his views were "a legitimate, biblically founded alternative."[61] Gerstner was still willing to respond to challenges to received orthodoxy, but not now in his denomination, instead in the wider evangelical movement.

Gerstner was speaking well into his seventies. One sign that Reformed evangelicalism was continuing to grow and become more self-conscious was that in 1994 the Alliance of Confessing Evangelicals (ACE) was formed. In 1996 ACE held that their goal was "the recovery of the biblical, apostolic witness by the evangelical movement."[62] In the early to mid-1990s Gerstner had triple-by-pass surgery, but he refused to allow his health to interfere with his speaking.[63] In March 1994 Gerstner spoke on the theme of "Revivals in American History" at Covenant Presbyterian Church (PCA) in Wexford, Pennsylvania. At this event Gerstner gave lectures on Edwards, Charles Finney, D. L. Moody, Billy Sunday, and Billy Graham.[64] Gerstner believed that Finney had done great damage to Edwards's evangelicalism, but Moody, Sunday, and Graham had partially restored Edwards's spiritual and evangelistic legacy. While Gerstner offered criticism of the evangelical movement he sought to be a part of it and did not reject it like some other conservative Presbyterians.[65] He was an evangelical Calvinist and his evangelical impulse reveals his large vision for the conservative Reformed tradition. Just as J. Gresham Machen helped lead the transdenominational League of Evangelical Students, Gerstner participated within the evangelical movement, even though he was not uncritical of it.

Church Society, and Westminster Theological Seminary.

60. Gerstner, *Repent or Perish*, 62.

61. Stott quoted by Gerstner, *Repent or Perish*, 62. Stott's biographer Chapman notes that Stott did not want to be brought into the controversy and that he "lost credibility among American evangelicals in particular": see Chapman, *Godly Ambition*, 145. Stott received an MA from Cambridge University and held several honorary doctorates including a Lambeth DD. Stott served as rector of All Souls Church, London, from 1945 to 1970. Stott founded the London Institute for Contemporary Christianity and served as a leader of the international evangelical movement.

62. On ACE, see Boice and Sasse eds., *Here We Stand*, dedication page.

63. Gerstner, Interview with the author, June 15, 2010.

64. Revivals in American History Lectures Flier, Covenant Presbyterian Church.

65. Some conservative Reformed Protestants have been resistant to the mainstream evangelical movement. On this point see Hart, *Between the Times*. Hart has not only chronicled Orthodox Presbyterian opposition to the larger evangelical movement, but he has also stated his objections to evangelicalism in *The Lost Soul of American Protestantism* and in *Deconstructing Evangelicalism*.

Gerstner's most thorough and intense criticism was lodged not against Hughes or Stott, however, but against Edward Fudge (1944–), author of *The Fire That Consumes* (1982).[66] Fudge, a Church of Christ minister and attorney, had contributed an important work that was intensifying the debate. Gerstner devoted sixty pages (two chapters) to what he called Fudge's "conditionalist attack on the traditional biblical doctrine of hell."[67] The conditionalist position, as formulated by Fudge, holds that a person is punished for a time that corresponds to a person's guilt, but then the person is "annihilated, only his ashes remaining in an ever burning hell."[68] Gerstner rejected this view because it denied the biblical concept of eternal punishment. Gerstner noted, "I know this [*Repent or Perish*] is a hard book." Nevertheless, he agreed to write it because he did not want to "shrink from declaring the whole counsel of God."[69] In a review, Robert Peterson, a Covenant Seminary theologian, noted that Gerstner came to the debate with "pistols flaring."[70] Gerstner showed little sympathy with those with whom he disagreed. He put down a heavy anchor on the conservative side of the debate. Of all of Gerstner's books, *Repent or Perish* received the fewest reviews.

In 1991 Gerstner produced another book, *Wrongly Dividing the Word of Truth*, which sought to analyze a key phenomenon within evangelical movement, the prophetic teaching known as dispensationalism.[71] Gerstner's family ties to dispensationalism, his own experience, and his theological concerns about the movement undoubtedly served as the impetus for writing on the topic. His 275-page book examined the history of dispensationalism and its philosophical, apologetic, and theological perspectives. Gerstner characterised dispensationalism as a "school of thought" offering a special form of prophetic interpretation that had "a penchant for dividing history into different epochs."[72] He noted that there had been "widespread neglect" of dispensationalism among scholars and that this "ignorance by large sections of the theological world" was quite "strange" due to the

---

66. Fudge, *The Fire that Consumes*. Fudge received his BA and MA degrees from Abilene Christian University and a JD from the University of Houston. Fudge has served as a Christian writer, pastor, and attorney.

67. Gerstner, *Repent or Perish*, 66.

68. Ibid.

69. Ibid., 215.

70. Peterson, "Undying Worm, Unquenchable Fire."

71. Gerstner, *Wrongly Dividing the Word of Truth*. For background information on the dispensationalist movement see Boyer, *When Time Shall Be No More* and Mangum, *The Dispensational Covenant Rift*.

72. Ibid., 7.

movement's importance to "American theological conservatism."[73] The bulk of the book was devoted to dispensationalism's theology, which Gerstner regarded as a "species of Arminianism." He also noted that dispensationalist theologians had been "preoccupied with eschatology rather than systematic theological concerns."[74] Dispensationalism had found its "strongest advocates in Calvinistic churches," but its theology, he asserted, was a "defection from Calvinism." Gerstner believed that dispensationalism denied basic Calvinist doctrines especially in regard to total depravity and unconditional election.[75] He also criticized dispensationalists's interpretation of Israel and their understanding of salvation. Moreover, he lamented the movement's views on sanctification, which Gerstner believed led to "desiccation of personal spirituality."[76] Gerstner's book offered exhaustive, but largely negative, analysis of dispensationalism.

The reviews of Gerstner's book, however, were scathing. John Witmer (1920–2007), a theologian at the leading dispensationalist institution Dallas Seminary, excoriated Gerstner in a two-part review that appeared in the pages of *Bibliotheca Sacra*. Witmer referred to the book as a "diatribe" which was "extreme" in its "false stereotypes" of dispensationalism.[77] He added that Gerstner's work "holds little hope of contributing significantly to the recent covenant-dispensational dialogue." Gerstner's "attitude" was blasted as "antagonistic, confrontational, denunciatory, and polemic." The review also revealed historical errors in the book including Gerstner's surprising contention that Wheaton College was founded at the turn of the century, instead of 1860 when it was actually begun.[78] Gerstner committed numerous other mistakes in the book, and Witmer, after careful examination, concluded that Gerstner also misquoted sources. Witmer wrote that his "check revealed multiplied examples where words in Gerstner's quotation were different from the source quoted."[79] This complaint corresponds to the concerns cited decades earlier by the Yale committee on Edwards's works. Moreover, Witmer added that Gerstner did not do justice to the "continu-

73. Ibid., 37–38.

74. Ibid., 106.

75. Ibid., 116.

76. Ibid., 247.

77. Witmer, "A Review of *Wrongly Dividing the Word of Truth*-Part 1," 131; "A Review of *Wrongly Dividing the Word of Truth*—Part 2," 259–76. Witmer served for many years on the faculty of Dallas Theological Seminary.

78. Gerstner, *Wrongly Dividing the Word of Truth*, 52. This historical misjudgement is compounded in light of the fact that Gerstner's wife was a Wheaton College graduate.

79. Witmer, "A Review of *Wrongly Dividing the Word of Truth*-Part 1," 135.

ing refinement of dispensational theology [at Dallas Seminary]."[80] In short, it was a devastating review. Bradley Hayton, a Christian psychologist, attempted to argue, however, that Gerstner's study was "definitely the most thorough" of any recent study "that disputes dispensationalist theology."[81] Ken Pulliam, a Baptist theologian, found Gerstner's book to be "weak in exegesis" and noted Gerstner included "[v]irtually no interaction with the biblical text."[82]

Richard Mayhue, dean of The Master's Seminary (California), criticised Gerstner for paying no attention to "current dispensational thinking."[83] Gerstner, he held, ignored dispensational theology after 1980. Zane Hodges (1932–2008), a dispensationalist theologian, argued that Gerstner "avoided pejorative rhetoric," but was guilty of ignoring the debate on "Calvin and Classical Calvinism" which "touches close to the dispensational/Reformed debate."[84] In 2000 Soli Deo Gloria Publications published a second edition of Gerstner's book that includes Gerstner's earlier response to Witmer, Mayhue, and Hodges. Gerstner felt that the historical inaccuracies were "petty matters" and that Witmer should be "ashamed" of his sharp language. Gerstner's entrance into the debates about dispensational theology reinforced tensions between Reformed theology and dispensationalism and established Gerstner as a virile critic of the movement.

By the end of the 1980s Gerstner had still yet to produce the study of Edwards's theology that he had first contemplated forty years earlier. In 1990 Gerstner was seventy-four years old and had decided that he did not want to publish his extensive analysis of Edwards's thought. He wrote that he was "incapable or at least inadequate" to finish what he had started. "I must give up my JET project," Gerstner noted. He added, "[t]he reason is that I cannot stand the pressure to do what I want to do as a scholar." He added that Edna might be right that "I am thinking too much of pecayune

80. Ibid., 260.

81. Hayton, "Review of Gerstner's *Wrongly Dividing the Word of God*," 186.

82. Pulliam, "Review of Gerstner's *Wrongly Dividing the Word of Truth*," 118.

83. Mayhue, "Who Is Wrong? A Review of Gerstner's *Wrongly Dividing the Word of Truth*," 73–94. Mayhue received his BS from Ohio State University and his MDiv, ThM and ThD degrees from Grace Theological Seminary. He has served as a professor of theology The Master's Seminary (California) from 1989.

84. Hodges, "Calvinism Ex Cathedra: A Review of John Gerstner's *Wrongly Dividing the Word of Truth: A Critique of Dispensationalism*." Hodges received his BA degree from Wheaton College and his ThM and ThD degrees from Dallas Theological Seminary. He served as a professor of New Testament Greek and Exegesis at Dallas from 1960 to 1987.

[sic] scholarship."[85] Apparently Edna, who was usually encouraging to her husband, believed that he was focusing too much on the minutia of the project and that this made the study picayune—meaning less important. Edna believed that the project was "unnecessarily depressing" her husband. He added that putting that "work together in three volumes is much more than I can envisage."[86] It was a painful admission.

Gerstner, who felt he had been unfairly treated by the Yale committee on Edwards's works, perhaps had some doubts about the legitimacy and reception of his labor of love. Despite once giving up the project and although he had his own misgivings, Gerstner was eventually persuaded by his former students like Coffin, Sproul, and Bogue, to publish his voluminous study of Edwards's theology.[87] David Coffin, who had studied with Gerstner at Pittsburgh Theological Seminary in the late 1970s, served as the editor for the three-volume work, which was entitled *The Rational Biblical Theology of Jonathan Edwards (RBTJE)*.[88] The study represented a milestone in Edwards studies because it was the first major systematic summary of Edwards's weighty theology. It was the culmination of Gerstner's "forty years" of research done "with an ever increasing fascination with the man's wisdom."[89] The three-volume set was funded by Ligonier Ministries, and Ligonier took a key role in the distribution and sale of the books.[90] The choice to pursue an editor and private publisher outside the mainstream of scholarly publishing, however, was a crucial mistake. One key issue was the length of the study, which rambled to over 1,600 pages. Coffin later claimed that vol. 1 was "the worst," but then noted that vol. 2 was "a little better" and that vol. 3 was in his view "pretty good."[91] Carl Bogue, who also helped with some of the editing, recalled "having a quick window to return material."[92] The whole project was rushed and lacked the necessary refinement it need.

Gerstner's supporters were pushing him to get the study finished before he was unable to complete the project. In 1991 he wrote that without

85. Coffin, Interview with the author, July 6, 2010.

86. Gerstner note, April 21 n.d. This note appears to be a personal devotional letter.

87. Gerstner, *The Rational Biblical Theology of Jonathan Edwards [RBTJE]*, 1:3. Bogue, Interview with the author, April 5, 2014.

88. Gerstner, *RBTJE*. Coffin, a former student of Gerstner at Pittsburgh Seminary, was the head of the Berea Center for Biblical and Theological Studies in Powhatan, Virginia.

89. Gerstner, *RBTJE*, 1:3.

90. Coffin, Interview with the author, July 6, 2010.

91. Ibid.

92. Bogue, Interview with the author, April 9, 2014.

their "godly goading and support these volumes may never have been produced."[93] The work was completed, but at a cost to its quality. What Gerstner needed, but did not receive, was professional editorial help. Despite these issues, Gerstner was finally—at last—able to demonstrate his vast knowledge of Edwards and his writings.

Volume one of *RBTJE* (1991) began with a brief biographical introduction of Edwards that spanned merely fifteen pages. Throughout his career Gerstner never seemed particularly interested in biographical details, choosing instead to concentrate on theology. Gerstner also gave an analysis of Edwards's place within the history of Christian theology. Edwards, according to Gerstner's analysis, was a classical apologist committed to common sense and to the reason and faith distinction.[94] He argued that "eliminating the theistic argument" in regards to faith was "logically absurd" and "intellectually futile."[95] Reason could not be separated from faith. Based on his historical examination he argued the mainstream of Christian scholars down through the centuries including Edwards affirmed that reason, scripture and faith created "perfect harmony"—they did not have to be hostile to each other.[96] Gerstner maintained that the classical Christian position of "theistic proofs" and "biblical evidences" was broken up in the post-Edwardsean period by Immanuel Kant (1724–1804), the German philosopher, who tried to show that knowledge of God as he is in himself is impossible. Against what Gerstner argued was the backdrop of Kantian irrationalism he attempted to show that Edwards was committed to the rational defence of the Christian faith and that he was "among the greatest systemizers of the reasonable Christian tradition."[97] He assured his readers that Edwards was committed to a rational defense of the faith because, as Gerstner noted, John Orr had clearly "shown in his *English Deism: Its Roots and Fruits*, [that] Edwards's century was the golden age of rational apologetics."[98] Gerstner lamented, however, that "for every one who has read John Orr probably ten have read John Dillenberger's *Protestant Thought and Natural Science* which reads the eighteenth century through twentieth century glasses."[99] From Gerstner's perspective, Edwards was a rational Christian theologian because he fitted his age.

93. Gerstner, *RBTJE*, vol. 1, "Dedication Page."

94. Ibid., 21–50.

95. Ibid., 22.

96. Ibid., 21.

97. Ibid., 56.

98. Ibid., 55.

99. Ibid.

Gerstner then turned from post-Edwardsean development to a discussion of twentieth-century theology and the rise of non-rational attempts to defend the faith. He identified the main twentieth-century "[o]pponents of the classical synthesis" of "faith and reason." Specifically, he analyzed and criticised Peter Bertocci, J. Oliver Buswell, Schubert Ogden, Karl Barth, Rudolph Bultmann, Ludwig Wittgenstein, and the "Amsterdam or Dooyeweerdian school."[100] The Dutch or Dutch-American scholars Gerstner cited and censured for the "most drastic attack on natural theology ever made" included Abraham Kuyper, Herman Dooyeweerd, and Cornelius Van Til.[101] His swift move to the twentieth-century theological scene reveals much about Gerstner's apologetic stance and how it influenced his understanding of history. Gerstner demonstrated his opposition to various forms of twentieth-century theology and how they were inconsistent with Edwards's theology. From Gerstner's vantage point, Edwards, "who saw solid reasons for faith," could be used as an important antidote to the irrationality Gerstner found so distressing in parts of contemporary theology, especially mainline Protestant thought.

Gerstner also analyzed different scholars's views of Edwards's epistemology and metaphysics. He held that Edwards was an "empirical noumenalist" who "taught that even natural, unregenerate man knows God speculatively."[102] He then discussed Edwards's position on reason and revelation. Specifically, he sought to challenge the views of those whom he accused of "reading Christian history through fideistically-colored glasses." He was troubled by scholars who viewed Edwards's reasoned defence of the Christian faith as an "occasional and unconscious anomaly."[103] He noted, "[i]t is clear that for Edwards man's reason—even fallen reason—can and does prove the being of God independently of special revelation."[104] Nevertheless, in the following chapter Gerstner laid out Edwards's argument on why special revelation, the Bible, is a still a necessity for the believer. Subsequent chapters in volume one explored Edwards's views of Scripture and its inspiration, interpretation, and illumination. Gerstner also provided comments on important Edwards sermons that dealt with the Bible. Chapter 7 in volume one was the most bizarre chapter, offering 232 pages of commentary on the remarks Edwards made on virtually every verse in the book of Hebrews. Gerstner noted that he wanted to "give the reader some

---

100. Ibid., 75. On Gerstner's criticisms of these thinkers, see 65–79.

101. Ibid., 75.

102. Ibid., 93.

103. Ibid., 97.

104. Ibid.

awareness of Edwards's depth and width of biblical comment" and for this reason "I have chosen, somewhat at random, the New Testament book of Hebrews."[105] Gerstner ended volume one by looking at Edwards's preaching of the Bible and Edwards's historical influence. His last chapter was a reworking of material Gerstner had produced thirty-four years earlier.[106]

Volume two of the *RBTJE* was better organized and examined Edwards's theological views on various key doctrines of the Christian faith. Gerstner analyzed Edwards's theology as it related to such topics as the covenants, creation, providence, imputation, sin, incarnation, and atonement, to name a few. Gerstner believed he had made a significant contribution to Edwards studies in his work on the colonial theologian and the covenant. He noted that "many of Edwards's interpreters" had "virtually eliminated the doctrine of the covenant" in his theology, "returning [Edwards] to the imagined purer Calvinism of Calvin."[107] Gerstner claimed that his own *Steps to Salvation* (1960) along with the work of Harry Stout and Carl Bouge had ended the "reign of [Perry] Miller's mistake concerning Calvinism, Edwards and the covenant."[108] Miller's error was not grasping the "covenant's compatibility with Calvinism and especially Jonathan Edwards."[109] While Gerstner's work interacts with various scholars, his evaluation of Edwards' theology is in many ways *sui generis* because his work was based on so many unpublished Edwards's sermons. Throughout his study, Gerstner quoted extensively from Edwards's own writings to formulate the colonial theologian's positions on various doctrines. Gerstner's strength was his knowledge of Edwards's own writings. In the 1970s Samuel Logan recalls Gerstner telling him that "he thought he was probably the only person living" who had "read all the Miscellanies."[110] The book included a seventeen-page index of the particular works of Edwards which Gerstner had utilized. While he was not uncritical of Edwards, Gerstner was clearly his vigorous advocate.

In volume three, Gerstner continued his analysis of Edwards's theology. Some of the issues Gerstner explored were Edwards's theology of evangelism, preparationism, regeneration, justification, sanctification, the church, and heaven. Gerstner noted that "perhaps the most distinctive thing

---

105. Ibid., 247.

106. Parts of the chapter on Edward's influence first appeared in Gerstner's essay "American Calvinism Until the Twentieth Century," 13–39.

107. Gerstner, *RBTJE*, 2:89.

108. Ibid., 90. Stout, "The Puritans and Edwards"; Bogue, *Jonathan Edwards and the Covenant of Grace.*

109. Gerstner, *RBTJE*, 2:80.

110. Samuel Logan email to the author.

about Jonathan Edwards's evangelistic message is his theory of seeking."[111] Edwards did not believe that sinners could do something to be saved (the Arminian position). Nevertheless, the Calvinist Edwards also rejected "those Calvinists who say there is nothing that the sinner can do." Gerstner maintained that "[a]ccording to Edwards, he [the person] can do something non-saving but promising and hopeful: namely seek." He held that "[a]fter Edwards, Puritan, Calvinistic seeking and preparation have just about perished from the face of America."[112] Even the great Princeton theologians had become "diffident toward preparationism." Despite the demise of preparationism, Gerstner hoped that Christians in his own day would "consider and appreciate anew" Edwards's view of seeking. In an effort to spark contemporary interest in the topic, Gerstner then inserted a twenty-eight page sermon by Edwards on the topic.[113]

In the *Evangelical Quarterly*, Michael McMullen, a Baptist historian, noted that Gerstner's *RBTJE* had presented "much that is new," especially in regards to the "substantial amount of unpublished manuscript material from the Edwards collection." He held that Gerstner's efforts will be "appreciated by those who have been involved in . . . painstaking" research on Edwards.[114] In 1993 M. X. Lesser, an Edwards scholar at Northeastern University (Massachusetts), held that *RBTJE* is "more an encyclopedia of Edwards's thought than a coherent narrative of it, and so, for all its thoroughness, a work of rather limited usefulness."[115] Charles Hambrick-Stowe, a Congregational historian, was also not very enthused. In a review for *Fides et Historia*, Hambrick-Stowe argued that Gerstner's "assertion that Edwards lived on 'most purely' in Old School Presbyterianism . . . is absurd." He added: "missing in the cranky lucubration is any glimpse of Edwards the evangelist of the Great Awakening." Moreover, he noted that *RBTJE* was "a rambling project never brought under control" and "full of typographical errors and grammatical idiosyncrasies." Perhaps most alarming was "the adulatory tone of Gerstner's prose" which "conveys the impression of hagiography."[116] It was a

111. Gerstner, *RBTJE*, 3:2.

112. Ibid., 95.

113. Ibid., 108–36

114. McMullen, Review of Gerstner's *The Rational Biblical Theology of Jonathan Edwards*, 58–59. McMullen, who earned his PhD from the University of Aberdeen, is currently professor of church history at Midwestern Baptist Seminary in Kansas City, Missouri.

115. Lesser, *Jonathan Edwards*, xxvi.

116. Hambrick-Stowe, Review of John Gerstner's *The Rational Biblical Theology of Jonathan Edwards*, 133. Hambrick-Stowe taught at Lancaster Seminary (PA), Pittsburgh Seminary, and Northern Seminary (IL).

stinging review. Because *RBTJE* was not recognized in academia as a scholarly work it was not widely reviewed. Perhaps Hambrick-Stowe's criticisms so marginalized the study in the minds of scholars that no one else reviewed the three-volume work.

Kenneth Minkema, director of the Jonathan Edwards Center at Yale University, observes that "Gerstner did not see" change over time in "Edwards's sayings" and that this led Gerstner's *RBTJE* to be "not very accurate" in its analysis of Edwards's theology.[117] In an effort to promote Edwards's theology Gerstner diminished the historical. Nonetheless, Minkema added that he "looks at Gerstner's work and uses it," acknowledging that *RBTJE* offers some "very impressive good points of biblical exposition and commentary" found nowhere else. Furthermore, he claims that Gerstner was responsible for "getting lots of people interested in Edwards."[118] Gerald McDermott, who has served as a theology professor at Roanoke College (Virginia) and at Beeson Divinity School (Alabama), holds that Gerstner's "rational" approach "becomes a bit 'rationalistic'". McDermott, a prolific Edwards scholar who co-authored the definitive survey of Edwards's theology, argues that Gerstner did "not leave enough room for Edwards's sense of mystery."[119] Nevertheless, McDermott maintains that,

> Gerstner was superb in his thoroughness, and his attention to JE's sermons, and overall, he was a meticulous and heroic repristinator of Edwards in a time when he might have known more about Edwards than anyone—Perry Miller included.[120]

While *RBTJE* was not originally widely acclaimed by Edwards scholars, the trilogy has left a legacy in the burgeoning field of Edwards studies. In addition, *RBTJE* has continued to exert influence within the Reformed evangelical subculture, where Edwards is intensely revered.[121] To be sure, *RBTJE* has been taken seriously by many. In 2010 W. Gary Crampton, a theologian at Whitefield Theological Seminary (Florida), produced an extensive study of *RBTJE* entitled *Interpreting Edwards: An Overview and Analysis of John H. Gerstner's* The Rational Biblical Theology of Jonathan

117. Minkema, Interview with the author.

118. Ibid.

119. McDermott email to the author. See McClymond and McDermott, *The Theology of Jonathan Edwards*.

120. McDermott email to the author.

121. On the contemporary Reformed evangelical reverence for Edwards, see Hansen, *Young, Restless, Reformed*; and Hart, "Before the Young, Restless, and Reformed: Edwards' Appeal to Post World War II Evangelicals."

Edwards.[122] The 470-page book closely examines each chapter in Gerstner's three-volume work and distils Gerstner's arguments. Crampton's work reveals the influence of Gerstner and the seriousness with which his work is taken in certain segments of Reformed evangelicalism.

Douglas Sweeney, a historian at Trinity Evangelical Divinity School, in a short notice of Crampton's book, points out that it "offers a summary of Gerstner's massive" study that has been "updated with helpful references to more recent Edwards scholarship." Sweeney also commented that "[y]ounger readers may need to know that Gerstner played a major role in fueling the Edwards renaissance and making its scholarly fruit accessible to evangelical Christians." He mentioned that Gerstner "promoted Edwards's writings with hundreds of pastors, seminarians, and evangelical laity."[123] Gerstner was indeed a leading promoter of Edwards.

In the 1990s Gerstner continued to work on Edwards, but he also continued to lecture and preach. The *Los Angeles Times* reported in October 1994 that Gerstner would be preaching at Valley Presbyterian Church on the topic of "Theology for the Layman."[124] Like Sproul, Gerstner sought to make theology accessible for the person in the pew, but his strength was gradually diminishing. By the summer of 1995 Gerstner was told by his doctor that he had pancreatic cancer. As Gerstner battled his final illness he took to his word processor. He wrote that "[o]ne month has passed" and that "I no longer feel the intensity of pain." "Yet it hurts more" he observed, "for I no longer feel anything." He was thankful that his "ritual of grief" had been "broken by the arrival of his oldest daughter." Then he wrote, "the first death was the death of my denomination."[125] Presumably Gerstner meant the PCUSA, but perhaps it was a reference to the UPCNA. Unfortunately, most parts of the last two lines of his note were smudged and therefore undecipherable. Despite the diagnosis, Gerstner moved forward and was determined to continue lecturing.

Two weeks before his death in March 1996 Gerstner departed for his last speaking engagement. He and his son Jonathan traveled from Pennsylvania to the Peniel Bible Church in Waverly, Kansas, to give lectures on Edwards. Darryl McNabb, Peniel's pastor, was committed to Reformed theology and had come to know Gerstner and his son Jonathan while attending the Burlington Reformed Conference in Iowa. He subsequently invited them to Peniel and remembers the response he received from those who

122. Crampton, *Interpreting Edwards.*

123. Sweeney, "Sweeney Booknotes: John Gerstner's *Rational Biblical Theology.*"

124. Dart, "Religion Notes."

125. Gerstner, Untitled Note.

attended the lectures. McNabb remembers Peniel members saying, "these guys are good!" Gerstner's son Jonathan helped his father during the trip and also lectured. Jonathan, who had earned a PhD from the University of Chicago (1985), was a strong advocate of his father's theological views. McNabb recalled Gerstner saying that they "needed to pray for the Yale Edwards scholarship" because "the Yale scholars did not believe in Edwards's theology." This comment signals that there was lasting bitterness over Gerstner's rejection by the Yale committee. In retrospect McNabb observed that Gerstner "could see different layers in things." "He was a very penetrating thinker," the Kansas pastor noted, who was "energized by Edwards."[126]

While on this trip to Kansas, Gerstner fell down at his hotel and injured his head. Struggling with the pain, he patched himself up with bandages and delivered his lectures on Edwards. McNabb remembers Gerstner lying down on a mattress several times during the conference. Despite the physical challenges, Gerstner persevered. In the same manner that J. Gresham Machen had in 1937 ended his career speaking to a few followers in Leith, North Dakota, Gerstner ended his life's work in another remote location far from the centers of academic influence or cultural prestige. Yet he did receive one last reward. A week before his death, Geneva College—the Reformed Presbyterian institution in Pennsylvania—formally recognized his achievements by awarding him an honorary doctorate at the Johnstown (Pennsylvania) Reformed Theology Conference. John White, the president of Geneva, presented the degree to Gerstner.[127] Gerstner died peacefully, while in a circle of prayer, at his home on March 24, 1996. A day later, Carl Bogue released an obituary noting that "[n]othing I can say here will adequately express what this man of God meant to me personally."[128] On March 27, the *Pittsburgh Post-Gazette* published an obituary of Gerstner entitled "John Gerstner-Longtime Seminary Professor, Passionate Scholar."[129] Gerstner's PTS colleague, Bob Kelley, was quoted saying that he remembered being told by another faculty member "[d]on't get into a debate with Gerstner . . . [h]e will win even if he's wrong."[130]

On March 28, Gerstner's funeral was held at the Pioneer Presbyterian Church in Ligonier, Pennsylvania. David Kenyon, Pioneer's pastor,

126. McNabb, Interview with the author.

127. Gerstner email to the author, March 8, 2014.

128. Bogue, "Dr. John Gerstner, Defender of the Faith."

129. Rodgers-Melnick, "John Gerstner-Longtime Seminary Professor, Passionate Scholar," B-4.

130. Kelley quoted by Rodgers-Melnick, "John Gerstner-Longtime Seminary Professor, Passionate Scholar," B-4.

delivered the funeral sermon and described Gerstner as a "life changing teacher." Kenyon encouraged those assembled to "pick up the mantle" of Gerstner as they moved forward in their own lives.[131] R. C. Sproul also spoke at his mentor's funeral and proclaimed, "our captain has fallen."[132] Another former student, Mark Ross, reported that a leader in the southern Associate Reformed Presbyterian Church had told him that one of main reasons for growth and revival in the ARP was Gerstner's ministry. John Kennedy told the crowded church that Gerstner inspired him to be a missionary, and Arthur Lindsley said that Gerstner was "the greatest teacher I ever had."[133] Carl Bogue then rose and spoke about the importance of John Orr to Gerstner's life, reminding those present that Gerstner too had a mentor. The public celebration of Gerstner's life was also carried over to print media. In the April 6 edition of *World* magazine, George Grant noted that Gerstner "was undoubtedly one of the most influential Reformed apologists and teachers of our time."[134]

Tabletalk, a monthly magazine published by Ligonier Ministries, devoted its October 1997 issue to Gerstner. A fine portrait of Gerstner appeared on the front cover with books and a bust of Edwards in the background. The October *Tabletalk* contained five essays on Gerstner's life, career, and thought. R.C. Sproul Jr. wrote that Gerstner "has not been widely recognized," but that he deserved to be. R.C. Sproul commented on the "The Gerstner I Remember" by recounting their friendship and ministry together.[135] Gerstner's disciples were working to ensure that their mentor would be remembered and that his "mantle" would be carried on well into the future.

Beyond Gerstner's devotees there were few appraisals of his life's work. The lack of commentary on Gerstner's death indicates that by 1996 obscurity had befallen the church historian. He finished his career outside the mainline Presbyterian church, mainstream academia, and even traditional evangelical scholarship. In the 1990s his books were not published with the usual evangelical publishing houses. The absence of critical evaluations of his life suggests that by the 1990s the reputation of the seasoned evangelical Presbyterian churchman was at a low ebb. Perhaps Gerstner's life symbolized past battles they would rather forget. From a different perspective, maybe the lack of attention to Gerstner by the PCUSA, where he was so

---

131. Kenyon's words transcribed from the Gerstner Funeral Service Video.

132. Sproul's words transcribed from the Gerstner Funeral Service Video.

133. Kennedy's and Lindsley's words transcribed from the John Gerstner Funeral Service Video.

134. Grant, "A Thirst For Gerstner," 23.

135. Sproul, "The Gerstner I Remember," 4–7.

widely known, was a small confirmation of Leith's claim that the PCUSA had been neglecting its own history.[136]

In the last phase of Gerstner's life, he had pursued a new ecclesiastical life in the PCA. His theological opposition to the PCUSA and its seminaries went through a process of maturation over many years. In the end, it is clear that the seeds for his final analysis of the PCUSA were planted many decades earlier while he was a student at Westminster College and at Westminster Seminary in the late 1930s during the tail end of the "Presbyterian Controversy." Despite teaching in two different mainline Presbyterian seminaries, he never strayed from a Machenesque understanding of theological liberalism. The concerns of Bloesch and Leith, two noted theologians, reveal that Gestner was not alone in his criticism of PCUSA seminary education. Throughout the 1990s Gerstner remained an active participant in the rise of non-mainline Reformed evangelical seminaries. His desire to teach at Knox was motivated by a desire to infuse energy into the new school, provide some stature, and promote his brand of Reformed apologetics and theology. Gerstner's involvement with the expanding Ligonier Ministries through the distribution of his books, audiocassettes, and videos raised his profile and made him even better known. After leaving the PCUSA he fought equivalent battles for the soul of evangelicalism. The books Gerstner published in the 1990s addressed difficult topics, but ensured that a conservative Reformed perspective was visible in such debates.

Gerstner's study of Edwards's theology was in various ways flawed. The three-volume series which began in 1991 was an accomplishment marred by Gerstner's own idiosyncratic interpretation of Edwards and the problems associated with its production. Connecting Edwards to Old Princeton was problematic because the New England theologian does not easily fit into the rational/evidentialist apologetic paradigm. No doubt many simply dismissed his work as a failed and unscholarly attempt to summarize Edwards's theology; *RBTJE* was not widely reviewed. And yet it must be recognized that *RBTJE* remains a valuable resource for Edwards's students simply because it reveals a massive analysis of Edwards's own writings. In addition, Gerstner inspired many evangelicals to study the colonial New England theologian. His teaching and lecturing on Edwards and his fervency for "the man" led to new interest in Edwards and the Calvinistic faith he proclaimed.

136. Leith, *Crisis in the Church*, 13–15.

8

Conclusion

ANY ASSESSMENT OF JOHN GERSTNER'S LIFE AND THOUGHT MUST HIGH-
light his resilience and persevering spirit. As a runner on the Westminster
College cross country team, Gerstner learned what it took to go the distance.
He wrote, taught, and lectured until the very end of his life. This study has
demonstrated that his persistence led him to make significant contributions
in changing proportion over time to both mainline Presbyterianism *and*
to the evangelical movement. Gerstner battled through major changes at
his seminary and in his denomination. He challenged those who sought
to change the doctrinal character of the PCUSA. At almost every point he
faced adversity and opposition and yet he kept going. His family provided
loving support, but as a parent he was uneasy with how the 1960s counterculture affected his children. He shaped the evangelical movement by
seeking to interpret its past and its historic theological boundaries. He also
played an important role in the debate over inerrancy. Moreover, his promotion of Jonathan Edwards in evangelical circles left an important legacy.
However, inadequacies were apparent in his scholarship. His termination as
the editor of the Yale volume on Edwards's sermons was profoundly disappointing to him. In addition, his evangelical renewal efforts in the PCUSA
were largely a failure. Even though Gerstner, was for the most part, defeated
in academia and in the PCUSA, he is important because he successfully
propelled Presbyterian and Reformed evangelicalism into his own day. The
surprising resurgence of this movement in modern America can be partly
attributed to Gerstner's energetic and tireless efforts.

Gerstner's early religious experiences proved highly transformative in
his life. He was greatly shaped by his involvement in an evangelical UPCNA
church, his conversion at the Philadelphia School of the Bible, and his period of study at Westminster College under John Orr. These events led to a
personal faith that was molded within evangelical United Presbyterianism

and strengthened by a liberal arts education at a UPCNA college. At Westminster, Orr helped Gerstner come to accept a Calvinist theological position and provided Gerstner with a model of informed evangelical scholarship. The spiritual and intellectual context of these formative events left their mark on the young student. The anti-modernist impulse within the UPCNA molded his young mind. Gerstner subsequently went on to pursue ordination by studying at the UP seminary, Pitt-Xenia. The Reformed evangelicalism that Gerstner had imbibed in his undergraduate years led him to reject the more moderate evangelicalism he encountered at Pitt-Xenia. As a result, Gerstner withdrew from Pitt-Xenia after one semester and entered Westminster Theological Seminary in Philadelphia, an institution known for its Reformed conservatism. At Westminster in the late 1930s, Gerstner observed the aftermath of the great "Presbyterian Controversy" that had engulfed the Presbyterian Church (USA) from 1922 to 1936. Gerstner did not share Westminster's separatist viewpoint, but he did embrace Machen's critique of theological liberalism in the PCUSA. Westminster provided Gerstner with a thorough biblical and theological education. Even though Westminster adhered to a conservative orthodox theological position, it did not steer its students away from more progressive institutions. Paul Woolley, Westminster's church historian, encouraged Gerstner to pursue a Ph.D. at Harvard University. Gerstner's marriage to the daughter of a key evangelical Mennonite leader, just prior to his arriving at Harvard, provided Gerstner with a wife who shared his religious commitments. At Harvard, Gerstner deepened his grasp of philosophy and intellectual history, but remained committed to his evangelical beliefs. In 1945 after earning his Ph.D. in the history and philosophy of religion, Gerstner continued to serve as the pastor of two Pittsburgh area UP churches. Gerstner thus retained his evangelical UP identity through seminary and graduate school and this faith tradition shaped his intellectual outlook, his commitment to pastoral ministry, and his scholarship in service of the church.

As Gerstner entered the 1950s, he made the transition from UP pastoral ministry to professor of church history at the UP seminary. At Pitt-Xenia, Gerstner was part of a cadre of scholars, led by Addison Leitch, who helped intensify the school's evangelical commitment. These efforts made Gerstner more widely known in the American evangelical movement and led to his service as a contributing editor of *Christianity Today* magazine. During the 1950s, Gerstner and his wife added two girls to their family. While Gerstner's home life remained calm, he encountered and addressed challenges at Pitt-Xenia and in the UPCNA. The evangelical character of Pitt-Xenia Seminary faced a serious threat when the UPCNA merged with the PCUSA in 1958. The coming together of these two denominations meant that

Pitt-Xenia would not be able to remain separate from the PCUSA's seminary in Pittsburgh, Western Theological Seminary. Gerstner opposed the merger of the two denominations and the consolidation of the two seminaries, but to no avail. He could not resist these juggernauts. As Gerstner dealt with these setbacks, he continued to write articles and essays and made progress on three books that would establish him as an evangelical scholar and apologist. In the 1950s Gerstner became intensely interested in the thought of Jonathan Edwards, the revered colonial theologian. In an effort to resurrect the illustrious Christian thinker and his theology, Gerstner taught courses on Edwards to Pitt-Xenia students and labored to produce a book on Edwards's view of salvation. His study of Edwards, *Steps to Salvation* (1960), cast him as an evangelical pioneer in Edwards studies. Against the backdrop of Billy Graham's decision-orientated evangelism and the need for improved evangelical intellectual life Gerstner promoted Edwards. The eighteenth-century theologian's brilliant mind and theory of seeking needed to be emulated. In his work, Gerstner blazed a trail in Edwards studies, which many evangelicals would later travel down. Thus by 1959, Gerstner had emerged as a noteworthy scholar in the newly formed UPCUSA *and* in the evangelical movement. Although Gerstner was certainly not alone in his efforts, his UP convictions led him to assert his own evangelical positions, thus making Pitt-Xenia a more explicit evangelical institution. As an indirect result, this led to Gerstner's becoming a notable leader in the wider American evangelical movement (via *Christianity Today*).

During the 1960s, Gerstner's work as a scholar and popular writer became better known with the publication of three of his books. He wrote on the theology of the sects, a popular theological work for laypeople and an apologetic treatise. In addition, he continued to write for *Christianity Today*, thus exercising his reputation over that magazine's growing evangelical readership. He also influenced the burgeoning evangelical movement through his adjunct teaching at Trinity Evangelical Divinity School (TEDS). At the newly formed Pittsburgh Theological Seminary (PTS), Gerstner continued his teaching and provided leadership for the school's evangelical student group. One of Gerstner's protégés at PTS, R. C. Sproul, would later play a key role in the renewal of Reformed evangelicalism. While Gerstner achieved much in the decade of the 1960s, he also faced challenges. On a personal level, Gerstner welcomed a son in 1960, but the 1960s counterculture disrupted his family life. His loving, but strict, parenting appears to have corresponded to his theological conservatism. Another problem Gerstner faced was that his evangelical viewpoint did not mesh well with the stance of the new consolidated PTS faculty. To make matters worse, Gerstner's closest evangelical ally at PTS, Addison Leitch, abruptly abandoned the seminary in 1961 and accused the school of "taking the road to liberalism."[1] Early on in the consolidation the former Western Seminary professors had achieved a more dominant role at PTS, and Gerstner subsequently had become marginalized as a faculty member. In many ways, the former Western professors had shaped PTS in the mold of the old Western Seminary. While Gerstner struggled in this new institutional milieu, he also had to deal with the theological changes that were taking place in the newly created UPCUSA. He vigorously opposed the revision of the Westminster Confession of Faith that produced the *Confession of 1967* (C-67) and a new *Book of Confessions*. He became the most visible UPCUSA seminary professor to oppose the confession. Despite his protests, the UPCUSA passed these doctrinal revisions overwhelmingly. Even though Gerstner was largely marginalized at PTS and in the UPCUSA, he seized on opportunities to express his evangelicalism.

In the 1970s Gerstner became a shaper of modern evangelicalism. He continued to teach at PTS and at TEDS, but expanded his teaching duties to the Ligonier Valley Study Center, which was founded in 1971 by his former student R. C. Sproul. As a Presbyterian churchman, he defended in church courts his former student, Wynn Kenyon, who was denied ordination because he would not participate in women's ordination. Even though Gerstner lost the Kenyon case, the controversy raised serious questions about the limits of tolerance in the UPCUSA. Gerstner actively participated in the "Battle of the Bible" by helping to launch the International Council of Biblical Inerrancy (ICBI). The creation of the ICBI by other evangelical scholars and church leaders was an attempt to counter evangelicals who were moving away from the inerrancy position. Gerstner also engaged in several important writing projects that defended inerrancy and defined evangelical identity. Gerstner's article entitled "The Theological Boundaries of Evangelical Faith," which appeared in the landmark book *The Evangelicals* (1975), gives evidence that Gerstner was playing a significant role within the movement.[2] Subsequent disagreement over his article, however, revealed the diverse nature of evangelicalism. In addition, Gerstner continued to write, teach, and lecture on Jonathan Edwards. Even though Gerstner was removed, in 1977, as the editor of the Yale volume on Edwards's sermons, he still continued to study and promote Edwards. According to Wilson Kimnach, a noted Edwards scholar, Gerstner became "an apostle of Jonathan Edwards."[3] He promoted Edwards at PTS, TEDS, the Ligonier Valley Study Center, and in numerous churches and at various events. As

1. Leitch quoted by Rimmel, "Seminary Too Liberal, Professor Says, Quits," 1.

2. Gerstner, "The Theological Boundaries of Evangelical Faith."

3. Kimnach, Interview with the author, 10 December 2010.

a result of Gerstner's passionate interest in the life, theology, and writings of Edwards, he motivated many students and colleagues to read and study and even pursue scholarship in this area. The negative side to his fervor, however, was that Gerstner could not offer the critical analyses required in an editor of Edwards's sermons. He struggled to transcribe Edwards's manuscripts and was too much of an advocate of Edwards's theology for many of the mainstream Edwards scholars. His struggle, as an evangelical outsider, to penetrate into the world of mainstream academic scholarship proved unsuccessful. Like Fuller Seminary's George Ladd, Gerstner failed to gain widespread respect within the academy and yet he did succeed in reviving interest in Edwards among American evangelicals, the country's most important constituency for Edwards studies. In the 1970s Gerstner became a shaper of modern evangelicalism through his teaching, lecturing, writing, and church leadership.

In 1980, after thirty years of teaching, Gerstner retired from PTS. As he moved forward, he would face both new challenges and new opportunities. He was unsuccessful in his attempt to prosecute Mansfield Kaseman, a UCC/Presbyterian minister whose heterodox theology many Presbyterians opposed. In 1981, however, as a direct result of the Kaseman conflict, the UPCUSA General Assembly issued a statement that affirmed a traditional understanding of Christ's divine and human natures. Gerstner pursued Kaseman because he believed strongly that liberal theology could never be ignored; in fact he believed that the church should always confront it. Gerstner's warnings to the UPCNA in 1956 about the doctrinal laxity of the PCUSA were realized in the Kaseman case. No doubt, Gerstner was deeply disturbed that although Wynn Kenyon had been denied ordination, Kaseman was accepted into the ministry of the UPCUSA. The denomination's failure to address Kaseman's views directly and opting instead for a General Assembly statement on the theological issues raised in the controversy appear to have exacerbated the conflict in the UPCUSA. The argument that Gerstner advanced early in the process, which was that the denomination's acceptance of Kaseman made the UPCUSA apostate, was taken seriously by some evangelicals. The reception of Gerstner's strong language even significantly contributed to the founding of the Evangelical Presbyterian Church (EPC). This new denomination became a haven for many disaffected mainline Presbyterians. As some members of the UPCUSA fled the denomination over the alleged apostasy, Gerstner later retracted his charge that the church was apostate. He continued to serve in the UPCUSA until the end of the decade. As theologian-in-residence at Eastminster Presbyterian Church (PCUSA) in Wichita, Kansas, Gerstner lectured and helped members grow in their knowledge of Reformed theology. Gerstner continued to write and lecture on Edwards and helped to found a publishing company, Soli Deo Gloria, which would republish work by Edwards and other books about him. Gerstner further established himself as an evangelical scholar by delivering numerous lectures at various evangelical colleges and seminaries. Moreover, he continued in his role as professor-at-large of Ligonier Ministries, and further expanded his evangelical influence. Gerstner's energy and uncompromising evangelicalism thus played significant roles in the increasingly polarised environment of Presbyterianism, most notably in the formation of the EPC and in the development of Presbyterian and Reformed evangelicalism for the late twentieth-century American church.

By 1990 Gerstner had reached a breaking point with his denomination. Gerstner withdrew from the PCUSA and joined the Presbyterian Church in America (PCA). His departure from the PCUSA was barely noticed in a church that had experienced a massive loss of over 1.2 million members from 1966 to 1987.[4] The conservative dissent that Gerstner had fomented within the denomination no doubt contributed to the PCUSA's continued loss of membership. The neglect Gerstner and other UPCNA evangelicals have received is problematic for Presbyterian history because it ignores a *bona fide* evangelical tradition within the church and skews the denomination's past. The lack of history written on UPCNA evangelicals has hurt the historical analysis of the controversies of the 1920s and 1930s and how that conflict reverberated throughout the church's subsequent history. A far too narrow view of the Machen conflict has led to a less than adequate interpretation of Presbyterian history after 1936. One of the reasons Gerstner is so important to Presbyterian history is because his influence extended into so many branches of American Presbyterianism and therefore played a leading role in developing the Presbyterian and Reformed evangelical movement. What is perhaps most remarkable about Gerstner's career is that he stayed with the PCUSA for so long, from 1958 to 1990. He was repeatedly ignored and marginalized and yet he consistently found ways to respond actively to controversy and to further evangelicalism.

It seems clear that the reason it took Gerstner so long to leave the denomination is that he lived his life on two tracks. He operated within his denomination, but also in the wider evangelical movement. The lack of encouragement he received from other PTS faculty members and administrators and other PCUSA scholars was mitigated by his evangelical contacts outside the PCUSA and PTS. Indeed, conservative Presbyterians, spurned by mainline Presbyterianism, helped establish the modern evangelical movement, and one of its subgroups, Presbyterian and Reformed

---

4. This statistic is found in Longfield's *The Presbyterian Controversy*, 3.

evangelicalism. Gerstner was a man, not unlike other evangelical leaders such as J. I. Packer and W. Stanford Reid, who lived between two worlds. One of the results of marginalization was that evangelical energy (including Gerstner's) was channeled into new evangelical ventures, organizations, and movements. Another key reason Gerstner stayed in the denomination was the influence of his mentor John Orr, who repeatedly encouraged his protégé to stay in the church. While mainline Presbyterianism had experienced serious decline in the last third of the twentieth century, evidence indicates that Presbyterian and Reformed evangelicalism was blossoming. Ligonier Ministries continued to grow and expanded its outreach through the use of radio, the Internet, and other forms of multi-media. Importantly, Gerstner's lectures were preserved and disseminated via audiocassette, VHS, and later as Internet and DVD resources. In addition, Reformed University Fellowship (RUF) mushroomed to over a hundred college and university campuses.

Significantly, the number of seminaries aligned with the Presbyterian and Reformed evangelical movement also continued to rise. Gerstner's lecturing and teaching in a number of these schools furthered his influence. His writings during the last six years of his life tackled thorny issues; one work dealt with the doctrine of hell and another with dispensationalism. Neither of these works nor his three-volume summary of Edwards's theology, however, was well written or edited, resulting in mostly devastating reviews. Nevertheless, his *RBTJE* offered comprehensive analysis of the colonial theologian's doctrinal views. The lasting contribution Gerstner made to the field of Edwards studies was a passionate promotion of Edwards to all who would listen; this active campaign lasted nearly fifty years. In many ways, Gerstner was a pioneer in Edwards studies, as he started to write and teach about the colonial theologian in the 1950s and early 1960s; this was a period prior to the dramatic rise of Edwards studies during the late 1960s.[5] Gerstner played an important role in the resurgence of Presbyterian and Reformed evangelicalism in the 1990s, as evidenced by his leadership and participation in growing institutions and in his reviving interest in Jonathan Edwards among the evangelical subculture.

One of the key aspects of his career was his work in the various smaller conservative Presbyterian bodies. Gerstner left a legacy in these denominations and in their institutions. He was active in speaking, debating, and teaching at Geneva College (Pennsylvania), an institution of the Reformed Presbyterian Church in North America (RPCNA). He also spoke at the RPCNA seminary in Pittsburgh and currently one of his former students,

5. On this point, see Hart, "Before the Young, Restless, and Reformed," 239–42.

Richard Gamble, is the professor of theology at this school. In addition, Gerstner was involved with RPCNA churches. The Pittsburgh church historian also had connections with the Associate Reformed Presbyterian Church (ARP) and preached in their congregations. His legacy in the ARP is detected by the fact that one of his protégés, Mark Ross, served for many years at the flagship ARP church and now serves as a professor of theology at Erskine Theological Seminary (South Carolina), the ARP'S only seminary. Furthermore, Gerstner also had a strong influence in the Presbyterian Church in America (PCA), of which he became a minister near the end of his life. His former students founded the PCA's first northern presbytery in 1975 and R. C. Sproul taught for many years at several of the Reformed Theological Seminary (RTS) campuses. While RTS is not directly affiliated with the PCA, it is strongly connected to it. Significantly, by 2014 another one of Gerstner's evangelical students from PTS, Mark Dalby, served as president of the PCA's national seminary, Covenant, in St. Louis, Missouri. Gerstner also influenced many of the founders of the Evangelical Presbyterian Church (EPC). Gerstner's fame as a scholarly evangelical leader in the mainline church opened many doors for him that perhaps would not have been open if he had spent his entire career in one of the smaller bodies.

Gerstner also participated in numerous ways in the wider evangelical movement. He preached at various evangelical churches and served as a contributing editor of *Christianity Today*, evangelicalism's chief periodical. In addition, he taught at the burgeoning Trinity Evangelical Divinity School (TEDS) and exerted some measure of influence over the students he taught there. At TEDS Gerstner appears to have had at least some influence on Mark Noll, who has subsequently become one of America's leading historians. Gerstner was not afraid to be counted as an evangelical and provided some support to the new Coalition for Christian Outreach, an upstart evangelical campus ministry. He spoke on the evangelical heritage at a meeting of the Evangelical Theological Society and helped lead a discussion at a conference that explored the future of evangelicalism. It is indeed notable that John White, one of Gerstner's Reformed Presbyterian colleagues, whom he had influenced when White was a student at Geneva College, became president of the National Association of Evangelicals (NAE). Gerstner's legacy with Ligonier Ministries was strong and the long durability of this group indicates the continued presence of a Reformed voice within the wider evangelical world.

The renewal of Reformed evangelicalism in the twentieth century can be partially traced to Gerstner's work. He participated in renewal movements in the mainline church that exist even to this day.[6] The revitalization that Edwards has brought to Reformed evangelicalism is in some measure attributable to Gerstner. Moreover, Ligonier's steady growth and expansion into radio, various forms of multi-media, national conferences, and most recently Ligonier Academy and Reformation Bible College offer some evidence of a Reformed evangelical revival. The rise of Reformed theology in the Southern Baptist Convention and in other churches and organizations such as the ACTs 29 network also reveals continued vitality. Gerstner's founding of Soli Deo Gloria books and the rise of other Reformed publishing houses has also been important and the continued expansion of Reformed evangelical seminaries is another sign of renewal. The momentous growth of Reformed University Fellowship, now on over 100 college campuses, shows a surge of interest in Reformed theology among young people. The publication of Colin Hansen's *Young, Restless, and Reformed* (2008) chronicles the various ways in which evangelical Calvinism is flourishing in contemporary America.[7] In 2009 *Time* magazine even dubbed the "New Calvinism" one of the top ideas changing the world today.[8] Furthermore, the rise of leading Reformed evangelical preachers such as Tim Keller and John Piper, signals a Reformed renaissance. While Gerstner is not necessarily connected to all of the movements mentioned, he did make solid contributions to the rebirth of Presbyterian and Reformed evangelicalism in modern America and should be considered one of the most influential Reformed evangelicals of the twentieth century.

One of the main currents in Gerstner's thought was his commitment to evidentialist apologetics. John Orr taught this form of apologetic method at Westminster College from 1928 to 1954 and Gerstner adopted this position as an undergraduate. The UPCNA's emphasis on a form of apologetic archaeology and Orr's evidentialism were strong influences on Gerstner's mind. His subsequent graduate studies with Cornelius Van Til and with various Harvard scholars did not change his mind on the issue of apologetics. In fact, Ralph Barton Perry, Gerstner's Ph.D. adviser, even seems to have reinforced the idea that Christians need to be able to provide answers to those who have questions. Perry told his student that he himself had decided to turn away from the ministry and study philosophy when some pastors refused to answer questions that he had about faith. Gerstner's dissertation on James McCosh allowed him to analyze the key challenges

---

6. Gerstner worked with Presbyterians United for Biblical Concerns (PUBC). This renewal group became Presbyterians for Renewal in 1988.

7. Colin Hansen, *The Young, the Restless, and the Reformed.*

8. Biema, "10 Ideas Changing the World Right Now: The New Calvinism."

facing the Christian faith and how a leading Christian philosopher astutely handled them. His study of McCosh reinforced his high view of reason and stimulated the idea that modern thought could be reconciled with evangelical Christian belief. Christian scholars, he believed, could effectively answer the most serious intellectual problems facing the faith. Even though, Gerstner had a high view of reason he still believed that spiritual factors still came into play in a person's faith. Gerstner was the last mainline Presbyterian seminary professor to hold to the Old Princeton apologetic and his dissemination of that viewpoint lives on in the Presbyterian and Reformed Evangelical movement.

Gerstner appears to have possessed a largely congenial personality throughout his life. His faculty colleagues in the 1950s and 1960s indicated that Gerstner was a friendly person and easy to get along with. This finding was somewhat unexpected given the turbulent events at Pittsburgh Seminary in the 1960s. As Gerstner entered the 1970s, however, he seems to have become less patient with colleagues at PTS. For him the development of the new PTS was a great disappointment and by retirement Gerstner appeared frustrated. C-67, the Kenyon case, and then the Kaseman case all seemed to have taken their toll on the scholar. Gerstner could be courteous, but he could also be somewhat brusque with those who shared a different theological perspective. This quality, although unappealing to most people (especially scholars), actually endeared him to many Presbyterian and Reformed conservatives, who cast him as a champion of the faith.

This book has sought to argue that Gerstner was deeply affected by his early religious experiences and that this led to his lifelong efforts to renew and revive Presbyterian and Reformed evangelicalism. It has been shown that his attendance at a UP church, his conversion at a dispensationalist Bible school, the Reformed mentoring of John Orr, and his seminary experience at Westminster all played significant roles in his distinct identity as a leader in the twentieth-century church. The combination of all these different influences produced an individual who both transcended his mainline denominational affiliation and also helped to develop an evangelical Calvinism that drew adherents from numerous denominations. This study of Gerstner's life and thought shows that an identifiable network of scholars, institutions and ministries, of which Gerstner was a crucial part, coalesced to form an observable American evangelical Calvinist subculture. Indeed, Gerstner, along with Francis Schaeffer and J. I. Packer, played a leading role in developing the Reformed evangelical movement after 1950. His position as a church history professor at the mainline PTS provided him with a platform to speak across the denominational spectrum. His voice was not confined to one church. Furthermore, the number of schools where he taught and lectured offers evidence of his influence. He taught courses at Pitt-Xenia, the consolidated Pittsburgh, TEDS, Geneva College and Knox Seminary, and with Ligonier ministries. He lectured widely at colleges, universities, seminaries, churches, and ministry events. His influence can partly be attributed to the vast number of places where he was willing to travel or to reside in order to further his goals, but it is also observed in the longevity of his tireless defence of his understanding of evangelicalism despite severe opposition at times. In the end, Gerstner's own evangelical conversion and Reformed education played a lasting role in his commitment to strengthening evangelical Calvinism. He never wavered from his early theological commitments. Even though evangelical United Presbyterianism is firmly in the past, new forms of the movement live on in the contemporary Presbyterian and Reformed evangelicalism that Gerstner labored so vigorosly to help create, promote, and defend. Most certainly, it was because of Gerstner's UP formation that he was able to foster the resurgent Reformed movement.

One of the conclusions of this book is that Gerstner did not have a stellar academic career. He was able to produce some popular books and some other works that represented industriousness, but they were not of high academic quality. His three-volume work on Edwards's theology provided a large-scale analysis of Edwards's thought and yet it was blemished by the lack of professional editing and his overemphasis on Edwards's use of reason. Gerstner's extensive knowledge of Edwards was impressive, but slanted because he viewed Edwards through the lens of Old Princeton. These problems contributed to his inability to demonstrate his decades of research in a scholarly fashion. An added problem was his strong advocacy of the colonial theologian. In short, his passion for Edwards caused him to be unable to step back and offer a more critical evaluation. His own personal theological agreement and intense love for Edwards clouded his academic work. His removal from the Yale committee on Edwards's works is a clear indication of his troubled scholarly career. However, there are parts of his scholarship which are helpful. In Gerstner's *RBTJE* he provided assessments of some parts of Edwards's theology that no other scholar has given. The new comprehensive survey of Edwards's theology written by Michael McClymond and Gerald McDermott interacts with Gerstner's work in numerous places.[9] While his Edwards's scholarship was clearly not top flight, it should be noted that it does have some value for the field of Edwards studies.

In the area of apologetics Gerstner represented an evidentialist approach that had been strongly marginalized in mainstream Protestant

9. See McClymond and McDermott, *The Theology of Jonathan Edwards.*

theology. The work of Karl Barth, the great Swiss theologian, had dealt a serious blow to the apologetic systems that stressed the importance of reason. The continuation of liberal theology in mainline Presbyterianism was also problematic for his position. Moreover, his evidentialism was somewhat maligned within conservative Presbyterianism because of the influence of Cornelius Van Til's presuppositonalism. Nonetheless, Gerstner's apologetic position persisted because of his own writing and teaching and as the result the work of his protégé R. C. Sproul. Gerstner's two apologetic books *Reasons for Faith* (1960) and *Classical Apologetics* (1984) did not represent the most advanced apologetic work, but did reinforce an evidentialism that has continued to be maintained by some evangelicals. In 1976 Gordon Lewis, a philosopher at Denver Seminary (Colorado), provided an examination of Gerstner's apologetic argument, thus highlighting the point that Gerstner had some apologetic influence.[10] It seems clear that Gerstner's apologetic extended largely to the laity and not to the scholarly arena. Gerstner was not a leading apologist, but he did play a role in keeping alive an evidentialism among the laity that had been spurned by many academics.

In the realm of mainline Presbyterian church politics Gerstner was almost completely unsuccessful. He failed to stop the 1958 merger of the UPCNA and the PCUSA, and he also could not halt the consolidation of Pitt-Xenia and Western seminaries. Moreover, in the 1960s Gerstner campaigned vigorously against the proposed Confession of 1967. He also failed to win this battle, but he and his fellow evangelicals were able to get some theologically orthodox statements into the new confession. Moreover, he lost both the Kenyon and Kaseman cases. These were very disappointing losses. The mainline Presbyterian church continued to veer to the theological left in the second half of the twentieth century and there was little Gerstner could do to stem the tide. These ecclesiastical setbacks, however, did not stop Gerstner in his efforts for evangelical renewal. Surprisingly, just as the UPUCSA became more progressive in its doctrine, the evangelical movement continued to expand. In the 1970s Gerstner became a shaper of the evangelical movement and sought to strengthen evangelicalism's theological boundaries. He argued for inerrancy and for a doctrinally conservative expression of evangelicalism. From his perspective, he did not want the evangelical movement to succumb to the theological liberalism that the mainline Presbyterian church had. He propelled his conservative evangelical vision forward through his teaching, lecturing, and mentoring. His involvement in various seminaries and other ministries reveal the extent of his influence. The continued growth of Ligonier Ministries offers

10. Lewis, *Testing Christianity's Truth Claims*, 60–71.

some evidence of the appeal of his theological perspective among the laity and some clergy. Moreover, the expansion of the Presbyterian Church in America and the Evangelical Presbyterian Church indicate the advance of a Calvinist orientated evangelicalism. The growth of Presbyterian and Reformed evangelicalism coincided with dramatic membership decline in the mainline Presbyterian church. Even though he lost his battles in the UPCUSA, it seems clear that he was successful in helping spawn the renewal of Presbyterian and Reformed evangelicalism in the last three decades of the century.

One of Gerstner's strength's was his ability as a classroom instructor. Many of his former students commented, in the oral interviews, on how impressive they thought Gerstner was as a teacher. His use of the Socratic method led to engaging classroom discussions and caused his students to study the assigned readings prior to class. Other students spoke of how amazed they were with Gerstner's knowledge of Jonathan Edwards. In a class on the cults Gerstner would play the role of a cult member, which led his students to defend traditional Christian doctrine. As a teacher Gerstner excelled in sparking conversation and comparing and contrasting different theological positions. During his career he developed a following of evangelical students whom he influenced. He did this in the classroom, but also by serving as the faculty advisor for an evangelical student group at Pittsburgh Theological Seminary. He became a mentor to many students and encouraged some to attend graduate school. One student even remembered Gerstner sending him money every month for the first year of graduate school. The number of Gerstner protégés who play a leading role in Presbyterian and Reformed evangelicalism today is a clear sign of Gerstner's importance to the movement he helped create. By all accounts he appears to have been a stimulating and caring teacher who engaged his students and pushed them to master course material. It must be said that part of Gerstner's influence stems from his work as an inspiring professor who left a lasting impression on his students.

Another arena where Gerstner excelled was in his work as a preacher and speaker. Even many people who disagreed with his theology commented on his outstanding lecturing abilities. Gerstner spoke forcefully and with conviction and he articulated a clear theological position. While he did not win many mainline Presbyterian scholars over to his side, evidence does suggest that he was able to reach some seminarians and laypeople. When Gerstner preached at the Pittsburgh Seminary chapel it was usually well attended. In addition, his popular lecturing on Jonathan Edwards established him as one of the leading promoters of the great American theologian. Part of contemporary evangelicalism's fascination with Edwards can be traced to Gerstner's efforts. Moreover, his participation in debates allowed him to advocate for an evangelical theological viewpoint in both ecclesiastical and university settings. Gerstner worked hard to ensure that conservative evangelical positions were part of the theological discussions in American church life. Video and audiocassette recordings of his lectures and debates were produced and ultimately put on the internet by Ligonier Ministries. This has served to continue his legacy into the present. Overall, Gerstner was a clear and effective communicator and this contributed to the renewal of the Presbyterian and Reformed evangelicalism.

Despite his flaws, Gerstner deserves to be regarded as an important evangelical and Presbyterian figure in post-World War II America. He was not a great apologist nor was he a leading Edwards scholar in his era. Likewise, his forays into Presbyterian church politics reveal that he was not a successful mainline Presbyterian church politician. Nevertheless, this book has demonstrated that Gerstner played a leading role in the development of the Presbyterian and Reformed evangelical movement. He was a constant promoter of evangelical theology and Jonathan Edwards. Throughout his career he tried to encourage others to study, learn, and embrace the Reformed tradition in all its richness. The scope of his activities was extensive. He lectured widely and was often willing to guest preach or offer a lecture on a wide range of topics. His energy can be detected even in the last years of his life. He also taught numerous students at various schools, engaged in important doctrinal controversies, and did whatever was necessary to ensure that his perspective was heard. As an evangelical leader he left an important legacy that continues to this very day in contemporary Presbyterian and Reformed evangelicalism. Part of the reason that he has a left such an inheritance is that Gerstner spoke for so many evangelicals who believed that their denomination was marginalizing their views. He was a theological leader for many disaffected Presbyterians who were troubled by the direction of their church. What this study has revealed is that their marginalization—and Gerstner's—was not ruinous and in fact helped provide the necessary energy that has led to the expansion of Presbyterian and Reformed evangelicalism. The rise of this movement in modern America can in many ways be linked to the life and thought of John Gerstner.

Bibliography

"About Chuck Colson (1931–2012)." Chuck Colson Center for Christian Worldview. www.colsoncenter.org/the-center/the-chuck-colson/center/about-chuck-colson. Accessed 8 April 2014.

"About Elisabeth." www.elisabethelliot.org/about.html. Accessed February 4, 2014.

Abrams, Richard. *America Transformed*. New York: Cambridge University Press, 2008.

"A Call To Every United Presbyterian . . ." *The Milwaukee Journal*. 27 December 1966, 12.

"A Confession? In 1967?" *Christianity Today*. December 1967, 36–37.

Adams, James L. "Its Debate and Decision Day for Presbyterians." *Cincinnati Post*. May 17, 1975, 28.

Adams, Jay. *The Homiletical Innovations of Andrew Blackwood*. Grand Rapids: Baker, 1976.

Ahvio, Juha. *Theological Epistemology of Contemporary American Confessional Reformed Apologetics*. Helsinki: Luther-Agricola Society, 2005.

Aitken, Jonathan. *Charles W. Colson*. Colorado Springs: WaterBook, 2005.

Annual Catalog of the Pittsburgh Theological Seminary 1961–1962. Pittsburgh: Pittsburgh Theological Seminary, 1961.

Annual Catalogue of the Pittsburgh Theological Seminary 1967–1968. Pittsburgh: Pittsburgh Theological Seminary, 1967.

Argo. 1936 Westminster College Yearbook. New Wilmington, PA: Westminster College, 1936.

Armstrong, John H. Interview with the author. December 29, 2010.

"Ascension Presbytery (PCA)." PCA Historical Center, St. Louis, Missouri. www.pcahistory.org.findingaids/presbyterariesAM/ascension.html. Accessed April 5, 2014.

Arnal, Oscar. Review of *Jonathan Edwards*, by John Gerstner. *Consensus* 13 no. 2 (1987) 94–95.

Ault, John. Email correspondence with the author. September 13, 2011.

Bahnsen, Greg, "A Critique of Classical Apologetics." *Presbyterian Journal* 44, no. 32, December 4, 1985. Accessed February 14, 2013. http://www.cmfnow.com/articles/PA061.htm.

Barbour, Clifford. *Annual Catalog of the Pittsburgh Theological Seminary of the United Presbyterian Church in the United States of America 1961–1962*, 4.

Barbour, Clifford. Letter to Buck. August 15, 1960. Barbour Papers, Pittsburgh Theological Seminary Archives.

Barr, Joe. Interview with the author. October 3, 2011.

Beal, Margaret. Interview with the author. September 7, 2013.

Beatty, William. Interview with the author. December 2, 2010.

Bebbington, David. *Evangelicalism in Modern Britain*. London: Routledge, 1993.

"Belhaven College Professor Presents Humanities Council Lecture." www.belhaven. edu/news/200304/Kenyon_lecture.pdf. Accessed March 14, 2014.

Bibby, Reginald. Review of *The Evangelicals*, *Sociological Analysis* 37, no. 4 (1976) 363–64.

Birney, Leroy. Email correspondence with the author. September 14, 2011.

Blake, Eugene Carson. "Anxiety, Frustration and Subconscious Hatred." *Pittsburgh Perspective* 2, no. 2 (1961) 11–16.

Bloesch, Donald G. Review of *The Evangelicals*, by David F. Wells and John D. Woodbridge. *Christian Scholars Review* 6, no. 1 (1976) 81–83.

———. Review of *Reasons for Faith*, by John Gerstner. *Theology and Life* 3, no. 4 (1960) 332.

———. *Theology of Word and Spirit*. Christian Foundations 1. Downers Grove, IL: InterVarsity, 1992.

Bogue, Carl. "Dr. John Gerstner Withdraws from the Presbyterian Church (USA)." *Christian Observer*, June 8, 1990, 20.

———. Interview with the author, July 7, 2010.

———. Interview with the author, April 9, 2014.

———. "Jonathan Edwards on the Covenant of Grace." In *Soli Deo Gloria*, edited by R. C. Sproul, 134–45. Philipsburg, NJ: P & R, 1976.

Bogue, Carl. Letter to John Gerstner, 6 December 1993. Bogue Papers, Scottsdale, AZ.

Bodamer, W. "Luther Stellung zur Lehre von der Verbalinspiration." *Theologische Quartalschrift* 33 (1936) 240–69.

Boice, James Montgomery, ed. *The Foundation of Biblical Authority*. Grand Rapids: Zondervan, 1978.

Borger, Byron. Interview with the author. May 23, 2014.

———. "Pete Steen—Legend or Legacy?" Accessed May 23, 2014. www.cardus.ca/comment/article/343/pete-steen-legend-or-legacy/.

Borstlemann, Thomas. *The 1970s*. Princeton: Princeton University Press, 2012.

Boyd, Lois, and R. Douglas Brackenridge. "Presbyterian Women Ministers: A Historical Overview and Study of the Current Status of Women Pastors." In *The Pluralistic Vision*, edited by Milton Coalter et al., 289–307. Louisville: Westminster John Knox, 1991.

Boyer, Paul. *When Time Shall Be No More*. Cambridge, MA: Harvard University Press, 1992.

Brackenridge, R. Douglas. Interview with the author. February 9, 2013.

"A Brief History of IBR." https://www.ibr-bbr.org/brief-history-ibr. Accessed May 24, 2014.

Brown, David. Letter to Gerstner. April 27, 1981. Gerstner Papers, Chandler, Arizona.

Bundy, D. D. "McQuilkin, Robert Crawford." In *Dictionary of the Presbyterian and Reformed Tradition*, edited by D. G. Hart and Mark Noll, 157–58. Downers Grove, IL: InterVarsity, 1999.

Buschart, David. Email correspondence sent to author. September 13, 2011.

Buchanan, Tom, and Christine Buchanan. *Sterling College*. Sterling, KS: Sterling College, 1987.

Bulletin, Founder's Day Celebration Service, Sterling College, October 25, 1987, John Gerstner Papers,Chandler, Arizona.

Bulletin, First Presbyterian Church Thornwell Lectureship, November 22–24, 1987, John Gerstner Papers, Chandler, Arizona.

Calhoun, David. *Princeton Seminary.* 2 vols. Edinburgh: Banner of Truth Trust, 1994, 1996.

Calovich, Annie, "Eastminster Church Decides to Break From Denomination." *Wichita Eagle,* 30 October 2011. Accessed April 3, 2014. www.kansas.com/2011/10/30/2083117/eastminster-decides-to-break-from.html.

Carpenter, Joel A. *Revive Us Again.* New York: Oxford University Press, 1997.

Carter, John. "On Leadership and Calling." Accessed January 4, 2011. http://www.rzim.org/default.aspx?TabId=602&articleid=6636&cbmoduleid=881.

Celebrating the CCO. Pittsburgh: Coalition for Christian Outreach, 2011.

Chapman, Alister. *Godly Ambition.* New York: Oxford University Press, 2012.

Christy, Wayne. "The United Presbyterian Church and Church Union." PhD diss., University of Pittsburgh, 1947.

Churchill, R. K. Review of *Reasons for Faith,* by John Gerstner. *Westminster Theological Journal* 23, no. 1 (1960) 50–54.

Clark, David K. Review of *Classical Apologetics,* by R.C. Sproul, John Gerstner, and Arthur Lindsley. *Journal of the Evangelical Theological Society* 29, no.3 (1986) 326.

Clark, Gordon H. "The Auburn Heresy." *Southern Presbyterian Journal,* July 15, 1946, 7.

"Clergyman Withdraws Charge That Church Betrayed Faith," June 27, 1981, *Milwaukee Journal,* 4.

Clowney, Edmund *Another Foundation.* Philipsburg, NJ: Presbyterian and Reformed, 1965.

Coalter, Milton. "Confession of 1967," In *Dictionary of the Presbyterian and Reformed Tradition in America,* edited by D. G. Hart et al., 65. Downers Grove, IL: InterVarsity, 1999.

Milton Coalter, John M. Mulder, Louis B. Weeks. *The Re-Forming Tradition: Presbyterians and Mainstream Protestantism.* Louisville: Westminster John Knox, 1992.

Cochrane, Arthur. "Barmen and the Confession of 1967." *McCormick Quarterly* 19, no. 2 (1966) 135–48.

Coffey, John, and Alister Chapman. "Introduction," In *Seeing Things Their Way,* edited by Alister Chapman et al., 1–23. Notre Dame, IN: University of Notre Dame Press, 2009.

Coffin, David F., Jr. "Gerstner on Edwards." *Tabletalk* 21, no. 10 (1997) 8–10, 52–53.

———. Interview with the author. July 6, 2010.

Coho, Frank, et al. *Ordination and Subordination.* Butler, PA: Concerned Group of United Presbyterians, 1975.

Coleman, Paul. "The Life and Works of John McNaugher." PhD diss., University of Pittsburgh, 1961.

Colson, Charles. "Keynote Address." In *Evangelical Affirmations,* edited by Kenneth Kantzer et al., 41–66. Grand Rapids: Academie, 1990.

"Committee on the Study of Religion, PhD Introduction." Accessed on July 3, 2013. http://studyofreligion.fas.harvard.edu/icb/icb.do?keyword=k70796&tabgroupid=icb.tabgrou106950.

Cornell, George W. "Presbyterian 'Court' Backs Minister in Christ Dispute." *Toledo Blade*, 7 February 1981, 10.

Coughenour, Robert A., ed. *For Me to Live*. Cleveland: Dillion/Liederbach, 1972.

Crampton, W. Gary. *Interpreting Edwards*. Lakeland, FL: Whitefield Theological Seminary, 2010.

Crocco, Steve. "Edward's Intellectual Legacy." In *The Cambridge Companion to Jonathan Edwards*, edited by Stephen J. Stein, 300–324. New York: Cambridge University Press, 2007.

———. "Whose Calvin, Which Calvinism? John Calvin and the Development of Twentieth Century American Theology." In *John Calvin's American Legacy*, edited by Thomas J. Davis, 165–88. New York: Oxford University Press, 2010.

Dart, John. "Religion Notes." *Los Angeles Times*, October 8, 1994. Accessed September 15, 2011. http://articles.latimes.com/1994-10-08/local/me-48001_1_san-fernando-valley.

Dayton, Donald. *Discovering an Evangelical Heritage*. New York: Harper & Row, 1976.

Davis, Edward. Interview with the author. February 11, 2013.

Davis, Mary Lou. *The Truth That Transformed Me*. Ross-Shire, Scotland: Christian Focus, 2006.

Davison, James. Letter to Gerstner, June 14, 1970. Gerstner Papers, Chandler, Arizona.

Dayton, Donald. *Discovering an Evangelical Heritage*. San Francisco: Harper & Row, 1976.

———. "'The Search for the Historical Evangelicalism': George Marsden's History of Fuller Seminary as a Case Study." *Christian Scholars Review* 23, no. 1 (1993) 12–33.

D'Elia, John. *A Place at the Table*. New York: Oxford University Press, 2008.

Delaney, C. F. "New Realism." In *The Cambridge Dictionary of Philosophy*, edited by Robert Audi, 610. 2nd ed. New York: Cambridge University Press, 1999.

Dennison, James. "John McNaugher and the Confessional Revision of 1925." In *Pressing toward the Mark,* edited by Charles G. Dennison and Richard C. Gamble, 221–31. Philadelphia: Committee for the Historian of the Orthodox Presbyterian Church, 1986.

———. Interview with the author, August 4, 2010.

———. Interview with the author, June 19, 2013.

———. Letter to Gerstner, November 4, 1983, Gerstner Papers, Chandler, Arizona.

DeWitt, H. Dewey. Interview with the author. July 6, 2010.

"Dispute over the Deity of Christ: The United Presbyterian Church is Disunited over a Heresy Case." *Time*, February 16, 1981, 78.

Dornbusch, Sanford M., and Roger D. Irle. "The Failure of Presbyterian Union." *American Journal of Sociology* 64, no. 4 (1959) 352–55.

Dorrien, Gary. *The Making of American Liberal Theology: Crisis, Irony, and Postmodernity*. Louisville: Westminster John Knox, 2006.

———. *The Remaking of Evangelical Theology*. Louisville: Westminster/John Knox, 1998.

Dorst, David. Letter to Gerstner, March 30, 1981, Gerstner Papers, Chandler, Arizona.

———. To the Session of Mt Lebanon U.P. Church and MacDonald, May 4, 1981, Gerstner Papers, Chandler, Arizona.

Dowey, Edward. "Revelation and Faith in the Protestant Confessions." *Pittsburgh Perspective* 2, no. 1 (1961) 9–26.

"Draft of Part of the JE Editorial Committee Meeting." April 8, 1977, Jonathan Edwards Center, Yale University.

"Dr. Carl W. Bogue Jr." Reformation International Theological Seminary. Accessed February 5 2014. www.reformation.edu/people/pages/carl-boguehtm.

"Dr. John Gerstner, Defender of the Faith." United Reformed News Service. Accessed April 9, 2014. www.iclnet.org/pub/resources/text/reformed/archive96/nr96-042.txt.

"Dr. John Gerstner Withdraws from the Presbyterian Church (USA)." *Christian Observer*, June 8, 1990, 20.

"Edna Suckau Wed to John Gerstner in Local Church." *Berne Witness*, September 9, 1940, 1.

Eller, Gary. "Special Interest Groups and American Presbyterianism." In *The Organizational Revolution*, edited Milton J. Coalter et al., 254–78. Louisville: Westminster John Knox, 1992.

Eshbaugh Howard, and James Arthur Walther. "Western Seminary." In *Ever a Frontier*, edited by James Arthur Walther, 133–58. Grand Rapids: Eerdmans, 1994.

Eskridge, Larry. "John Howard Pew." In *The Biographical Dictionary of Evangelicals*, edited by Timothy Larsen, 522–23. Downers Grove, IL: InterVarsity, 2003.

The Evangelical Student 1, no. 1 (1926) 1–12.

The Evangelical Student 3, no. 1 (1928) 1–24.

The Evangelical Student 9 and 10, no. 1 (1935) 1–40.

Evangelical Theological Society: 27th Annual Meeting Program, December 29–31, 1975.

Eveson, Phillip. "Lloyd-Jones and Ministerial Education." In *Engaging with Martyn Lloyd-Jones*, edited by Andrew Atherstone and David Ceri Jones, 176–96. Nottingham, UK: Apollos, 2011.

Farley, Edward. Interview with the author. August 14, 2012.

Fisk, William L. *A History of Muskingum College*. New Concord, OH: Muskingum College, 1978.

———. "Addison H. Leitch." In *Dictionary of the Presbyterian and Reformed Tradition in America,* edited by D. G. Hart et al., 142. Downers Grove, IL: InterVarsity, 1999.

———. "The United Presbyterian Church of North America." In *Dictionary of the Presbyterian and Reformed Tradition in America*, edited by D. G. Hart and Mark Noll, 264–65. Downers Grove, IL: InterVarsity, 1999.

Fitzwater, P. B. Review of *English Deism: Its Roots and Fruits,* by John Orr. *Moody Monthly* (1937) 598.

Flynn, Tyler. "Calvinism and Public Life: A Case Study of Western Pennsylvania 1900–1955." PhD diss., Pennsylvania State University, 2006.

"Founding." Reformed Theological Seminary. Accessed May 2, 2013. http://www.rts.edu/site/about/founding.aspx.

"4 Presidents' is Distance Runner." *Philadelphia Evening Bulletin.* December 7, 1935, n.p.

Fortson, Donald. *Liberty in Non-Essentials*. Livonia, MI: Evangelical Presbyterian Church, 2016.

"40+ Years of Ministry—A Testimony of Grace (Video)." LigonierMinistries. www.ligonier.org/blog/40-years-ministry-testimony-grace/. Accessed, February 30, 2013.

Franks, Rick. Interview with the author. April 3, 2014.

Freundt, A. H. "Presbyterian Church in America." In *Dictionary of the Presbyterian and Reformed Tradition in America,* edited by D. G. Hart, 198–99. Downers Grove, IL: InterVarsity, 1999.

Frame, John. *Cornelius Van Til.* Philipsburg, NJ: P & R, 1995.

———. "Cornelius Van Til." In *Handbook of Evangelical Theologians,* edited by Walter Elwell, 156–67. Grand Rapids: Baker, 1993.

———. "Machen's Warrior Children." In *Alister E. McGrath and Evangelical Theology,* edited by Sung Wook Chung, 113–46. Grand Rapids: Baker, 2003.

———. "Van Til and the Ligonier Apologetic." *Westminster Theological Journal* 47, no. 2 (1985) 279–99.

Frost, Ron. Email correspondence sent to the author, September 13, 2011.

Fudge, Edward. *The Fire That Consumes.* Houston: Providential, 1982.

G-6.0106b (1) UPC, 1081, Rankin v. National Capital Union Presbytery (Rem.Case 193–10) *PCUSA Annotated Book of Order,* 113. Accessed January 30, 2013. http://index.pcusa.org/NXT/gateway.dll/Constitution/CONST0930/level1000192/level1009.

Gage, Daniel S. "Dr. Lingle and the Auburn Affirmation." Accessed on January 11, 2014. www.pcahistory.org/documents/auburn/gage-1944lingle.html.

———. "The Auburn Affirmation." *Southern Presbyterian Journal* (1942) 19.

Gaitens, Robert J. "The Presbyterian Dispute." *Pittsburgh Post-Gazette,* January 7, 1967, 4.

Gamble, W. Paul. *The Westminster Story.* New Wilmington, PA: Westminster College, 2002.

Geisler, Norman L., and William Roach. *Defending Inerrancy.* Grand Rapids: Baker, 2011.

Geneva College Course Flier. "Dispensationalism." 1986, Gerstner Papers, Chandler, Arizona.

Geneva College Course Flier. "Jonathan Edwards: Model for Renewal and Reformation in Church and Nation." 1987, Gerstner Papers, Chandler, Arizona.

Gensch, Gary. Interview with the author. April 3, 2014.

Gerhardt, Andy. Interview with the author. January 5, 2011.

Gerstner, John. "20th Century: Theological Liberalism." Handout Church History Video, Ligonier Ministries, 1989. Accessed April 23, 2013. www.ligonier.org/learn/series/handout-church-history/20th-century-theological-liberalism/.

———. "American Calvinism until the Twentieth Century." *American Calvinism,* edited by Jacob Hoogstra, 13–39. Grand Rapids: Baker, 1957.

———. *The Apostasy of the United Presbyterian Church in the United States of America.* Westmoreland County, PA: privately published, 1981.

———. *A Biblical Inerrancy Primer.* Grand Rapids: Baker, 1965.

———. "Can Anyone Drink and Harm Only Himself." *United Presbyterian,* March 5, 1945, 21.

———. "Candidate Denied Ordination." *Presbyterian Layman* 7, no. 3 (1975) 1–2.

———. Letter to Carl Bogue. April 20, 1966, Carl Bogue Papers, Scottsdale, Arizona.

———. Letter to Carl Bogue. December 13, 1993, Bogue Papers, Scottsdale, AZ.

———. "Christian Science." *Christianity Today* 5, December 9, 1960, 5–7.

———. "A Church Historian Warns: Presbyterians Are Demoting the Bible." *Christianity Today,* December 3, 1965, 11–14.

———. "The Church's Doctrine of Biblical Inspiration." *The Foundations of Biblical Authority*, edited by James Montgomery Boice, 23–58. Grand Rapids: Zondervan, 1978.

———. "The Contributions of Charles Hodge, B. B. Warfield, and J. Gresham Machen to the Doctrine of Inspiration." In *Challenges to Inerrancy*, edited by Gordon Lewis and Bruce Demarest, 347–81. Chicago: Moody, 1984.

———. Curriculum Vitae. Carl F. H. Henry Papers, 1959, Billy Graham Center Archives, Wheaton College.

———. "Enlightenment." Handout Church History, Ligonier Ministries, 1989. Accessed May 23, 2014. www.ligonier.org/learn/series/handout-church-history/enlightenment-root-and-branch-attack-on-reformers.

———. *The Epistle to the Ephesians*. Grand Rapids: Eerdmans, 1958.

———. Letter to John Frame. July 21, 1990, Frame Papers, Orlando, Florida.

———. Friends of the Gerstner Project, November 1982, Gerstner Papers, Chandler, Arizona.

———. "Harvard." In *John H Gerstner: The Early Writings*, edited by Don Kistler, 2:108–10. Morgaintown, PA: Solo Deo Gloria, 1999.

———. Interview with David Coffin, June 15, 1992, PCA Historical Center, St. Louis, Missouri.

———. Interview with R. C. Sproul. Accessed July 1, 2013. http://www.ligonier.org/learn/series/silencing_the_Devil/an-interview-with-dr-gerstner/.

———. "Is Our Civilization Worth Keeping." *United Presbyterian*, February 5, 1945, 25.

———. *Jonathan Edwards*. Wheaton, IL: Tyndale, 1987.

———. "The Message of the Word." *The Bible*, edited by Merril C. Tenney, 165–76. Grand Rapids: Zondervan, 1968.

———. "New Light on the Confession of 1967." *Christianity Today*, December 9, 1966, 4–6.

———. "An Outline of the Apologetics of Jonathan Edwards, Part 1: The Argument of Being." *Bibliotheca Sacra* 133, no. 529 (1976) 3–10.

———. "An Outline of the Apologetics of Jonathan Edwards, Part II: The Unity of God." *Bibliotheca Sacra* 133, no. 530 (1976) 99–107.

———. "An Outline of the Apologetics of Jonathan Edwards, Part III: The Proof of God's Special Revelation, The Bible." *Bibliotheca Sacra* 133, no 531 (1976) 195–201.

———. "An Outline of the Apologetics of Jonathan Edwards, Part IV: The Proof of God's Special Revelation, The Bible—Continued." *Bibliotheca Sacra* 133, no. 532 (1976) 291–98.

———. "A Protestant View of Biblical Authority." In *Scripture in the Jewish and Christian Traditions*, edited by Frederick E. Greenspahn, 41–63. Nashville: Abingdon, 1982.

———. *Reasons for Faith*. New York: Harper's Bros., 1960.

———. *Repent or Perish*. Morgan, PA: Soli Deo Gloria, 1990.

———. "A Response to the Role of Logic in Biblical Interpretation." In *Hermeneutics, Inerrancy, and the Bible*, edited by Earl D. Radacmacher and Robert D. Preus, 873–78. Grand Rapids: Zondervan, 1984.

———. Review of *Therefore Stand*, by Wilbur Smith. *United Presbyterian*, November 12, 1945, 9, 11.

————. Review of *The New Modernism*, by Cornelius Van Til. *United Presbyterian*, December 30, 1946, 2.

————. Review of *Scottish Seceders in Victoria*, by Maxwell Bradshaw, *United Presbyterian*, January 9, 1950, 17.

————. Review of *Trends in Protestant Social Idealism*, by Neal J. Hughley. *United Presbyterian*, December 10, 1951, 3.

————. Review of *Luther and His Times*, by E. G. Schwiebert. *Interpretation* 5, no. 2 (1951) 240–42.

————. Review of *On This Rock*, by G. Bromley Oxnam. *United Presbyterian*, June 30, 1952, 2–3.

————. Review of *Faith and Sanctification* and *The Providence of God*, by Gerrit C. Berkouwer. *The United Presbyterian*, June 30, 1952, 3.

————. Review of *The Drift of Western Thought*, by Carl F. H. Henry. *The United Presbyterian*, June 23, 1952, 21.

————. Review of *The Theology of Reinhold Niebuhr*, by Edward Carnell. *United Presbyterian*, February 9, 1953, 20.

————. Review of *The Main Traits of Calvin's Theology*, by Bela Vasady. *United Presbyterian*, June 22, 1953, 22.

————. Review of *The Doctrine of God*, by Herman Bavinck. *United Presbyterian*, March 29, 1954, 22.

————. Review of *The History and Character of Calvinism*, by John T. McNeill. *United Presbyterian*, October 25, 1954, 22.

————. Review of *The Church and Infallibility*, by B. C. Butler. *Interpretation* 9, no. 1 (1955) 110–12.

————. Review of *Protestant Christianity*, by John Dillenberger and Claude Welch. *Interpretation* 9, no. 2 (1955) 219.

————. Review of *The Philosophy of Jonathan Edwards from His Private Notebooks*, edited by Harvey G. Townsend. *New England Quarterly* 29, no. 3 (1956) 423.

————. Review of *The Incomparable James Henry Snowden*, edited by W. W. McKinney. *Western Pennsylvania Historical Magazine* 45 (1962) 69–71.

————. Review of *Christian Dilemma*, by W. H. de Pol. *Interpretation* 7, no. 3 (1953) 376–77.

————. "Scotch Realism, Kant, and Darwin in the Philosophy of James McCosh." PhD diss., Harvard University, 1945.

————. Letter to Tom Stark, April 20, 1967, Gerstner Papers, Chandler, Arizona.

————. *Steps to Salvation*. Philadelphia: Westminster, 1959.

————. "The Contributions of Charles Hodge, B. B. Warfield, and J. Gresham Machen to the Doctrine of Inspiration." In *Challenges to Inerrancy*, edited by Gordon Lewis and Bruce Demarest, 347–81. Chicago: Moody.

————. *The Rational Biblical Theology of Jonathan Edwards*. Vols. 1–3. Powhatan, VA: Berea; Orlando, FL: Ligonier Ministries, 1991–1993.

————. "The Relation of White to Colored People." *United Presbyterian*, January 29, 1945, 20.

————. "The Theological Boundaries of Evangelical Faith." *The Evangelicals*, edited by David F. Wells and John D. Woodbridge, 21–37. Nashville: Abingdon, 1975.

————. *The Theology of the Major Sects*. Grand Rapids: Baker, 1960.

————. *Theology for Everyman*. Chicago: Moody, 1965.

————. Undergraduate Transcript, Registrar's Office, Westminster College.

————. Letter to Cornelius Van Til, February 20, 1960, Van Til Archives, Westminster Theological Seminary.

————. "Warfield's Case for Biblical Inerrancy." In *God's Inerrant Word*, edited by John W. Montgomery, 115–42. Minneapolis: Bethany Fellowship, 1974.

————. "Why Did Presbyterianism Not Win in England between 1640 and 1660?" [1950 Inauguration Address]. In *John Gerstner: The Early Writings*, edited by Don Kistler, 2:95–107. Morgan, PA: Soli Deo Gloria, 1998.

————. *Wrongly Dividing the Word of Truth*. Brentwood, TN: Wolgemuth & Hyatt, 1991.

Gerstner, John, R. C. Sproul, and Arthur Lindsley. *Classical Apologetics*. Grand Rapids: Academie, 1984.

Gerstner, John, and Paul C. Kemeny, "The Presbyterian Controversy." Fundamentalists, Modernists and Moderates [audiocassette]. Philadelphia: Westminster Media, 1992.

"Gerstner Speaks For Spiritual Life Week." *Ye Sterling Stir*, Sterling College, October 22, 1956, 1.

Gerstner Lectures Flier, First Presbyterian Church, Akron, Ohio, September 30, 1990, Carl Bogue Papers, Scottsdale, AZ.

Gerstner, Jonathan. Email to the author, March 8, 2014.

————. Interview with the author, June 15, 2010.

————. Interview with the author, April 30, 2012.

————. Interview with the author, September 10, 2012.

————. Interview with the author, May 2, 2013.

————. Interview with the author, August 8, 2013.

————. Interview with the author, June 9, 2010.

Gilliand, Thomas Matthew, Jr., ed. *Truth and Love*. Maryville, TN: United Presbyterian Conservancy of North America, 2008.

Glass, William Robert. *Strangers in Zion*. Macon, GA: Mercer University Press, 2000.

Gohrum, Dick. Interview with the author. 6 July 2010.

————. Interview with the author, 15 November 2011.

Graham, W. Fred. Letter to Gerstner, April 16, 1981, Gerstner Papers, Chandler, Arizona.

Grant, George. "A Thirst For Gerstner." *World*, April 6, 1996, 23.

Gregory, Thomas. Letter to Gerstner, April 1981, Gerstner Papers, Chandler, Arizona.

————. "The Presbyterian Doctrine of Total Depravity." In *Soli Deo Gloria*, edited by R.C. Sproul, 36–45. Philipsburg, NJ: P & R, 1976.

Grimstead, Jay. "How the International Council on Biblical Inerrancy Began." Accessed on November 6, 2012. http://65.175.91.69/Reformation_net/Pages/ICBI_Background.htm.

————. Interview with the author, January 20, 2014.

————. Interview with the author, November 6, 2012.

Gundlach, Bradley. *Process and Providence*. Grand Rapids: Eerdmans, 2013.

Gutjahr, Paul. *Charles Hodge*. New York: Oxford University Press, 2011.

Halverson, Richard. Letter to Gerstner, April 7, 1981, Gerstner Papers, Chandler, Arizona.

Hambrick-Stowe, Charles. Review of *The Rational Biblical Theology of Jonathan Edwards*, by John Gerstner. *Fides et Historia* 25, no. 2 (1993) 132–34.

Hamilton, Floyd. *Basis of the Christian Faith*. Rev. ed. New York: Harper & Row, 1964.

Hankins, Barry. *Francis Schaeffer*. Grand Rapids: Eerdmans, 2008.

Hannah, John. *An Uncommon Union*. Grand Rapids: Zondervan, 2009.

Hansen, Colin. *Young, Restless, Reformed*. Wheaton, IL: Crossway, 2008.

Hart, D. G. "Before the Young, Restless and Reformed: Edwards' Appeal to Post-World War II Evangelicals." In *After Jonathan Edwards*, edited by Oliver D. Crisp and Douglas A. Sweeney, 237–53. New York: Oxford University Press, 2012.

———. "Beyond the Battle for the Bible: What Evangelicals Missed in Van Til's Critique of Barth." In *Karl Barth and American Evangelicalism*, edited by Bruce McCormack and Clifford Anderson, 42–70. Grand Rapids: Eerdmans, 2011.

———. *Between The Times*. Willow Grove, PA: The Committee for the Historian of the Orthodox Presbyterian Church, 2011.

———. *Calvinism*. New Haven: Yale University Press, 2013.

———. *Defending the Faith*. Baltimore: John Hopkins University Press, 1994.

———. "Defending the Faith." April 21, 2010. Accessed May 16, 2014. www.vimeo.com/11406692.

"Make War No More? The Rise, Fall, and Resurrection of Machen's Warrior Children." In *Always Reformed*, edited by R. Scott Clark and Joel E. Kim, 37–55. Escondido, CA: Westminster Theological Seminary, 2010.

Hayton, Bradley. Review of *Wrongly Dividing the Word of Truth*, by John Gerstner. *Journal of Psychology and Christianity* 12, no. 2 (1993) 186–87.

Heidbrecht, Paul. "Evangelical Presbyterian Church." In *Dictionary of the Presbyterian and Reformed Tradition in Modern America*, edited by D. G. Hart and Mark Noll, 94. Downers Grove, IL: InterVarsity, 1999.

Heimert, Alan D. Review of *Steps to Salvation*, by John Gerstner. *American Literature* 32, no. 4 (1961) 473.

Heinze, Frank. "PUBC Meets in Chicago to Discuss Confession." *Presbyterian Life*, January 1, 1966, 26–27.

Henry, Carl F. H. *God, Revelation and Authority*. Vols. 1–6. Waco: Word, 1976–1983.

Herchenroether Jr., Henry C. "Pittsburgh Theological Seminary 1959–1999." Unpublished paper, August, 1999.

"History." Fellowship of Christian Athletes. Accessed May 27, 2014. www.fca.org/about-fellowship-of-christian-athletes/history/.

"History of the Harvard PhD program in the History and Philosophy of Religion," Committee on the Study of

"Religion, PhD, Introduction." Accessed on July 3, 2013. http://studyofreligion.fas.harvard.edu/icb/icb.do?keyword=k70796&tabgroupid=icb.tabgrou106950.

Hodges, Zane. "Calvinism Ex Cathedra: A Review of John Gerstner's *Wrongly Dividing the Word of Truth: A Critique of Dispensationalism*." *Journal of the Grace Evangelical Society* 4, no. 2 (1991). Accessed May 4, 2013. http://www.faithalone.org/journal/1991b/Calvin.html.

Hodiak, Bohdan. "Assembly Soothes Presbyterian Rift." *Pittsburgh Post-Gazette*, June 6, 1981, 5.

———. "Ministry Presbyterians Cite Biblical Authority Loss." *Pittsburgh Post-Gazette*, November 22, 1980, 16.

———. "Theological Seminary Seeks an Image." *Pittsburgh Post-Gazette*, June 26, 1976, 16.

———. "U. P. Church Vote: Apostate." *Pittsburgh Post-Gazette*, June 12, 1981, 9.

Hoeveler, J. David. *James McCosh and the Scottish Intellectual Tradition*. Princeton: Princeton University Press, 1981.

Hoffecker, Andrew. "Beauty and the Princeton Piety." In *Soli Deo Gloria*, edited by R.C. Sproul, 118–33. Philipsburg, NJ: P & R, 1976.

———. *Charles Hodge*. Philipsburg, NJ: Presbyterian and Reformed, 2011.

———. *Piety and the Princeton Theologians*. Philipsburg, NJ: P & R, 1981.

———. "Princeton Theology." In *Dictionary of the Presbyterian and Reformed Tradition in America*, edited by D.G. Hart and Mark Noll, 202. Downers Grove, IL: InterVarsity, 1999.

Hoke, Donald E. "Consultation on Future Evangelical Concerns." Workshop pamphlet, C-5, December 14–17, 1977.

Howard, Robert L. Interview with the author. February 7, 2013.

Hoop, John. Interview with the author. September 16, 2011.

Hopkins, Joseph M. "'Concerned' Faction Spurns Presbyterian Accommodation." *Christianity Today*, July 1981, 96–97.

Horton, Michael. "Is Evangelicalism Reformed or Wesleyan? Re-Opening the Marsden-Dayton Debate." *Christian Scholars Review* 31, no. 2 (2001) 137–55.

———. "Response to Roger E. Olson's Reply." *Christian Scholars Review* 31, no. 2 (2001) 163–68.

Hughes, Philip. "The Sovereignty of God—Has God Lost Control?" In *Soli Deo Gloria*, edited by R.C. Sproul, 26–35. Philipsburg, NJ: P & R, 1976.

Hui, Tim. Interview with the author. June 20, 2013.

Hunter, James Davidson. *American Evangelicalism* . New Brunswick, NJ: Rutgers University Press, 1983.

Hurlbutt, Robert H. *Hume, Newton and the Design Argument*. Lincoln: University of Nebraska Press, 1965.

Inauguration Bulletin of the Reverend Dr. John Gerstner, Jr., Ph.D., Thursday Evening, 16 November 1950. John Gerstner Papers, Chandler, Arizona.

Jamison, Wallace N. "Associate and Associate Reformed Seminaries." In *Ever a Frontier*, edited by James Arthur Walther, 83–95. Grand Rapids: Eerdmans, 1994.

———. "The United Presbyterian Seminaries." In *Ever a Frontier*, edited by James Arthur Walther, 97–116. Grand Rapids: Eerdmans, 1994.

———. *The United Presbyterian Story*. Pittsburgh: Geneva, 1958.

Johnson, A. Wetherall. *Created for Commitment*. Wheaton, IL: Tyndale, 1982.

Johnston Reformed Conference Flier. "The Christian Church." October 8–10, 1993, John Gerstner Papers, Chandler, Arizona.

"Judicial Commission Upholds Presbytery's Reception of Minister." *The Presbyterian Layman* 14, no. 2 (1981) 1.

Jumper, Mark. Interview with the author. February 6, 2013.

Kaiser, Walter. Letter to Gerstner. April 9, 1981, Gerstner Papers, Chandler, Arizona.

Kantzer, Kenneth. "John Calvin's Theory of the Knowledge of God and the Word of God." PhD diss., Harvard University, 1950.

———. Letter to Gerstner. January 31, 1966, Gerstner Papers, Chandler, Arizona.

Kaseman, Mansfield. Interview with the author. January 29, 2013.

Kehm, George. Interview with the author. August 14, 2012.

Kelly, Carl Robert. "The History of Religious Instruction in United Presbyterian Colleges." PhD diss., University of Pittsburgh, 1952.

Kelley, Bob. Interview with the author. December 2, 2010.

————. Interview with the author, May 22, 2012.

————. "Pittsburgh-Xenia Seminary." In *Ever a Frontier*, edited by James Arthur Walther, 117–32. Grand Rapids: Eerdmans, 1994.

Kelsey, Hugh A. "Enrichment of the Spiritual Life." *The Evangelical Student* 5, no. 2 (1931) 7–8.

————. *The Life Story of a Garden Variety Preacher*. Sterling, KS: Sterling College, 2007.

Kemeny, Paul C. Interview with the author. March 15, 2012.

Kilpatrick, Ron. Interview with the author. September 22, 2011.

Kimnach, Wilson. Interview with the author. December 10, 2010.

————. Interview with the author, December 6, 2012.

Kistler, Don, ed. *John H Gerstner: Early Writings*. Vols. 1–2. Morgantown, PA: Solo Deo Gloria, 1997, 1999.

————. Interview with the author, July 13. 2010.

————. Interview with the author, July 14 2012.

Klein, Douglas. "Letter to the Editor." *Pittsburgh Press*, March 1, 1981, B-4.

Kuhlman, Paul. *The Story of Grace*. Omaha: Grace College of the Bible, 1980.

Kyle, Melvin Grove. "The Bible in the Light of Archaeological Discoveries." *Bibliotheca Sacra* 74, no. 293 (1917) 1–19.

————. *The Deciding Voice of the Monuments in Biblical Criticism*. Oberlin, OH: Bibliotheca Sacra, 1912.

————. "The Recent Testimony of Archaeology." In *The Fundamentals*, edited by R. A. Torrey and A. C. Dixson, 1:315–33. Grand Rapids: Baker Book House, 2000.

Kyle, Richard, and Dale Johnson. *John Knox*. Eugene, OR: Wipf and Stock, 2009.

Lamerson, Samuel. Interview with the author. September 16, 2011.

Larsen, Robert. Interview with the author. July 23, 2012.

"Launching Seminary Probe Denied." *Pittsburgh Post-Gazette*, June 25, 1961, section 1, page 3.

"Lay Committee Advertisements Assail Proposed Confession," *Presbyterian Life*, February 1, 1967, 23–24.

Lehrer, Keith. "Reid, Thomas." In *Cambridge Dictionary of Philosophy*, edited by Robert Audi, 783–87. 2nd ed. New York: Cambridge University Press, 1999.

Leitch, Addison. *Interpreting Basic Theology*. Great Neck, NY: Channel, 1961.

————. *A Layman's Guide to Presbyterian Beliefs*. Grand Rapids: Zondervan, 1967.

————. Review of *Reasons for Faith*, by John Gerstner. *Pittsburgh Perspective* 1, no. 3 (1960) 24–27.

————. "The Relevancy of Calvin to Modern Issues within Protestantism." PhD diss., Cambridge University, 1941.

————. Review of *The Theology of the Major Sects*, by John Gerstner. *Pittsburgh Perspective* 1, no. 3 (1960) 27–29.

————. *Winds of Doctrine*. Westwood, NJ: Revell, 1966.

Leith, John. *Crisis in the Church*. Louisville: Westminster John Knox, 1997.

————. *Introduction to the Reformed Tradition*. Richmond, VA: John Knox, 1981.

Lesser, M. X. *Jonathan Edwards*. Westport, CT: Greenwood, 1994.

Lemos, Noah M. "Perry, Ralph Barton." In *The Cambridge Dictionary of Philosophy*, edited by Robert Audi, 660. 2nd ed. New York: Cambridge University Press, 1999.

Lewis, Gordon. *Testing Christianity's Truth Claims*. Chicago: Moody, 1976.

Lieber, David. "U. Darby Chronicle From Farm to Suburb." *Philadelphia Inquirer*, 12 June 1988. Accessed July 2, 2013. http://articles.philly.com/1988–06–12/news/26268776_1_log-cabin-upper-darby-township-paperback.

Linder, Dale. "Preaching the Whole Counsel." Edited by R. C. Sproul Jr. *Tabletalk* 21, no. 10 (1997) 54–55.

Lindsley, Arthur. John Gerstner Funeral Service Video. March 28, 1996, John Gerstner Papers, Chandler, Arizona.

Livingstone, David N. *Darwin's Forgotten Defenders*. Edinburgh: Scottish Academic, 1987.

Logan, Samuel. Email to the author. July 15, 2012.

———. Email to the author, July 16, 2012.

Long, Burke O. *Planting and Reaping Albright*. University Park: Pennsylvania State University Press, 1997.

Long, William. Interview with the author. January 6, 2011.

Longfield, Bradley J. *Presbyterians and American Culture*. Louisville: Westminster/John Knox, 2013

———. *The Presbyterian Controversy*. New York: Oxford University Press, 1991.

Luidens, Donald A. "Numbering the Presbyterian Branches: Membership Trends since Colonial Times." In *The Mainstrean Protestant "Decline*," edited by Milton Coalter et al., 29–65. Louisville: Knox, 1990.

MacDonald, Myles W. Letter to John H. Gerstner, 15 May 1981, Gerstner Papers, Chandler, Arizona.

Machen, J. Gresham. *Christianity and Liberalism*. New York: Macmillan, 1923.

MacLeod, A. Donald. *George Murray of the "U.P."* Boston: Newton Presbyterian Church, 1996.

———. *W. Stanford Reid*. Montreal: McGill-Queen's University Press, 2004.

Mangum, R. Todd. *The Dispensational Covenantal Rift*. Milton Keynes, UK: Paternoster, 2007.

Marietta College Athletic Department Obituary for Wynn Kenyon. Accessed October 22, 2012. http://pioneers.marietta.edu/sports/2012/2/27/FB_0227124538.aspx?id=166.

Marsden, George. Email correspondence to the author. July 14, 2011.

———. *The Evangelical Mind and the New School Presbyterian Experience*. New Haven: Yale University Press, 1970.

———. "From Fundamentalism to Evangelicalism: A Historical Analysis." In *The Evangelicals*, edited by David Wells and John Woodbridge, 122–42. Nashville: Abingdon, 1975.

———. *Fundamentalism and American Culture*. New York: Oxford University Press, 1980.

———. *Reforming Fundamentalism*. Grand Rapids: Eerdmans, 1987.

Marston, George W. Review of *The Theology of The Major Sects*. by John Gerstner. *Westminster Theological Journal* 23, no. 2 (1961) 239–42.

Martin, David V., ed. *Trinity International University 1897–1997*. Deerfield, IL: University Press, 1998.

Martin, Walter. Review of *The Theology of The Major Sects*, by John Gerstner. *Christianity Today*, November 21, 1960, 174–75.

Masthead for *Christianity Today* 1, no. 1 (October 15, 1956) 2.

Mawhinney, Bruce. Interview with the author. October 13, 2010.

Maxwell, Jack Martin. Interview with the author. October 25, 2012.

Maxwell v. Presbytery of Pittsburgh. Remedial Case 1, 1975. Accessed October 25, 2012. http://index.pcusa.org/NXT/gateway.dll/Constitution/CONST09-30/level1000278.htm/leve.

Mayhue, Richard L. "Who Is Wrong? A Review of John Gerstner's *Wrongly Dividing the Word of Truth.*" *The Master's Journal* 3, no. 1 (1992) 73–94.

McCallum, Ed. Interview with the author. February 11, 2012.

McCrea, Earle. Letter to Gerstner, March 27, 1981, Gerstner Papers, Chandler, Arizona.

McCrory, James Thomas. "A Message From the Past to the Present and the Future." In *Testimonial and Memorial to William Gallogly Moorehead for Forty One Years Professor in the Xenia Theological Seminary,* 47–52. Xenia, OH: Smith, 1913.

McCulloch, W. E. *The United Presbyterian Church and Its Work in America.* Pittsburgh: Board of Home Missions of the United Presbyterian Church of North America, 1925.

McDermott, Gerald. Email to the author. April 9, 2014.

McDonald, Jeffrey S. Interview with White—TEDS assistant registrar, January 20, 2013.

McKim, Donald. *Ever a Vision.* Grand Rapids: Eerdmans, 2009.

———. Interview with the author. October 18, 2010.

McKinney, William W. "Many Streams One River." In *The Presbyterian Valley,* edited by William W. McKinney, 528–59. Pittsburgh: Davis & Warde, 1958.

McKinney, William W., ed. *The Incomparable Snowden.* Pittsburgh: Davis and Warde, 1961.

McMullen, Michael. Review of *The Rational Biblical Theology of Jonathan Edwards, vol. 1,* by John Gerstner. *Evangelical Quarterly* 65, no. 1 (1993) 58–59.

McNabb, Darryl. Interview with the author. July 26, 2011.

McNaugher, John. *Theological Education in the United Presbyterian Church and Its Ancestries.* Pittsburgh: United Presbyterian Board of Publication and Bible School Work, 1931.

McQuilkin, Marguerite. *Always in Triumph.* Columbia, SC: Columbia Bible College, 1955.

Medsger, Betty. "Presbyterians Examine Confession of Faith." *Johnstown Tribune-Democrat,* n.d., Gerstner Papers, Chandler, Arizona.

Metzger, John Mackay. *The Hand and the Road.* Louisville: Westminster, 2010.

Middlekauff, Robert. "Perry Miller." In *Pastmasters,* edited by Marcus Cunliffe and Robin W. Winks, 167–90. New York: Harper & Row, 1969.

Minkema, Kenneth. Email to the author, May 15, 2014.

———. Interview with the author. October 13, 2011.

———. "Jonathan Edwards in the Twentieth Century." *Journal of the Evangelical Theological Society* 47 (2004) 659–87.

Miglorie, Daniel L. "A Conversation with Edward A. Dowey." *The Princeton Seminary Bulletin* 9, no.2 (1988) 89–103.

Miller, Glenn T. *Piety and Profession.* Grand Rapids: Eerdmans, 2007.

Minutes of an Adjourned Meeting of the Board of Directors, Pittsburgh Theological Seminary of the United Presbyterian Church in the United States of America. June 19, 1961. Pittsburgh, PA, Pittsburgh Theological Seminary Archives.

Montgomery, John W., ed. *God's Inerrant Word.* Minneapolis: Bethany Fellowship, 1974.

Moody, Suzanne. Interview with the author. February 9, 2013.

Moore, James R. *The Post-Darwinian Controversies*. Cambridge: Cambridge University Press, 1979.

Moore, Joseph. *Founding Sins*. New York: Oxford University Press, 2016.

Moore, Louis. "Presbyterians Affirm Deity of Christ, Vow to Be Led By Historic Confessions." *Christianity Today*, June 26, 1981, 32–33.

Moorhead, James H. *Princeton Seminary in American Religion and Culture*. Grand Rapids: Eerdmans, 2012.

———. "Redefining Confessionalism: American Presbyterians in the Twentieth Century." *Journal of Presbyterian History* 79, no. 1 (2001) 72–86.

Moorehead, William G. "Millennial Dawn: A Counterfeit of Christianity." In *The Fundamentals*, edited by R. A. Torrey and A. C. Dixon, 4:109–130. Grand Rapids: Baker, 2000.

———. "The Moral Glory of Jesus Christ A Proof of Inspiration." In *The Fundamentals*, edited by R. A. Torrey and A. C. Dixon, 2:61–79. Grand Rapids: Baker, 2000.

Morgan, D. Densil. *Barth Reception in Britain*. London: T. & T. Clark, 2010.

Muether, John. *Cornelius Van Til*. Philipsburg, NJ: P & R, 2008.

———. "The Significance of Paul Wooley Today." In *Confident of Better Things*, edited by John R. Muether and Danny E. Olinger, 7–23. William Grove, PA: Committee for the Historian of the Orthodox Presbyterian Church.

Murphy, Martin. "Defender of the Faith." *Tabletalk* 21, no. 10 (1997) 11–13.

Murray, Iain. *The Life of John Murray*. Edinburgh: Banner of Truth Trust, 2007.

Nelson, Rudolph. *The Making and Unmaking of an Evangelical Mind*. New York: Cambridge University Press, 1987.

1930 United States Census. s.v. "John Gustner [John Gerstner]." Philadelphia, accessed through *Ancestry.com*.

Noll, Mark A. *America's God*. New York: Oxford University Press, 2002.

———. "Catching Up with the Evangelicals." *Christianity Today*, December 5, 1975, 18–21.

———. "Edwards Theology After Edwards." In *The Princeton Companion to Jonathan Edwards*, edited by Sang Hyun Lee, 292–308. Princeton: Princeton University Press, 2005.

———. *A History of Christianity in the United States and Canada*. Grand Rapids: Eerdmans, 1992.

———. "Jonathan Edwards and Nineteenth-Century Theology." In *Jonathan Edwards and the American Experience,* edited by Nathan Hatch and Harry Stout, 260–87. New York: Oxford University Press, 1988.

———. Interview with the author. September 13, 2011.

———. *The Old Religion in the New World*. Grand Rapids: Eerdmans, 2001.

———. "Princeton Theology." In *New Dictionary of Theology,* edited by Sinclair Ferguson et al., 532–33. Downers Grove, IL: InterVarsity, 1988.

Noll, Mark A., ed. *The Princeton Theology*. Grand Rapids: Baker, 1983.

Noll, Mark, and George Rawlyk. *Amazing Grace*. Grand Rapids: Baker, 1993.

Nutt, Rick. "The Tie That No Longer Binds: The Origins of the Presbyterian Church in America." In *The Confessional Mosaic,* edited by Milton Coalter, John Mulder, and Louis Weeks, 236–58. Louisville: Westminster John Knox, 1990.

Okholm, Dennis. Interview with the author. January 13, 2011.

Olson, Roger E. "The Reality of Evangelicalism: A Response to Michael S. Horton." *Christian Scholars Review* 31, no. 2 (2001) 157–62.

"Once in a Century." *United Presbyterian* 116, no. 22 (1958) 9.

Orr, James, and Melvin Grove Kyle, eds. *International Standard Bible Encyclopaedia*. 5 vols. Chicago: Howard-Severance, 1929.

Orr, John, *English Deism: Its Roots and Fruits*. Grand Rapids: Eerdmans, 1934.

Packer, J. I. "Sola Fide: The Reformed Doctrine of Justification." In *Soli Deo Gloria*, edited by R. C. Sproul, 11–25. Philipsburg, NJ: P & R, 1976.

Parsons, Buck. "R.C. Sproul: A Man Called by God." Accessed December 1, 2012. http://www.ligonier.org/learn/articles/r-c-sproul-man-called-god.

Patterson, Bob, *Carl F. H. Henry*. Waco: Word, 1983.

Patterson, James. Review of *Jonathan Edwards*, by Bob E. Patterson. *Eternity* 39 (1989) 36–37.

Partee, Charles. *Adventure in Africa*. Grand Rapids: Zondervan, 1990.

———. Interview with the author. October 13, 2010.

Perspectives 7, no. 6 (1973) 19.

Peterson, Robert A. "Undying Worm, Unquenchable Fire." *Christianity Today*, October 23, 2000. Accessed May 1, 2013. www.christianitytoday.com/ct/2000/october23/1.20html?paging=off.

Peterson, Rodney L., and George Williams, eds. *The "Augustan Age."* Vol. 2. Gottingen: Vandenhoeck and Ruprecht, 2014.

Philbrick, Richard. "Presbyterian Doctrine Plan Is Criticized." *Chicago Tribune*, November 23, 1965, B11.

Philosophy B1hf 1941–1942. Harvard University Reading Assignments, Gerstner Papers, Chandler, Arizona.

Pittsburgh-Xenia Theological Seminary: Annual Catalogue 1949–1950. Pittsburgh: Pittsburgh-Xenia Theological Seminary, 1949–1950.

Pittsburgh-Xenia Theological Seminary: Annual Catalogue 1950–1951. Pittsburgh: Pittsburgh-Xenia Theological Seminary, 1950–1951.

Pittsburgh-Xenia Theological Seminary: Annual Catalogue 1952–1953. Pittsburgh: Pittsburgh-Xenia Theological Seminary, 1952–1953.

"Pittsburgh-Xenia Seminary Holds Inauguration Service." *United Presbyterian*, December 4, 1950, 7.

Pope, Liston. "The 1960 Commencement Address." *Pittsburgh Perspective* 1, no. 5 (1960) 13–18.

"Presbyterians Debate Jesus' Divinity." *Rock Hill Herald*, May 25, 1981, 3.

Presbyterian Church in America Historical Center. Statistical Tables. Accessed April 23, 2013. www.pcahistory.org/main/pcastats.html.

"The Presbyterian League of Faith." *Christianity Today*, May 1931, 19.

"Public Education: High Schools." *The Encyclopedia of Greater Philadelphia*. Accessed May 28, 2014. www.philadelphiaencyclopedia.org/archive/public-education-high-schools/.

Pulliam, Ken. Review of *Wrongly Dividing the Word of Truth*, by John Gerstner. *Journal of the Evangelical Theological Society* 38, no. 1 (1995) 118.

Purdy, Richard A. "Carl F. H. Henry." In *Handbook of Evangelical Theologians*, edited by Walter Elwell, 260–75. Grand Rapids: Baker, 1993.

Quirk, Charles Evans. "The Auburn Affirmation." PhD diss., University of Iowa, 1967.

"Ralph Barton Perry." *Encyclopaedia Britannica.* Accessed May 29, 2014. www. britannica.com/EBchecked/topic/452626/Ralph-Barton-Perry.

Reeves, Thomas. *Twentieth-Century America.* New York: Oxford University Press, 2000.

Reid, Thomas G. Interview with the author. February 20, 2013.

"Revivals in American History." Lectures Flier, Covenant Presbyterian Church, March 12–13, 1994, Gerstner Papers, Chandler, Arizona.

"Reasons for Faith Seminar." Flier. Coral Ridge Presbyterian Church, April 28–30, 1989, Gerstner Papers, Chandler, Arizona.

Report of the Special Committee on a Brief Contemporary Statement of Faith. Philadelphia: Office of the General Assembly, 1965.

Richardson, Michael. *Amazing Faith.* Colorado Springs: WaterBrook, 2000.

Rimmel, William. "Seminary Too Liberal, Professor Says, Quits." *Pittsburgh Post-Gazette,* June 20, 1961, 1, 6.

Roberts, John H. *Darwinism and the Divine in America.* Madison: University of Wisconsin Press, 1988.

Rodgers, Ann. "Obituary: Wynn Kenyon/Became Beloved Philosophy Professor After Ordination Ordeal." *Pittsburgh Post-Gazette.* February 15, 2012. Accessed March 18, 2014. www.postgazette.com/news/obituaries/2012/02/15/Obiturary-Wynn-Kenyon-Became-beloved-philosophy-professor-after-ordinationordeal/stories/201202150985.

Rodgers-Melnick, Ann. "John Gerstner-Longtime Seminary Professor, Passionate Scholar." *Pittsburgh Post-Gazette,* March 27, 1996, B-4.

Rogers, Jack B. Interview with the author. December 2, 2010.

Rogers, Jack, and Donald McKim. *The Authority and Interpretation of the Bible.* San Francisco: Harper & Row, 1979.

Ross, Alexander. Review of *English Deism: Its Roots and Fruits,* by John Orr. *Evangelical Quarterly* 6, no. 4 (1934) 440–42.

Ross, Mark. Interview with the author. July 6, 2010.

Rowley, Jack. Email to the author. March 8, 2014.

———. Interview with the author. July 29, 2010.

———. "The Ligonier Valley Study Center Early Years." Accessed November 17, 2012. http://www.ligonier.org/blog/ligonier-valley-study-center-early-years/.

Sandeen, Ernest. *The Roots of Fundamentalism.* Chicago: University of Chicago Press, 1970.

"Says Bible Unhurt by Archaeologists." *The Daily Princetonian,* February 16, 1928, 1, 5.

Schlect, Chris. "J. Gresham Machen, Roy T. Brumbaugh, and the Presbyterian Schism of 1934–1936." MA thesis, University of Idaho, 2005.

Scholer, David M. "My Fifty Journey with Women and Ministry in the New Testament and in the Church Today." Accessed 29 November 2012. http://www.eewc.com/Articles/women-minsitry-scholer/.

Scorgie, Glen. *A Call for Continuity.* Macon, GA: Mercer University Press, 1988.

Sell, Alan P. F. *Defending and Declaring the Faith.* Exeter, UK: Paternoster, 1987.

Shackleford, Dennis. Interview with the author. May 9, 2013.

Sharpe, Jerry. "Presbytery Bids to Heal Rift." *Pittsburgh Press,* March 22, 1981, A-4.

Showalter, Jean S. Letter to Edna Gerstner. July 22, 1978, Gerstner Papers, Chandler, Arizona.

Sidwell, Mark. Review of *Jonathan Edwards,* by John Gerstner. *Biblical Viewpoint* 23 (1989) 104–5.

Smith, Elwyn A. *The Presbyterian Ministry in American Culture.* Philadelphia: Westminster, 1960.

Smith, Morton. *How the Gold Has Become Dim.* Jackson, MS: Steering Committee for a Continuing Presbyterian Church, 1973.

Snowman, Daniel. *America Since 1920.* London: Heinemann Education, 1978.

Soden, Dale. *Reverend Mark Matthews.* Seattle: University of Washington Press, 2000.

Spear, Wayne. Interview with the author. August 9, 2011

———. Interview with the author. September 9, 2011.

Spitz, Lewis. Review of *The Theology of the Major Sects*, by John Gerstner. *Concordia Theological Monthly* 31, no. 10 (1960) 655.

Sproul, R. C. "Foreword." In *God's Inerrant Word*, edited by John Warwick Montgomery, 9. Minneapolis: Bethany Fellowship, 1974.

———. Interview with the author. December 1, 2010.

———. "The Gerstner I Remember." *Tabletalk* 21, no. 10 (1997) 4–7.

———. Statement on the back of John Gerstner's "The Theology of Jonathan Edwards." Audiotape series. Orlando: Ligonier Ministries, 1994.

Sproul, R. C., ed. *Soli Deo Gloria.* Philipsburg, NJ: Presbyterian and Reformed, 1976.

Sproul, R. C., and John Gerstner. "Silencing the Devil." Video. Orlando: Ligonier Ministries, 1992.

Stark, Tom. Interview with the author. August 15, 2011.

Steely, Jeff A. "Cornelius Herman Suckau: Mennonite Fundamentalist?" *Mennonite Life* 44, no. 1 (1989) 15–21.

Stendahl, Krister. "Uses and Misuses of the Bible." *Pittsburgh Perspective* 1, no. 4 (1960) 22–32.

Stonehouse, Ned. *J. Gresham Machen.* Grand Rapids: Eerdmans, 1954.

Strong, D. M. "Kyle, Melvin Grove." In *Dictionary of the Presbyterian and Reformed Tradition in America*, edited by D. G. Hart and Mark Noll, 140–41. Downers Grove, IL: InterVarsity, 1999.

Stuart, Albert. "Diminishing Distinctives: A Study of the Ingestion of the United Presbyterian Church in North America by the Presbyterian Church in the United States of America." Self-published, 2000.

Suckau, Edna. Wheaton College Transcript. Gerstner Papers, Chandler, Arizona.

Sweeney, Douglas. "Evangelical Tradition in America." In *Cambridge Companion to Jonathan Edwards*, edited by Stephen J. Stein, 217–38. Cambridge: Cambridge University Press, 2007.

———. "Sweeney Booknotes: John Gerstner's *Rational Biblical Theology*." Jonathan Edwards Center at Trinity Evangelical Divinity School. Accessed May 7, 2013. http://jecteds.org/blog/tag/gary-crampton/.

Talbot, Mark. Interview with the author. June 11, 2013.

"The Presbyterian League of Faith." *Christianity Today*, May 1931, 19.

"The Presbyterian Predicament" [Advertisement]. *Christianity Today*, February 18, 1966, 27.

"The Third Annual Soli Deo Gloria Conference on The Mercy of God." Brochure. April, 24–25, 1992, John Gerstner Papers, Chandler, Arizona.

Thompson, Ernest Trice. *Presbyterians In the South.* Vol. 3. Richmond: John Knox, 1973.

Todd, Richard. Interview with the author. February 9, 2013.

Trippert, Daniel. "Wild, John Daniel, Jr. (1902–1972)." In *Dictionary of Modern American Philosophers*, edited by John R. Shook, 1:2596–600. Bristol, UK: Thoemmes, 2005.

Trollinger, William Vance. "William Gallogly Moorehead." In *Dictionary of the Presbyterian and Reformed Tradition*, edited by D. G. Hart and Mark A. Noll, 164. Downers Grove, IL: InterVarsity, 1999.

Turner, John. *Bill Bright and Campus Crusade for Christ*. Chapel Hill: University of North Carolina Press, 2008.

Turner, John, and Jennifer Goetz. Review of *Jonathan Edwards*, by John Gerstner. *Journal of the Evangelical Theological Society* 32, no. 3 (1989) 410–11

Van Biema, Dave. "The New Calvinism." *Time*, 12 March 2009. Accessed May 10, 2013. http://www.time.com/time/specials/packages/article/0,28804,1884779_1884 782_1884760,00.html.

Van Til, Cornelius. "Calvin the Controversialist." In *Soli Deo Gloria*, edited by R. C. Sproul, 1–10. Philipsburg, NJ: P and R, 1976.

———. *The Confession of 1967*. Philipsburg, NJ: P and R, 1967.

———. Letter to Gerstner. February 26, 1960, Van Til Archives, Westminster Theological Seminary.

———. Review of *English Deism: Its Roots and Fruits*, by John Orr. *Christianity Today*, August 1934, 73.

Vandoodewaard, William. *The Marrow Controversy and the Seceder Tradition*. Grand Rapids: Reformation Heritage, 2011.

Vos, Johnannes S. Letter to John Gerstner, n.d. John Gerstner Papers, Chandler, Arizona.

Walther, James Arthur, ed. *Ever a Frontier: The Bicentennial History of the Pittsburgh Theological Seminary*. Grand Rapids: Eerdmans, 1994.

Weeks, Louis. "Presbyterian Church (U.S.A.)." In *Dictionary of Christianity in America*. edited by Daniel Reid et al., 931–32. Downers Grove, IL: InterVarsity, 1990.

Weir, D. A. "Reformed Presbyterian Church of North America, Covenanter Synod." In *Dictionary of the Presbyterian and Reformed Tradition in America*, edited by D. G. Hart and Mark A. Noll, 211–12 Downers Grove, IL: InterVarsity, 1999.

Wells, David. Interview with the author. November 3, 2010.

Wells, David F., and John D. Woodbridge eds. *The Evangelicals*. Nashville: Abingdon, 1975.

Weston, William. *Presbyterian Pluralism*. Knoxville: University of Tennessee Press, 1997.

"Whale, John Seldon." In *Twentieth Century Encyclopedia of Religious Knowledge*, edited by Lefferts Loetscher, 1171. Grand Rapids: Baker, 1955.

Whale, J. S. *Christian Doctrine*. Cambridge: Cambridge University Press, 1941.

"What Does It Mean to Be Evangelical?" *Christianity Today*, 16 June 1989, 60, 63.

White, Becky. Interview with the author. January 20, 2013.

White, Ed. Interview with the author. February 7, 2013.

White, John. *Black Leadership in America*. London: Longman, 1990.

White, John H. "Foreword." In *Repent or Perish*, by John Gerstner. Ligonier, PA: Soli Deo Gloria, 1990.

———. Interview with the author, May 15, 2012.

Wibbels, Alan, and Mariana Caro. Email to the author. March 5, 2013.

Wiest, Walter. Interview with the author. August 13, 2012.

Wilkinson, John. "Edward A. Dowey, Jr. and the Making of the Confession of 1967." *Journal of Presbyterian History* 81, no. 1 (2004) 5–22.

Wilshire, Leland. "United Church of Christ." In *Dictionary of Christianity in America,* edited by Daniel G. Reid et al., 1199–1201. Downers Grove, IL: InterVarsity, 1990.

Wilson, Talmage. Letter to Carl Henry. March 2, 1956, Graham Center Archives, Wheaton College, IL.

Witmer, John. "A Review of *Wrongly Dividing the Word of Truth*-Part 1." *Bibliotheca Sacra* 149, no. 594 (1992) 131–45.

———. "A Review of *Wrongly Dividing the Word of Truth*—Part 2." *Bibliotheca Sacra* 149, no. 595 (1992) 259–76.

Woodbridge, John, and Tom McComiskey, eds. *Doing Theology in Today's World.* Grand Rapids: Zondervan, 1991.

Worthen, Molly. *Apostles of Reason.* New York: Oxford University Press, 2014.

Wright, J. Stafford. Review of *The Theology of the Major Sects,* by John Gerstner. *The Evangelical Quarterly* 33, no. 2 (1961) 119–20.

Zacharias, Ravi. "On Leadership and Calling." Interview with John Carter. Accessed January 4, 2011. http://www.rzim.org/default.aspx?TabId=602&articleid=6636&cbmoduleid=881.

Zemek, George J., Jr. Review of *Classical Apologetics,* by John Gerstner. *Grace Theological Journal* 7, no. 1 (1986) 111.

Zikmund, Barbara Brown. "Ministry of Word and Sacrament: Women and Changing Understandings of Ordination." In *The Presbyterian Predicament,* edited by Milton J. Coalter, John M. Mulder, and Louis B. Weeks, 134–58. Louisville: Westminster John Knox, 1990.

Subject Index

UPCUSA. *See* United Presbyterian Church USA (UPCUSA)
"Uses and Misuses of the Bible" (Stendahl), 83

Van Til, Cornelius
    arguments supporting, 161–62
    on Barth, 91–92n74
    career, 97n102
    contribution to *Soli Deo Gloria*, 141
    critique of Dutch theologians, 64
    Gerstner's disagreements with, 34–35
    The New Modernism, Gerstner's review, 48
    praise for *English Deism*, 31
    presuppositional apologetics, 88–89, 113, 157–59, 210
    on the Westminster standards, 97
Vasady, Bela, 65, 73n132
virgin birth, 8
von Harnack, Adolf, 23
Von Waldow, H. Eberhard, 101
Vos, Gerhardus, 10, 10n36, 145
Vos, Johannes, 145

Wallace, W. Charles, 24
Warfield, Benjamin B.
    importance of personal religion to true theological understanding, 114
    McCosh's influence on, 46
    position on inerrancy, 112–14, 124–25, 164–65
    and the Reformed apologetic approach, 87
    at Westminster Seminary, 10
Warren, Earl, 15

Weisiger, Cary N. III, 59
Welch, Claude, 65–66
Wells, David, 131–32, 137–38, 138n174
Wesley, John, 5, 133
Western Baptist Seminary, Portland, Oregon, 167
Western Seminary, Pittsburgh, 74, 78–79, 201
Westminster College, New Wilmington, PA, 22–23, 31, 127n119
Westminster Confession of Faith. *See also* Confession of 1967 (C-67), UPCUSA
    as basis for conservative theology, 86, 95–96
    and the Confession of 1967 (C-67), UPCUSA, 92
    Dowey's views on, 94–95
    McNaugher's views on, 32
    position on inerrancy, 124
Westminster Theological Seminary, Montgomery County, PA (WTS)
    conservative theology at, 7, 86
    founding, 9
    Gerstner's continuing association with, 169, 177
    Gerstner's studies at, 3, 9–10, 33–35, 49, 199–200
    Jubilee Lecture, 1980, 167
    Orr's teaching career at, 210
    Van Til's leadership at, 89
    Gerstner's graduate studies at, 3
West Philadelphia High School, 20
Whale, J.S., 53–54
"What Is Wrong With the Auburn Affirmation?" (Gerstner), 71

Name Index

Aaron, Hank, 84
Adams, J. D., 21
Ahlstrom, Sydney, 128, 131
Albright, William F., 26
Alexander, Archibald, 10
Alexander, Eric, 170
Alexander, Malcolm S., 75n141
Anderson, J. Lowrie, 51
Archer, Gleason, 127n120
Armstrong, William Park, 10
Armstrong, John, 166, 166n118
Ault, John, 104

Bahnsen, Greg, 121, 160–61
Bald, John M., 75n141
Ballantyne, Agnes, 76
Barbour, Clifford E., 80–82
Barr, James, 165
Barr, Joe, 56
Barrick, J. Louis, 20
Barth, Karl, 48, 54, 65, 91, 91n74,
    113, 133, 135, 191, 210
Barth, Markus, 104, 162
Bavinck, Herman, 65, 158–59
Bebbington, David, 5–6
Berkeley, George, 40
Berkouwer, G. C., 64
Bertocci, Peter, 191
Bibby, Reginald, 135, 135n161
Birney, Leroy, 103–4

Bixler, Julius, 39–40
Blackwood, Andrew, 10, 82
Blake, Eugene Carson, 73,
    73n132, 74, 83, 94
Bloesch, Donald G., 89, 135,
    135n159, 178, 178n22, 198
Bodamer, Walter K., 123
Bogue, Carl, 101–2, 142, 176, 189,
    196, 197
Boice, James Montgomery,
    122–23, 122n93
Bonhoeffer, Dietrich, 92
Brackenridge, R. Douglas, 60–61
Bradshaw, F. Maxwell, 64
Briggs, Charles, 8
Brown, David, 145
Brumbaugh, Roy, 13n54
Brunner, Emil, 54, 92, 124, 133
Buck, Pearl S., 82
Bultmann, Rudolph, 91–92, 191
Burggraff, Winfield, 62
Burrows, Bessie, 75n141
Burtt, Edwin, 39
Buschart, David, 137
Buswell, J. Oliver, 33–34, 191
Butler, BISHOP, 129
Butterfield, Lyman, 128

Cadbury, Henry Joel, 39, 44, 165
Calvin, John, 4, 123–24, 141, 192